D1918324

The Limits of Transnationalism

The Limits of Transnationalism

NANCY L. GREEN

The University of Chicago Press ❋ Chicago and London

The University of Chicago Press, Chicago 60637
The University of Chicago Press, Ltd., London

Published 2019
Printed in the United States of America

28 27 26 25 24 23 22 21 20 19   1 2 3 4 5

ISBN-13: 978-0-226-60814-3 (cloth)
ISBN-13: 978-0-226-60828-0 (paper)
ISBN-13: 978-0-226-60831-0 (e-book)
DOI: https://doi.org/10.7208/chicago/9780226608310.001.0001

Library of Congress Cataloging-in-Publication Data

Names: Green, Nancy L., author.
Title: The limits of transnationalism / Nancy L. Green.
Description: Chicago : The University of Chicago Press, 2019. | Includes bibliographical references and index.
Identifiers: LCCN 2018052445 | ISBN 9780226608143 (cloth : alk. paper) | ISBN 9780226608280 (pbk. : alk. paper) | ISBN 9780226608310 (e-book)
Subjects: LCSH: Transnationalism.
Classification: LCC JZ1320 .G74 2019 | DDC 303.48/2—dc23
LC record available at https://lccn.loc.gov/2018052445

♾ This paper meets the requirements of ANSI/NISO Z39.48-1992 (Permanence of Paper).

For Pierre,
toujours

Contents

Introduction

The "Transnational Moment" and Its Limits

I do not find that I have gained any point in either country, except that of rendering myself suspected by my impartiality; in England of being too much an American, and in America of being too much an Englishman.
—Benjamin Franklin[1]

It has been over a quarter of a century since "transnationalism" was born—as a perspective, as a concept, as a research agenda. US political scientists in the early 1970s may have been the first academics to use the term, but cultural anthropologists, migration anthropologists, and US historians, separately but enthusiastically, "discovered" transnationalism in the early 1990s. They made it into a veritable scholarly success story. It fit easily into the globalization talk of the late twentieth century and seemed obvious once revealed.

Transnationalism means many things to many people, from crossing physical borders to crossing intellectual ones. For individuals it may mean a legal status—two or more passports—and/or multiple identities. For institutions or corporations, it means stretching activities across borders. For researchers, a newly wrought study of international relations is having a comeback, and the histories of international nongovernmental organizations (NGOs) are getting new attention. Many scholars use transnationalism, like global history, to argue that we cannot do history in one country. Others use it to seek the international or extranational in local contexts, the question then being whether to put the accent on the global, the local, or the unfortunate but evocative neologism, the "glocal." Indeed, the frequent interchangeability of "transnationalism" with the terms "globalization," "comparative history," "connected history," or the history of circulation, shows its own "flexibility," the latter idea being indeed intrinsic to the epistemological cause. "Transnationalism," "global history," and "comparative history" are frequently used in overlapping ways, despite valiant efforts to specify their distinctiveness.[2] ("Transnationalism" is rarely used on a truly global scale, but are two countries enough, four too many to study? "Comparative history" may or may not include actual connections, etc.) The use of each term may depend on discipline, on country, on historiographic posturing, but transnationalism has galvanized conference papers, book titles, a dictionary, a reader, and journals in the United States and Europe.[3] For historians, transnationalism has become a historiographic perspective and a search for, as well as an analysis of, transnationals/transnationalisms past, be they in the form of the movement of ideas, goods, or people. And certain forms of transnational mobility and networks have been celebrated (e.g., international organizations, study abroad programs), while others have not (e.g., mafias, trafficking).[4] As Pierre-Yves Saunier notes, there is a certain "prejudice against evil" and a "positive moral value that we tend to give to connections and circulations."[5] This helps explain the initial formulation of transnationalism as a positive affirmation of human agency.

This book proposes to question this "transnational moment," in particular as it relates to human mobility. I do not argue that transnationalism does not exist. It has become and should remain a fruitful line of study. However, I raise two criticisms. On the one hand, as many scholars have by now amply shown, it is not necessarily a new phenomenon. Migration historians have suffered déjà vu and argued that the modern migrants we have been studying have been acting as transnationals since at least the nineteenth century; we thus have been studying transnationalism all along, albeit without designating it as such. On the other hand, as this book explores, transnationalism is not as easy as it looks. Insofar as transnationalism has come to emphasize a somewhat heroic sense of individual opportunity and mobility, the difficulties of transnational activities have been lost from sight. While the idea of transnationalism arose as an understandably powerful antidote to the older Sturm und Drang of migration studies, it has led too often to an overly optimistic vision of migrant agency, ignoring the state's capacity for interference and "the very different and unequal ways in which people experience transnationality."[6] The notion of unfettered movement—particularly since the fall of the Berlin Wall—has perhaps now run its own useful turn and not just due to the threat of new walls. It is time to take a closer look at the metaphoric and real obstacles to transnational mobility from a historical perspective.

The book starts with the tragi-comic story of an American in France at the turn of the twentieth century (chapter 1). Frank Gueydan, a.k.a. François Gueydan de Roussel, was condemned in France for having manufactured artificial wine. He fled to Switzerland and spent the following years writing to friends and officials on both sides of the Atlantic, bemoaning the fact that, as an American, he was helpless to receive a proper hearing in France. The literal and figurative trials of François Gueydan de Roussel serve as an illuminating example of the limits of transnationalism. Gueydan tried to draw upon powerful networks in both the United States and France, to the point of exasperation—of himself and of his contacts. His travails highlight two oft-ignored aspects of transnationalism: the perspective—and doubts—of the country of origin with regard to its absent citizens and the ways in which citizens abroad may try to use their citizenship of origin to plead their causes, even though this strategy does not always work. Gueydan's story thus tells a cautionary tale about both the weakness of networks and the home state's relationship to its tempestuous citizens abroad. It serves to introduce more general questions about contrasting views of protection and citizenship, both from the perspective of the home state and that of individuals trying to mobilize their citizenship while living transnational lives.

Thus, if individual transnationalism has been largely defined by the liberty of movement and the innovative use of cross-boundary ties it permits, Gueydan's life highlights three aspects of transnationalism that have often been absent from the discussion: first, the perspective of the country of origin; second, the sometimes frantic ways in which transnational citizens turn to their home countries for help; and third, and perhaps most notably, Gueydan's story reminds us of a part of the story seldom told—the complications and the eventual failure of networks.

Before further examining the friction in the transnational experience, chapter 2 provides an overview of the varied analyses of transnationalism over the past quarter century. Different terms have been used to describe transnational activities, and different disciplines have approached the topic. Reviewing what I call the "newness debate," chapter 2 shows how migration historians have pointed out that transnationalism, as a practice, is not that new, contrary to what many more present-oriented anthropologists and sociologists have claimed. However, the "discovery" of transnationalism, or rather the historiographic turn to writing about transnationalism, *is* new. Its advent, I argue, is linked not only to the political and economic environment of the late twentieth century but also to larger epistemological trends, notably poststructuralism. The question then is, to what extent has the emphasis on flexibility, mobility, and individual agency, as fundamental elements of transnationalism, blinded us to other, more constraining aspects of international movement?

The subsequent chapters pursue the questions raised by Gueydan's case. How does the country of origin see its wayward flock—even to the point of expatriating its birthright citizens (chapter 3)? It happened that while Gueydan was living in France, the United States started looking more closely at its citizens abroad. The 1907 Expatriation Act was passed just as Gueydan fled to Switzerland. While immigration history has mostly focused on those who arrive, I argue that we need to incorporate departure and expatriation into migration studies. The perspective of the home state is important for understanding its relation to its transnational citizens and the ways it encourages or raises obstacles to their lives abroad. Women were particularly at risk of losing their birthright citizenship from the transnational activity of mixed marriage, as the case of Natalie (Lily) Oelrichs, a.k.a. the Duchess of Mecklenburg, illustrates. She was an American citizen who, after a life lived largely between France and Germany, left her lawyers to grapple with meanings of domicile and citizenship in order to settle her will. Chapter 3 shows how the meaning of expatriation shifted in the United States from the early nineteenth to the early twentieth century. The earlier period's inclusive view stressed the individual's right to expatriate voluntarily to another country, focusing on those coming *to* the US, with first British nationals in the US, and then the immigrants of the mid-nineteenth century in mind. In the later period, a more troubled view emerged as suspicion arose concerning a new, more worrisome figure: those *leaving* the United States. For those transnational citizens, the acts that potentially could incur citizenship loss were codified and lengthened from 1907 to 1967. Expatriation law reflects ideas about transnationalism, while it also can act to constrain it.

However, as chapter 4 shows, many countries have also tried to hang on to their citizens through a modernized form of perpetual allegiance that in effect both abets and impedes transnationalism. Beyond the US, other countries—notably those with much higher rates of emigration in the nineteenth century—all debated the issue of departures, with considerable concern. Chapter 4 continues to look at emigration from the perspective of the home state, to see the ways in which it can have an impact on transnational ties. Focusing on several European countries of emigration over the nineteenth century—Germany, Italy, Great

Britain, and Hungary—this chapter shows how their policies affected the possibilities of mobility. Attitudes ranged—from country to country and within each country over time—from a fear of loss of both labor and soldier manpower to an encouragement of departure if it could be helpful to national stature across borders. Emigration, after all, could help spread a country's culture abroad and, importantly, result in remittances. But concerns about the loss of and the protection of citizens overseas mean that, at different moments, homeland policies could also create obstacles to transnational movement.

Chapter 5 returns to the ways in which citizens draw upon transnational networks via that hub of transnational activity, the consulate, to plead their causes when they find themselves in trouble far from their native soil. Their homeland ties may prove to be efficacious. Or not. Mobile lives create their own problems, most notably at the crossroads of different legal systems, but also due to the very fact of having to cope with life crises while living abroad. Returning to the perspective of individual experience, this chapter highlights the life trajectories of Gertrude Moulton and Clara Steichen, two American women living abroad who, in turning to their lawyer in Paris for help with their divorce settlements, expressed the twists and turns of transnational existence in Paris, Salzburg, and Majorca. Many others went to the US consulate for aid. Chapter 5 shows how, in times of both war and peace, even well-heeled transnationals can be constrained by the legal systems in which they are embedded. Calling upon home networks for help, they first need to prove their citizenship when seeking US government protection. Letters from grateful citizens to the State Department show how the homeland can help out at its best, but other letters, from irate citizens, reveal the dashed expectations of some and the fact that public, like private, transnational ties do not always work.

This book aims to serve as a resounding reminder of the complexities of transnationalism, with a call for greater attention to the bumps along the road.

1

Fake Wine and Future Cadaver: The Trials of an American in France

"There is no Justice in France for an American citizen!"[1] In the years preceding World War I, an American from Louisiana who had moved to France protested his innocence to all who would listen. Yet on November 12, 1907, François Gueydan de Roussel was condemned by an appeals court in Nîmes to six months in prison and charged 7,500 francs in fines and damages. His crime? Having manufactured artificial wine. The sentence was rendered in his absence, for Gueydan de Roussel had fled to Switzerland with his wife and five children.[2] Having already been condemned twice that year on what he insisted were trumped-up charges, he despaired of a fair trial. He spent the following years proclaiming, increasingly desperately, that a helpless American could get no justice in France. Ever fond of capital letters, italics, and exclamation marks to advance his cause, he even compared himself to that other high-profile wronged man of his era, Alfred Dreyfus.[3]

Gueydan's thick file in the US State Department archives is an eye-opening example of the limits of transnationalism. A

Franco-American by heritage, but a US citizen by birth and education, he moved to France at the age of twenty-five. From there, he tried to draw upon powerful networks on both sides of the Atlantic. His efforts show the mechanics of transnationalism at work while exuding the exasperation of it. Gueydan's story may be in large part sui generis, but at the same time it reveals larger questions about transnationalism. Assumptions about the ease and benefits of traversing borders need to confront the frequent frictions of such mobility.

How did Frank Gueydan, formerly of New Orleans and San Diego, Texas, come to be François Gueydan de Roussel, enmeshed in local and national French politics, hero to his family, thorn in the side of the US embassy, and fly in the ointment of the French judicial system? An American accused of making fake wine in France is enough to raise American eyebrows and deepen that disapproving French *moue* of the mouth. But the Gueydan Affair also offers a tale about the uses of citizenship in transnational times. Writing to his congressmen—that quintessential American reflex—is how Gueydan came to the attention of American authorities (and this historian), enlivening State Department (and French Ministry of Justice) correspondence with files thickened by his prolixity. His self-defense speaks to the indignation of a wronged American seeking justice. But, as the French would say, *ça se complique*. Gueydan was first an American *abroad*; second, of French ancestry; and third, linked by family to one of France's most influential politicians of his day. Pleading with both the French and US governments for help, as well as leaning on his US citizenship and his French and American connections as needed, Gueydan stayed out of jail, but his tale is a cautionary one for transnational biographies.

Born François Gueydan in 1861 in New Orleans, "Frank" was a Franco-Louisianan. His father, henceforth "François *père*," was French, while his American mother was born in New Orleans of French parents. Before Frank's eastward ho from the United States to France, his father's family had moved westward, from

France to the United States. In that nineteenth-century era of intense transatlantic travel, Frank's father was among those who had left France for the New World albeit not to trap furs or seek gold. Most of the nineteenth-century "Foreign French" emigrants to New Orleans (as distinct from the longer-settled Creoles) were fortune hunters of another sort, ranging from adventurers to a majority of merchants, lawyers, and everything from hairdressers to dancing masters.[4] François *père* arrived in the United States in 1844, at age thirteen; his younger brother, Jean-Pierre, followed four years later. The brothers were the sons of a prosperous hotel owner in Saint-Bonnet in the Hautes-Alpes who sent them to an uncle in New Orleans. The entrepreneurial young Gueydans tried their hands at everything from cotton to cattle in Louisiana and Texas. They are hailed with introducing cotton farming to south Texas, as well as inventing a machine to make cactus edible for sheep.

But it was during the Civil War that the pair ran into trouble. After three years of peddling goods along the Mississippi River, Jean-Pierre had settled down as a merchant in Vermillion Parish, but with the outbreak of war, he took to more itinerant trading. While driving a herd of 420 cattle, he was arrested by federal troops as a "guerilla" at Bayou Goula, some ninety-five miles north of New Orleans. His herd, as well as his bales of cotton, was confiscated, despite his protest that he was a French subject and had refused to fight for the Confederate cause. He was soon released and acquitted of trading across the lines; twenty years later he was awarded $20,000 with 5 percent interest for his losses. He went on to buy out his brother and consolidate his own holdings in Louisiana. Frenchman builds American town: Jean-Pierre became a pioneer rice farmer and, to this day, is fondly remembered as the founder of Gueydan, Louisiana, still proud of its French heritage, not to mention its renown as the "Duck Capital of America."[5]

Jean-Pierre's older brother, François ("François *père*"), father to Frank Gueydan, was not so lucky. He, too, was arrested, in November 1862. He was able to prove that he was only traveling on business and was eventually released. His sugar was not. Like his brother, he swore he had never belonged to the Confederate army, but his receipts had been confiscated and accidentally, or purposefully, destroyed at the time of his arrest; François was never able to prove that the sugar was his or where it had disappeared to. (Stolen by famished soldiers? Sold by the army to pay off same?) In *François Gueydan v. United States*, he sued the government, like his brother, under the French and American Claims Commission, for 200 hogsheads of sugar and 150 barrels of molasses.[6] Government counsel disputed Gueydan's ownership of the goods and the date of purchase. He was charged with having engaged in unlawful trafficking under the Civil War Non-intercourse Act of 1861. Gueydan's lawyer argued that Gueydan had a permit; the US government countered that the permit was to pass but not to trade. Gueydan's claim was disallowed.

François Gueydan had first come to the United States on a ship named the *Rubicon*; his Civil War experience was his American rubicon.[7] We do not know to what extent the father's disappointments prefigure those of his son. François *père* was disgusted with his American adventure, but his business kept him in the US, and he became a transatlantic regular. In 1875, he moved to Texas, where his brother had moved two years earlier. But at the same time, he sent his wife and six girls back to France for their education, and, like his brother, he continued to travel to France regularly. François *père* would stay in France for two or three months each time, visiting his family and purchasing merchandise for sale in Texas and Mexico. But he insisted to the Claims Commission in 1881, "My home is in San Diego, Texas."[8] In 1885, after forty-one years in the US, François *père* definitively joined his family in France, where French history books describe him variously as a Paris merchant or as a middling bank employee in Grenoble who had sought his fortune in America in vain.[9] To add pathos to disappointment, family lore has it that oil was found in Texas shortly after he had sold off his Texas lands, packed his bags, and returned to France.[10]

So where did that leave his son, François *fils*, a.k.a. Frank? Apparently in 1886, a year after his father had done so, Frank Gueydan, a US-born twenty-five-year-old, moved to France. He stayed for a short time in Grenoble and Paris, before going on business to the Midi (the French South). There this "very handsome boy, tall and distinguished-looking, with very big dark eyes"[11] met and married a local woman. Renée de Roussel was charming, intelligent, and the sole child of a prosperous winegrower. Frank won the girl, the vineyard, and the particle, taking over the management of her father's 800-hectare property, as well as his name. Frank Gueydan became François Gueydan de Roussel. By 1902, he was the proud father of five. But his legal troubles were about to entangle him in the reverse of his father's travails. As it happens, both were bound up in disputes over sugar. Whereas François *père* was a Frenchman who had filed a claim against the US government to reclaim his sugar, François *fils* would spend a good decade of his life as an American fighting the French government while denying that a certain cache of sugar was his.

The Case against Gueydan de Roussel

At 7:30 a.m. on September 21, 1904, a French bailiff showed up at the wine cellar of Gueydan de Roussel's Saint Jean vineyard to evict the tenant farmer, Louis Boyer. A menacing Boyer, seconded by his team of workers, barred the bailiff from entering. The bailiff tried again at noon, again with no success. Boyer still refused entry. Not until three days later was Boyer finally forced to hand over his keys. Needless to say, he and Gueydan de Roussel were no longer on speaking terms. In the following years, the insults would turn to death threats against the backdrop of the Great Wine Revolt and political turmoil in southern France.

In 1903, Gueydan de Roussel had sublet his father-in-law's land to Boyer, a forty-four-year-old local farmer, on very generous terms: Gueydan de Roussel lent Boyer 80,000 francs per year upfront to work the land. By the end of the first year, Boyer had only been able to pay back 70,000 francs. By the end of the second year, he owed Gueydan de Roussel almost 90,000 francs. Gueydan de Roussel tried to cancel the lease but could not do so legally, and he was condemned instead to pay damages to Boyer. Worse yet, the vineyard was sequestered by the state, and the elder Monsieur de Roussel retrieved his property only by canceling his son-in-law's lease. If Gueydan de Roussel's career as a winegrower was over, his legal troubles had just begun.

Within the first year that Gueydan de Roussel hired Boyer, Gueydan de Roussel became embroiled in two deals relating to serious charges of wine tampering. On October 2, 1903, Gueydan de Roussel and Boyer had entered into a verbal contract (as was customary) with the wine merchant Martel to sell him that year's coming vintage of an estimated 10,000 hectoliters. Some 8,000 hectoliters had been delivered by August 1904, but the following month Boyer refused to sign off on the remainder of the delivery. He argued that the wine was no longer his responsibility, that it had been adulterated, and that, as a result, it could no longer be sold. Martel sued Gueydan de Roussel and Boyer jointly for breach of contract, but Boyer argued that the fault could not lie with him since he no longer had the keys to the cellar. Experts declared that the wine was indeed fake, manufactured wine, which Gueydan de Roussel did not dispute. But he countered that it was Martel's own doing: that Martel had had his chemist give the first 8,000 hectoliters a boost with oenanthol and citric acid and had treated the subsequent 2,500 hectoliters with something stronger. One judge considered Gueydan de Roussel blaming Martel to be an audacious defense. In 1906, the Nîmes court acquitted Boyer and found Gueydan de Roussel guilty. Gueydan de Roussel appealed, but in June 1907 he was sentenced to pay Martel 37,280 francs in damages.[12]

What did happen in the Saint Jean wine cellar between August and September 1904? Had Martel's chemist snuck in? Had adulterated wine been delivered to Gueydan de Roussel's personal cellar and piped in clandestinely to the adjoining commercial cellar, as Boyer imagined?[13] Had perhaps the disgruntled Boyer sabotaged the lot? Or, as Boyer subsequently argued, had Gueydan de Roussel's neighbor and other tenant farmer, Louis Gout, substituted fake wine for good with Gueydan de Roussel's knowledge?

Gout (whose name, with the help of a circumflex [*goût*], means "taste" in French—and not some painful disease brought on by eating too much foie gras) was the farmer of a nearby property who also sublet a few hectares of vines from Gueydan de Roussel. In February 1904, a suspicious stash of 6,300 kilograms of sugar and 3,700 kilograms of syrup had been found in his cellar, complete with a bubbling cauldron. For the police of the wine country, this was clear evidence of manufacturing fake wine. Gout was found guilty, and he did not contest the sentence. He admitted that he was making sugar wine because part of his vines had frozen.

That was in 1904. By 1907 everyone had changed his story. Gout now blamed Gueydan de Roussel. Gout claimed that he had purchased the ingredients with Gueydan's backing and that Gueydan de Roussel had let him take the fall, forgetting his promise to help Gout financially. Gueydan de Roussel argued that Gout's fake wine wasn't even proven: the law prosecuted only the actual making of sugar wine, not its presumed preparatory stages.[14] But Gueydan de Roussel's most strenuous defense was to accuse the irascible Boyer of having set him up—of egging Gout on to accuse Gueydan de Roussel a good year after the initial sentence.

Who bought the sugar found on Gout's farm? Who stirred the pot? (Gueydan de Roussel, according to one witness.) When Gueydan de Roussel was sentenced in 1907 to pay damages to Gout, his exasperation knew no bounds. He argued in court papers that for him to pay Gout, an avowed manufacturer of sugar wine, was to allow Gout to benefit from his crime. This was contrary to law and public order, as the Ligue des droits de l'homme chimed in on Gueydan de Roussel's behalf.[15]

In June 1907, learning that more proceedings against him were about to reach the court, Gueydan de Roussel did two things. First, he called the US embassy in Paris to garner its support:

First Request
June 5th 1907
backed by the American Embassy at Paris,
"**warning**"
the French Government of what was
being plotted by the French Justice
at Nîmes, against an American
Citizen, Mr. Gueydan de Roussel

Then he fled to Switzerland. A Nîmes lawyer had advised him that he had no chance against Boyer's influence. On August 24, 2007, he registered at the US consulate in Geneva and settled in Lausanne, continuing his battles from there by copious letter. For the French judicial system, Gueydan de Roussel was henceforth a fugitive.

Winegrowers and the Great Wine Revolt

Gueydan de Roussel's implantation in the French vineyards could not have come at a worse time. From the phylloxera plague of the 1870s and 1880s to a crisis of overproduction twenty years later, winegrowing in southern France had gone from bust to boom to bust again. This, too, was, in part, a transatlantic story. The phylloxera insects that had destroyed so many vines undoubtedly had been imported via resistant American plants in the 1870s. Ultimately, the scourge was solved with the importation and grafting of more American plants. Gueydan arrived at a time when southern French vineyards were becoming more capital-intensive and laborer-landowners less numerous. At the same time, wine prices in the Gard region were practically at an all-time low from 1904 to 1906.[16] The relationship between Gueydan de Roussel and Boyer only grew worse as the situation around them deteriorated and accusations of fraudulent winemaking spread throughout the region.

Trace grapes? Grape wine cannot be made in the absence of grapes, but it can be made in the presence of very few grapes indeed. The practice of making fake wine from raisins or sugar has been known since ancient times and is described in Diderot and d'Alembert's eighteenth-century *Encyclopédie* article on wine, under the subheading "chemical," adding that the method for making artificial wine could be useful "in the American colonies and anywhere else where much sugar is grown."[17] Adding sugar to wine is common practice, and in certain regions of France, this chaptalization is legally used to increase the alcohol level of the fermented grapes. However, in the case of "sugar wine," the sugar is used to increase the quantity, not the quality, by adding huge quantities of sugar and hot water to the vat residue left over from the first or second grape press. Fake wine is nonetheless often difficult to detect. During the phylloxera crisis, the production of artificial wine had been largely tolerated and quite massively practiced. As the phylloxera threat receded, however, and southern wine growers sought to expand their market in the north of France, they insisted on the virtues of their "natural wine" in contrast to beer and other "unhealthy" drinks more common up north.[18]

A law against food fraud was passed in 1905, and, just as Gueydan de Roussel's legal cases came to trial, the Great Wine Revolt of 1907 rocked southern France. In the face of overproduction and dire want on the part of many winegrowers, farmers gathered in town squares shouting, "Long live natural wine!" and "War on the Cheaters."[19] Between March and June, escalating numbers of demonstrators turned out to hear Marcellin-Albert, the firebrand leader of the revolt.[20] The protesters demanded that the government crack down on fraudulent wine. The socialist Jean Jaurès called for the nationalization of the vineyards. While historians have argued that the actual production of fake wine had greatly decreased since the phylloxera period, that's not the way it looked to the men and women at the time, marching with bread on pikes and banners marked "the last crust."[21]

In Nîmes, where Gueydan de Roussel was sentenced in June, July, and November 1907, almost three hundred thousand people demonstrated on June 2; over five hundred thousand converged on Montpellier (thirty-six miles away) on June 9. Town halls were burned, and, when the council president Clemenceau called in the troops to maintain order, violence erupted. Six protesters died in Narbonne on June 19 and 20, and the 17th infantry battalion, of mostly local recruits, mutinied during the night of June 20–21, rather than turn on their neighbors; the regiment was immortalized in the popular French ditty "Gloire au 17ème" (Glory to the 17th), which apparently even Lenin hummed. On June 29, 1907, the government finally agreed to take measures. A law was passed limiting the amount of sugar allowed in the making of wine for family use; it required a special permit for the sale of more than twenty-five kilograms of sugar and raised the sugar surtax. Clearly, this was not the time to have a case pending for wine tampering.[22]

Gueydan de Roussel's French Strategy

Fake wine and the French wine revolt are the important background to François Gueydan de Roussel's troubles in the Midi. As a native-born and self-proclaimed American, he was undoubtedly an unusual figure in the French vineyards. It is unclear the extent to which he also passed himself off as an integrated local. In any case, his legal strategy, as attested by the archival traces he left on both sides of the Atlantic, was determinedly transnational, drawing on both French and American networks to attempt to clear his name. Gueydan de Roussel ardently protested his innocence and demanded a special appeals court in France, arguing that he could get no justice in the local courts. His transnational strategy was all-encompassing, writing heatedly, both in excellent French to French officials, politicians, and publicists, and in impeccable English to US officials. In late 1910, totally incensed, he printed 800 copies of a 188-page book entitled *La magistrature gangrenée* (The gangrened judicial system) in which he detailed every moment of his struggle, the people to whom he had written, the support he had garnered, and the frustrations he had suffered at the hands of the French government and the US embassy. He ended his long legalistic ranting with pathos, concluding that the affair had led his eighty-year-old father-in-law to die of a broken heart.[23]

Gueydan de Roussel's first quarrel was indeed with the French judicial system, which ignored his request for an appeal. "I insist on being judged!! . . . The French government refuses me MY judges!"[24] he wrote, using his typical full emphatic panoply of exclamation marks and capital letters. He wrote incessantly to the French minister of justice, imploring in the name of humanity and pity to be able to return to France to visit his dying father-in-law. He was refused. In September 1914, at the outbreak of the war, he sent a telegram asking for permission to take care of the grape harvest on his wife's property, and again in 1916 he wrote directly to the council president, Aristide Briand, asking humbly for a pardon to return to France to help the war effort. He was refused yet again. He continued to exasperate the French Ministry of Justice.[25]

He contacted everybody in France from Dreyfusards to anti-Dreyfusards. The Ligue des droits de l'homme (human rights league), created to defend Dreyfus, wrote up a five-page defense of Gueydan de Roussel's case, but in the end it, like other potential backers, told him it was helpless to do more.[26] An editor from the right-wing newspaper *La Libre Parole*, which had briefly covered Gueydan de Roussel's 1907 trials, traveled to Lausanne to meet the exiled American in December 1910.[27] Georges Thiébaud stayed an entire day discussing Gueydan de Roussel's case with him. Thiébaud apparently asserted that as a foreigner, Gueydan de Roussel would get no justice in France, and he even suggested that Gueydan de Roussel naturalize. ("Useless to tell my answer," Gueydan de Roussel commented in his letter to his cousin Eugene in Louisiana.) Gueydan de Roussel's best strategy, Thiébaud counseled, would be to find some dirt on Joseph Caillaux: it was better to be guilty but have political backing in France than to be innocent but isolated.[28] And *La Libre Parole* was out to get Caillaux.

Indeed, the American's most potentially powerful trump card was a Frenchman. Joseph Caillaux, a prominent French politician throughout the first part of the twentieth century, was minister of finance from 1899 to 1902 and again from 1906 to 1909. He also happened to be Gueydan de Roussel's brother-in-law via Caillaux's first marriage to Berthe Gueydan, François's sister. Caillaux urged passage of the sugar law against wine fraud in 1907, but he is best known in this period for two other things. He was the architect of the first French income tax law (1914), which was already being discussed heatedly in the press during the period of Gueydan de Roussel's trials. However, Caillaux is more often remembered because in 1914 his second wife shot and killed Gaston Calmette, the editor of the daily newspaper *Le Figaro*. The immediate cause was a 1901 letter by Caillaux to Berthe Gueydan, his mistress at the time, which *Le Figaro* printed on March 13, 1914. The letter was politically compromising, and Henriette Caillaux, infuriated by the paper's repeated attacks on her husband, decided to take matters into her own hands.

On March 16, Henriette went to the *Le Figaro* office. The editor was out, but she gave her calling card in an envelope to the secretary and waited calmly, cuff in muff, for Calmette to arrive. When he did and saw her card, Calmette agreed to receive her, commenting chivalrously to a skeptical colleague: "I cannot refuse to receive a woman." No sooner was the office door closed than she took the revolver from her sleeve and fired five shots. The first one hit the bookcase, but the other four made their mark. When a bailiff rushed in to restrain her, she coldly told him to take his hands off her: "I do not want to flee. My car is downstairs to go to the police station. Take your hands off of me. *I am a lady*."[29]

The famous 1901 letter, signed "Ton Jo" (Your Jo), had revealed the politician's early cynicism, as well as his behind-the-scenes private life. Several years before he pushed for the income tax, Caillaux had written in 1901 to Berthe: "I killed off the income tax while appearing to defend it." But why should such a letter lead his second wife to such drastic measures? As Henriette's biographer, Edward Berenson, has suggested, Caillaux could have just thrown down the gauntlet for a duel as did so many others when honor was at stake in early twentieth-century France.[30]

It wasn't just the politics or even jealousy of a former mistress/first wife that motivated Henriette Caillaux. It was also fear for her reputation. If the newspaper editor could stoop to publish a thirteen-year-old love letter, he could certainly have some more recent letters ready to print. Henriette feared that Caillaux's early amorous correspondence with *her* might be next to appear, proving hanky panky before their marriage and ruining her moral and his political reputations. Yes, even in permissive France, private dallying was supposed to remain so. Of course, if Henriette didn't want her past indiscretions revealed, shooting the potential revealer was hardly a way of keeping them out of the news, as the subsequent trial amply showed. But she took matters up her own sleeve, leading to her imprisonment, a sober hiatus in her husband's political career, and a serious diversion for France in the months running up to the First World War. Berthe Gueydan was called to the stand, and police investigators sought out her brother François in Lausanne.

Thanks to the famous 1901 "Ton Jo" letter, Berthe Gueydan has her own entry in many French history books as the first Madame Caillaux, but few pay more than passing attention to the fact that she was American by birth. The youngest of François *père*'s girls, Berthe was born in New Orleans in 1869. When she moved to France with her mother and five sisters in 1875, she was six years old. If her niece Isabelle Couturier de Chefdubois's memoirs are to be trusted (they are full of factual errors), Berthe was sent to a Catholic convent school in Grenoble, but to little effect. Couturier de Chefdubois criticizes her aunt's bad judgment, although apparently the sentiment was mutual; Berthe did not approve of Isabelle's marriage either. Berthe married for the first time at the young age of sixteen and had a son the following year. As she later confided to her niece, she agreed to the marriage not so much for the groom, but because she was fascinated with his father, the naturalist landscape painter Jules Dupré. Fifteen years later she met the "very elegant, very thin, and surprisingly vivacious" Joseph Caillaux. She divorced Dupré in 1904 and married Caillaux two years later.[31]

As Caillaux, also known as the "bald Don Juan," later described his marriage to Berthe, it was a "marriage of resignation." He claimed in his memoirs that he would have preferred to live his life alone, but Berthe "made an audacious move. She got divorced." And he chivalrously persuaded himself that he owed it to his mistress to marry her.[32] According to Couturier de Chefdubois, the ceremony was quite discreet, but it so upset Berthe's father, François *père*, that he went home and died "overcome by emotion."[33] American-born Berthe went on to be the belle of the Parisian balls and receptions that she organized, while Caillaux buried himself in his work.

In late 1907, shortly after Gueydan de Roussel's cases were judged and he had fled to Switzerland, Caillaux began a heated affair with Henriette Clarétie. He started writing *her* love letters, which Berthe discovered but then agreed to burn in 1909 in exchange for Caillaux's promise to remain faithful. But Berthe had kept copies of the burned letters, and Caillaux couldn't stay away from Henriette.

He divorced Berthe in 1911 and married Henriette later that year. Berthe attributed Caillaux's womanizing to his provincial background, his wanting to emulate his Parisian politician friends, and to the attraction of power: "As butterflies around a flame, women came to whirl around his power."[34] According to her niece, Berthe's troubles were the result of a weak moral upbringing, a too-early marriage, and a tragic fate. But she acknowledged that Berthe's saving grace was that she finally handed over the Henriette–Jo love letters at her successor's murder trial. The audience was stunned, the lawyer's voice trembled with emotion, and Berthe was congratulated for her "gesture of reparation."[35]

Eight years and an ocean apart, separated by upbringing and education, Berthe and Frank were probably not close. The identities of these two Gueydan children of a transnational family had diverged radically: Frank was an American in France claiming his innocence to all who would listen; his sister had become a very Parisian hostess, married to one of France's powerful politicians, who was, however, deaf to Frank's pleas for help. Nonetheless, the two siblings clearly remained in touch, and Berthe apparently did try to intervene with Caillaux on her brother's behalf.

Gueydan de Roussel had another "Ton Jo" letter to prove it. In yet one more missive addressed to "*Ma chère petite Berthe*," this one dated August 21, 1909, Caillaux had written to his (still, but not for long) wife:

> When your brother came to see me at the Ministry, was I able to obtain a clear, complete explanation [*aveux*] of his situation? No. Is that not correct? You know it, and you admitted it.
> NOW, IT IS CLEAR THAT THERE HAS BEEN VIOLENT PREJUDICE AGAINST HIM, AND THAT LOCAL PASSIONS HAVE BECOME INVOLVED AND THAT HE WAS MUCH TOO SEVERELY SENTENCED.[36]

Gueydan de Roussel would repeatedly reference the second (but not the first) phrase of this letter to prove, first, that the local cabal had done him in, and second, that Caillaux recognized the judicial wrong that Gueydan de Roussel had suffered. The caps, of course, are, as usual, HIS. But Caillaux refused to more actively involve himself. And by then Berthe's own relationship with her husband was on the rocks.

If Gueydan de Roussel's timing in going into farming in southern France was bad in terms of the wine business, it was even more unfortunate in relation to the timing of his potential backer's political and personal life. In 1904, when the sugar cache was found in Gout's basement, Caillaux had supported Gout; Caillaux was between two cabinet posts at the time. By the time that Gout in turn charged Gueydan de Roussel with being behind the boiling pot, Caillaux had become minister of finance for the second time, the winegrowers in the Midi were up in arms, and the French politician became more circumspect in supporting anyone accused of artificial winemaking, let alone an American. And he was getting involved with Henriette.

From 1907 through 1911, while Caillaux was wooing Henriette on the sly and then divorcing Berthe, Gueydan de Roussel was becoming increasingly desperate. In late December 1910, he even gave the right-wing Thiébaud a letter of introduction to his sister, saying that, as she was getting divorced from Caillaux, perhaps she might have the dirt on Caillaux that Thiébaud theorized was the path to Gueydan de Roussel's innocence. Apparently nothing came of this.[37] The 1909 "Ton Jo" letter came back to haunt Gueydan de Roussel in 1914; as a *New York Times* headline put it, "American Involved in Caillaux Case." The French police traveled to Lausanne to question Gueydan de Roussel in connection with Henriette's trial. He declared under oath that he knew nothing of the 1901 "Ton Jo" letter to his sister until it was published in *Le Figaro*, and that although he had possessed some "intimate" correspondence of Caillaux's in 1909, he had returned it and had nothing to do with the current affair. Gueydan de Roussel's wife, however, gave an interview to a Swiss paper to the effect that if her husband published the documents he *did* have in his possession, then "political scandal would result even more greatly to the detriment of Mr. Caillaux," clearly referring to Gueydan de Roussel's own legal troubles.[38] By then Gueydan de Roussel had alternately invoked the French politician's name to prove his innocence and castigated him for having dropped him. This did not help his case with the Ministry of Justice. Exit the Caillaux strategy.

US Strategy

François Gueydan de Roussel had one more card up his sleeve—the US government. The advantage of having two networks was having two audiences. To his American contacts, it was as an American that he protested energetically against French injustice, repeatedly invoking his US citizenship as a cornerstone of his defense. The insistent and earnest tone in his appeal to the

State Department is itself proof that he believed that the write-to-your-congressman strategy would work on the basis of nationality alone. He contrasted his disappointment with France with full expectation of US protection and help. Here, too, he was sorely frustrated.

As one of Gueydan de Roussel's supporters wrote to his congressman, "We are prone to believe in this country that no nation on the face of the earth defends so jealously the rights of its citizens as the United States."[39] Gueydan de Roussel styled himself as an "honest but helpless American citizen."[40] He used his citizenship as a critical part of his defense strategy, and he was outraged when it was brought into question. It seems clear that his French rivals, as well as the French courts, saw him as American. The French legal decisions against him had required him to post bond as an American citizen.[41] Many of his French sympathizers also believed, given French domestic politics, that his best chance for help was to get the US government's backing.

However, in spite of the clear support of two consul generals, formal protection never came. On March 29, 1911, Gueydan de Roussel complained to Arthur Bailly-Blanchard, secretary of the Paris embassy:

> My task is arduous enough in having to fight against the enmity of the French Government covering its magistracy, without having to fight against my own Embassy, who seems to care more for the interests and consideration of the French Government than for those of an American Citizen. . . .[42]

Confidentially, he worried to his cousin Henry in Louisiana: "Is our Embassy at Paris independent from our home Gov't?"[43]

Bailly-Blanchard was another Louisianan, born in New Orleans in 1855 and educated at the University of Louisiana (before it was renamed after benefactor Paul Tulane). He went into business and journalism before going into the diplomatic service. He was a private secretary to the US minister in France in 1885 before serving in Russia; he next served as secretary to the US delegation at the Hague Peace Conference. He was back in Paris as second secretary of the US embassy in Paris in 1909, when Gueydan de Roussel turned to it for help.[44] Did Bailly-Blanchard have something against Gueydan de Roussel, or was he simply doing his duty? Bailly-Blanchard initially answered that the embassy could not intervene directly in what was a personal matter, but he said that he had sent an officious letter to the French Ministry of Foreign Affairs anyway; he suggested that Gueydan de Roussel write directly to the ministry. Castigating "*le jeune snob*" Bailly-Blanchard for his French sympathies, Gueydan de Roussel suspected him of dual loyalties; he was rumored to have received a French decoration, proof if need be that he had gone over to the other side.[45] The frustrated Gueydan de Roussel contrasted his own true American roots to those of his obstructer:

> Is he a direct descendent of Black Hawk or some other Indian Chief, has he rendered as many services to America as I have done, is his family's name engraved, like mine, on our dear American soil?[46]

Furious at Bailly-Blanchard's foot-dragging, Gueydan de Roussel accused him:

> WHO spread those doubts concerning my citizenship, in order that the Dep't of State should abandon me to those french wolves?
>
> WHO solicited the Coudert freres' incomplete and consequently false consultation, . . . ?
>
> WHO refused to allow my dear wife to interview our Ambassador, . . . ?
>
> Mr. BAILLY-BLANCHARD![47]

By early 1910, despairing of help through the Paris embassy, Gueydan de Roussel took another tack by writing to two Louisiana congressmen whom he hoped could intercede directly with the State Department. One was his first cousin, Henry Gueydan, son of Jean-Pierre, living in the town founded by his father and now state senator of Louisiana. The other was Albert Estopinal, US House representative for Louisiana from 1908 to 1919. The argument was simple: a foreign government had wronged Gueydan de Roussel, and he deserved protection from the US government. But protection depends on citizenship, and his transnational itinerary seems to have led to some doubts. Was he really American?

Gueydan de Roussel saw himself as an American. So did the French authorities. Only the US embassy seems to have had some doubts. He considered his American identity as both the source of his troubles and his only hope for salvation. His foreignness had clearly not endeared him to his jealous French neighbors. Although little proof exists that he was accused of artificial wine production simply because he was American—"everyone was accusing everyone of fraud" at the time[48] and French newspaper reports of Gueydan de Roussel's problems were mostly interested in his identity as Caillaux's brother-in-law[49]—however, as one of his Texas friends opined, the local French "rubes" saw him as the foreigner who'd carried off the coveted prize of the girl and the vineyard.[50] Gueydan de Roussel himself referred to "a decided unbridled antipathy, for which there was apparently no reason, save my nationality!"[51] He repeated over and over the words of an American lawyer in Paris, Edmond Kelly, that there was no hope for foreigners—usually reprised as no hope for *Americans*—in France.[52] As Gueydan de Roussel wrote:

> The American Citizen, more than any frenchmen, on account of his nationality, is liable to be ill-treated, illegally despoiled, dishonored and sentenced to emprisonment as I have been, but contrarily to frenchmen, he has not the advantage of being protected by any political party.[53]

Caught between two legal systems, Gueydan de Roussel was not shy about trying to get help from any quarter, but he put his greatest faith in the United States. When, to add American insult to French injury, the very authoritites to whom he had turned questioned his American defense strategy, he reeled from disbelief to outrage.

In light of the US Expatriation Law of 1907, was Frank, born a Louisianan François, still an American citizen? As if three

French lawsuits, the Winegrowers' Revolt, and his brother-in-law's philandering were not enough for one year, the US Congress passed a law in 1907—Gueydan de Roussel's own *annus horribilis*—making explicit certain conditions for loss of citizenship. Among other things, naturalized citizens would lose their American citizenship if they returned to their native country for more than two years. Gueydan de Roussel was himself American-born, but he came from a Franco-Louisianan family whose ties to France remained strong. He clearly had an excellent bilingual education, and he wrote to his cousins and connections in Louisiana, sometimes in flawless French (peppered with English expressions: "*Tu me diras*: Well, break his jaw!"[54]) and at other times in vivid, if not livid, English (with but the occasional telltale trace of quirky French capitalization). Yet the State Department questioned his citizenship. The issue turned on whether François *père* had ever been naturalized in the United States (only the patrilineal line interested the citizenship bureau) and whether François *fils* had moved to France while he was a minor, therefore returning de facto to his father's citizenship.

The dates of Frank's goings and comings are crucial. Did Frank move to France in 1880, as his son, William, later claimed, or in 1886, as an affidavit by his Texas friends attests? His friends stated that Frank moved to San Diego, Texas, at age seventeen, where he lived for the next eight years, working with his father in sheep raising, general merchandising, and banking. (Father and son appear in the 1880 San Diego census as a dry goods merchant and a store clerk.) Frank had served on jury duty and had become second assistant postmaster of the town. As they stated, "He has always enjoyed public esteem and confidence."[55] An upstanding American citizen, in sum.

Three sources argued that Gueydan de Roussel was possibly French: a law firm, the Bureau of Citizenship, and later his youngest, Swiss-born son. The embassy solicited an opinion from its counsel, the American firm of Coudert Brothers (itself of Franco-American heritage).[56] The Coudert opinion instilled doubt: "The Papers show that Mr. Gueydan was an American citizen, but has expatriated himself." The lawyers concluded somewhat contradictorily: "We however fail to see how you can intervene in his case, even if he still retains his American citizenship."[57] A US Bureau of Citizenship memo by none other than expatriation expert Richard Flournoy argued along similar lines: although Gueydan's father apparently had moved to the US at age thirteen, "and was virtually American," according to Gueydan, the latter's own citizenship would depend on whether his father had been naturalized before his son's birth. If not, the son also would be a Frenchman under the French Civil Code. Furthermore,

> if he established himself in the native land of his father before or at about the time of attaining his majority it seems to me that the Department should hold that he practically elected French nationality rather than American.[58]

Nothing seems to indicate that François *père* became a naturalized US citizen, yet nothing shows that François *fils*, American by virtue of birth on US soil, opted for French citizenship upon moving to France. And, if the Texas affidavit is to be believed, he moved to France at age twenty-five. The Office of the Solicitor concluded that Gueydan should avail himself of all possible French legal remedies, "and there is no ground for the intervention of this government in the case, even if it be held that he has retained his American citizenship."[59] The ball was back in the court of French jurisdiction.

Another, more self-serving, argument for Gueydan de Roussel's Frenchness came in the late 1930s from his son, William Gueydan de Roussel. Gueydan de Roussel's last child, born in Lausanne in 1908, argued forcefully that his father had been French, and that he, William, should be able to recover *his* French citizenship and heritage. He stated that his father had come to France in 1880 and had never renounced his French citizenship (which was not incompatible with his American citizenship), and that his father's subsequent Swiss naturalization was insignificant.

By 1940, however, William was a Vichy collaborator. He had gone to work for the soon-to-be-infamous Bernard Faÿ, French historian of early Franco-American relations, appointed by the Vichy government to head the National Library in France, replacing his evicted Jewish predecessor. William Gueydan de Roussel's job was to help Faÿ compile lists of Freemasons. He seemed desperate to abandon any American or Swiss citizenship that might get in the way. His concerns over citizenship predate the outbreak of World War II. He had been battling the French administration on the subject of his citizenship for several years, insisting that he should be able to recover the French citizenship of his ancestors, to which he claimed he was "ethnically and legally" entitled. But the French government stubbornly refused to recognize him as a French citizen owing to, according to William, "a concept of legality and the incapacity to make a decision which is characteristic of the old French bureaucracy"[60]—William's swipe at republican France versus its "modern" Vichy incarnation.

François Gueydan de Roussel himself was incensed at any notion that he was *not* an American. He vigorously denied a rumor that he had only maintained his US citizenship to avoid French military service. He suspected that his sisters had spread the story to please Caillaux, "who didn't want it to be said that he was an ally of Americans!"[61] Gueydan de Roussel forcefully and fatiguingly repeated his American ancestry, using the language necessary to disprove expatriation: that his father had left France at a young age, "with no intent of return." As for his own situation, Gueydan de Roussel claimed the opposite: that he had never planned on settling in France, that he had educated his children in England with the idea of their ultimately going to the United States, that he always registered at the American embassy, and that he had always maintained commercial ties and relations with relatives and friends in the US.[62] In the end, the embassy and the State Department may have had their doubts, but no proof showed that Gueydan was not an American citizen.

Perhaps the symbolic clincher of Gueydan de Roussel's Americanness may be seen in the very "Ton Joe" letter that he reproduced. Whereas the signature on Caillaux's 1901 letter to Berthe published in *Le Figaro* made the spelling "Ton Jo" a standard figure in French history books, when Gueydan de Roussel retyped

Caillaux's 1909 letter to Berthe, he transformed Caillaux into an Americanized "Joe." Spelling can be a telltale identity giveaway. Hobbies can be just as telling. One of Gueydan de Roussel's grandsons (tracked down thanks to Patricia Heard, historian of Gueydan, Louisiana), an affable septuagenarian named Olivier Gueydan living in Switzerland, told me by telephone that he still remembered his grandfather as "American." Over his lifetime, François Gueydan de Roussel had been interested in everything from cactus food machines and new methods of tinning tomatoes to hot air balloons. This affinity for "modernité" and new techniques impressed his grandson and helped defined François *fils* turned *grand-père* as an American in his Swiss grandson's eyes.[63]

Insults aren't what they used to be. The Gueydan Affair was not only a tale of troubled transnational ties. It was also an affair of outrage reinvented several times by the main protagonists. Reading the French judicial files, one assumes Gueydan de Roussel was guilty of manufacturing fake wine.[64] As he may have been. In any case, the Ministry of Justice refused his request for a new appeal, leaving his fate in the hands of the local yokels. Yet Gueydan de Roussel was thoroughly convinced that they were in league against him. As indeed they may have been.

But it is the level of moral indignation in his copious justifications that make Gueydan de Roussel's papers compelling reading of failed networking. Bubbling with anger, the American used French language and font à la the Dreyfus Affair, peppering his *La magistrature gangrenée* with a thrice-invoked Zola-esque "*J'accuse*" to the French minister of justice.[65] He also had his own variant:

> I CLAIM [*J'AFFIRME*]
> that the Judges HAVE LIED
> and that they have lied KNOWINGLY! . . .
> I CLAIM
> that [the investigating judge] also LIED,
> and that he lied KNOWINGLY! . . .
> I CLAIM
> that [the attorney general] committed a "cowardly act" in ordering a lawsuit to go forward against me in February 1907.[66]

When not comparing himself to Dreyfus, with Truth, Justice, and Honor, each one emblazoned in capital letters throughout his writings, he styled himself as David challenging Goliath.[67] Increasingly desperate, even pitiful by the end, Gueydan de Roussel was exasperated, and he was undoubtedly exasperating others. When he had not heard from US House Representative Albert Estopinal in a timely fashion, he sent him two dollars and asked that he cable him with a one-word reply: "Helpless" or "Protected."[68]

By 1910, Gueydan de Roussel's French father-in-law had died, his Franco-American sister was about to be divorced from her powerful husband, the US embassy was not helping, and his American cousins did not seem to be making much headway with the State Department. Cousin Henry finally suggested that Gueydan de Roussel go to Washington himself to plead his case. But complaining of the wear and tear that this affair was having on himself and his family, he once again compared himself to Dreyfus:

> Do you suppose, dear Henry, that if Dreyfus had personally pleaded his case he would have vanquished his enemies, the french Judges?
>
> No, of course not, and he would still be in his island had not his relations and friends pleaded in his favor with all their hearts.[69]

Exhausted, sleeping but three or four hours a night, in a "deplorable state of health and enervation," "the most I can do is to keep from becoming insane, mad, furiously mad," he wrote four years after having fled to Lausanne.[70] Estopinal felt obliged to apologize for their tone as he transmitted yet more documents on Gueydan's behalf to the secretary of state: "It is very evident that Mr. F. Gueydan de Roussel is under considerable mental strain in this matter."[71]

Leading lives referenced between two republics, the Gueydans were ultimately among the disenchanted. While for years Gueydan de Roussel peppered his ire with statements of belief that justice would prevail, sister Berthe outdid her brother's 188-page *La magistrature gangrenée* by venting her anger against

Caillaux in an adept two-volume historical critique of French politics published in 1925.[72] *Les rois de la République* seems to have been a best seller, having had three printings in one year, as the spurned first wife included her telling of her murderous rival's shooting of the *Le Figaro* director. Neither was Gueydan de Roussel's son, William, a friend of the republic. He wrote in 1940 of "the little sympathy [*le peu de compréhension*] that our family has had for republican institutions."[73] He embellished his grandfather's emigration story, by pushing the tale of the two brothers' New World adventures back to the turn of the nineteenth century, implying that his grandfather and uncle were refugees from the French Revolution. After becoming a Vichy collaborator during the Second World War, he went into his own exile, first in Argentina and then later in Chile, where he died in 1996.[74]

Only one protagonist's ultimate fate remains obscure: the farmer Boyer. As enraged as Gueydan de Roussel was, his relentless enemy outdid him. While Gueydan de Roussel complained of the "implacable hatred of this domestic Boyer against me," Boyer returned the compliment, denouncing Gueydan as a "fraud, a poisoner, a counterfeiter, a thief, an assassin, in a word the most scurrilous of bandits."[75]

On September 15, 1909, Boyer sent the first of a long series of threatening postcards to "François Gueydan, refugee" in Lausanne. He demanded money he considered his due and called Gueydan a "dirty cretin, bandit, *escroc*, assassin. Give me my 100,000 francs or your brains. Choose." He said he had a revolver and was a keen marksman, ready to meet Gueydan at the train station. In another card, with undeniable panache and a rare play on words, he reiterated that he was ready to fry Gueydan's brains, and not just with butter (like the sautéed French delicacy). By March 26, 1910, Boyer was on his fifty-fifth numbered postcard, promising a fifty-sixth. He also published leaflets smearing Gueydan's reputation, which he sent to France, the US, and Switzerland. And on one of his postcards to Lausanne, he closed with the forewarning: "Awaiting your reply, future cadaver."[76]

Gueydan de Roussel survived Boyer's postcards, as did Boyer himself. (In a last legal round, Gueydan de Roussel in absentia attacked Boyer for the death threats, but the French court was once again easy on Boyer; Boyer said he didn't really mean to kill Gueydan, and he got off with a small fine.) And Gueydan de Roussel didn't do badly in Switzerland. Having clearly given up on both the United States and France, he became a Swiss citizen, due to the "thorns of uprootedness," as his niece, the very French patriotic Isabelle Couturier de Chefdubois, disconsolately explained it.[77] (Worse yet, in her devout Catholic view, most of the family in Switzerland became Protestant, with the exception of François's wife and one son, who returned to Catholicism.[78]) François Gueydan de Roussel died in 1938, a becalmed Swiss citizen, dividing a hardly inconsiderable inheritance among his hardly inconsiderable progeny.[79] The future cadaver had met his fate. Peacefully after all.

2

Old History, New Historiography

François Gueydan de Roussel's transatlantic troubles make for a great story—even if the *Wine Spectator* never answered my letter. His difficulties may be unique, his rhetoric and typography as well—although the latter may have been a somewhat common literary form of exasperation at the time.[1] And not everyone caught between two countries has a cabinet minister as a brother-in-law and a US House representative as a cousin. But, specifics aside, Gueydan de Roussel's story makes us think about transnational figures in a new way. First, as by now well recognized, transnational families and networks are not solely a recent phenomenon. Second, although many mobile individuals have loved the life of in-betweenness, one can be caught in the snares. Third, networks—even powerful ones—do not always work. Fourth, when problems arise, states may be suspicious of their own citizens abroad, especially when foreign parentage is involved. Finally, individuals may attempt to use their own citizenship strategically, but it does not always work. We thus need to think more carefully about how states see their citizens abroad and how individuals abroad use their citizenship—or try to—in times of trouble.

Before turning to the state's view of its citizens abroad (chapters 3 and 4) and individuals' use of their home state (chapter 5), a historiographic interlude is called for. We do not need a Google Ngram Viewer to note that the word "transnationalism" has become a favorite term among scholars in the last couple of decades. But is it a historic phenomenon, or is it a historiographic one? Is it a social "reality," a concept, or a methodological approach? Is it a political question that foresees and participates in the end of the nation-state? Or is it an intellectual fad?

Definitions and Use

The term "transnational" may be traced back to the nineteenth century, but then more poignantly (and more frequently) to Randolph Bourne, who, in 1916, used it to defend immigrant America against the xenophobic naysayers.[2] Political scientists Robert O. Keohane and Joseph S. Nye, Jr., launched the word in their field in the early 1970s as a way of going beyond interstate relations to include "intersocietal intercourse." In 1971, they first published a special issue of the journal *International Organization*, which quickly came out a year later as a separate book with the same name: *Transnational Relations and World Politics*.[3] Keohane and Nye had recently joined the journal as editors, and the project grew out of their dissatisfaction with the study of international organizations per se. They sought instead to start from "the patterns of interaction in the world." They noted that Raymond Aron (who used the term "transnational society") and others had already used a similar term, but Keohane and Nye argued for greater attention to the "interactions between governments and transnational society and in the transnational coalitions among subunits of governments."[4] The volume included studies of multinational businesses (crediting Raymond Vernon's work on the topic as inspiration for the volume), the Catholic Church, the Ford Foundation, revolutionary movements, trade unions, scientific networks, and even outer space (and the interaction of state, business, universities, and NGOs in exploration). James A. Field, Jr., began the volume with a breathless overview of transnationalism from the early nineteenth century onward, remarking that the last two centuries had been notable for their "great fluidity as capital, labor, and entrepreneurial and technological skills acquired a mobility never before approached." Field pointed to a variety of indicators, from the spread of potatoes and cotton to the importance of improved transportation and population movements, and he emphasized the "shrinking and linking" of the world thanks to philanthropists, missionaries, business, and the US government (which became a transnational actor via the Peace Corps).[5] But the overall question of the journal volume had to do with how transnational relations affect governments and international organizations. Which is more powerful in international/transnational relations: states or markets? As Keohane and others later explained it, their interest in transnationalism was based on contemporary assumptions about pluralism, positing not just economic challenges to state power, but also those coming from a variety of actors, including groups from civil society.[6]

However, in the end, transnational relations, as a research agenda for political scientists, flopped. Already, in the 1971 volume, Robert Gilpin raised a skeptical brow, arguing that both transnational actors and transnational processes are nonetheless dependent upon political and interstate relationships. (He added that multinationals are, after all, mostly American corporations, acting largely consistently with the political interest of the United States.) Gilpin did not see the nation-state as dissolving any time soon.[7] As some of the journal editors reflected twenty-five years later, transnational relations theory never took off for two reasons. On the one hand, state-centered theorists pushed back, like Steven Krasner, in 1976:

> In recent years, students of international relations have multinationalized, transnationalized, bureaucratized, and transgovernmentalized the state until it has virtually ceased to exist as an analytic construct. . . . This perspective is at best profoundly misleading.[8]

On the other hand, transnational relations theory was too hard to operationalize; cause and effect were too difficult to specify when too many variables were involved.[9]

The term straggled on in the 1970s and 1980s, most often in conjunction with a critique of "multinationals," the term of choice from the 1960s, relating to nonstate, private corporations straddling nations and continents, wheeling and dealing across borders. Joseph Camilleri, for example, argues in "Economic Transnationalism: The New Imperialism" (a chapter in *Civilization in Crisis*) that "by taking the philosophy of free enterprise and the concept of the division of labour to their ultimate and logical conclusion, multinationalism has helped to create a global political economy based on hierarchy and inequality."[10]

Thus drawing a straight line from Bourne to the present misreads transnationalism's rise. Political scientists of the 1970s never referenced Bourne's 1916 article. The term fizzled or came to be used briefly as a critical term for capitalism gone awry—which is a very different use than the heralding of transnationalism to come. Not until the early 1990s did the term "transnationalism" jog up the usage graph and well beyond Bourne, international relations, and political science to describe, among other things, new approaches to American history and migration studies. But now, it was used in a much more positive vein.

Multiple words are available to name the phenomenon, and other terms, both older and more recent, may transmit a similar meaning. The most obvious is "international" (a recurrent question among seminar students). Although "internationalism" was a self-avowed political slogan from the nineteenth century to the mid-twentieth century, the term today usually refers to (diplomatic) relations between states. "Inter," referring to *relations between* states, is not the same as "trans," which can imply *transcending* both states. Yet international organizations are happily being scrutinized anew through a more transnational lens that focuses on the links that helped construct and sustain them, rather than solely on the functioning of the organizations themselves.[11] When the topic is neither states nor firms, an older term, "cosmopolitanism," is sometimes still invoked to describe transnational individuals, but the term usually refers to an elite social class, be they *salonnières* or intellectuals, not to mention the fact that "cosmopolitanism" has also been used in different periods as an anti-Semitic euphemism.

Both parts of the term have been scrutinized. "Trans" can mean either *between* or *beyond*, as Rogers Brubaker has suggested in his analysis of (transgender and transracial) categories and individuals.[12] More problematic for historians is the "nation" at the heart of the concept. What about regions? And what about time periods before the nation-state? Studying transnationalism questions the nation while simultaneously calling attention to it, as Michael Werner has argued. And in that respect, transnationalism also clearly situates history in space.[13] While some have argued for the pertinence of translocality, the term "transnationalism" has not been limited to modern nation-state borders. It has recently been attributed to all sorts of border crossings throughout different periods, back to ancient and medieval times.[14]

The study of transnationalism, as it has developed since the 1990s, has been furthermore very interdisciplinary. Indeed, in 2004, Akira Iriye chided historians for being slower than scholars in other disciplines in disengaging from their parochial and national ways in these globalizing times.[15] Two decades after the political scientists, cultural studies scholars began to use the concept in the early 1990s: Arjun Appadurai in 1991, Paul Gilroy in 1993.[16] Anthropologists Nina Glick Schiller, Linda Basch, and Cristina Blanc-Szanton, as we will see, "invented" the term in migration studies at the same time.[17] In a very different field, Ian Tyrrell used the term in a 1991 article, arguing against the unbounded hubris of American exceptionalism.[18] More generally, transnationalism has helped expand horizons beyond the nation-state and exceptionalist narratives.

But transnationalism has not been without its detractors. A substantive critique was raised in France, not just as a question of chauvinism. On May 31, 2006, a heated dispute broke out at the annual general meeting of the Centre de recherches historiques (CRH), the major history research lab at the French graduate school, the École des Hautes Études en Sciences Sociales (EHESS).[19] The subject was transnationalism. Often a lively affair, the CRH meeting discussed, once again, the internal organization of the center. It was about *axes*, a frequent French bureaucratico-conceptual issue. *Axes* are supposed to represent the main intellectual priorities of a research lab; they are the way in which colleagues can get together for seminars and conferences; and they are also a way of allocating resources, being the rhetorical justification proffered to the funding agencies. So the debate was about how to best develop new priorities for the institutional and intellectual life of the wide-ranging CRH, where members include ancient, medieval, and contemporary historians with a core group of early modernists.

Transnationalism was one suggestion among others, but in this case, the proposed "axe transnational" led to a verbal fistfight. There were those who were for it; there were those dead against it, including one historian who claimed that it was simply one more unnecessary trendy American import.[20] In the end, the *axe* was created, a CRH conference was subsequently held, and a book was published, including a minority report on the part of some of the skeptics.[21]

Ultimately the question came down to a larger and more important question: what is the best way of investigating the history of a place: by conducting in-depth research into its political, economic, social, and/or cultural ways and manners, or by expanding the breadth to take into account external and interactive factors? The debate is an ongoing one between the value of deeply foraged local knowledge and more general approaches that may extend to the global in reach. In the end, the debate also turns around questions of scale and scope: small research topics versus large research topics; micro approaches versus macro approaches; and more recently, the local versus the global. Fortunately, as we will see, these are not stiff or stuffy dichotomies, as some heated discussions may have it. It is rather, in Jacques Revel's felicitous phrase, a question of "*jeux d'échelles*" (differing historical scales).[22]

Other problems beset the "transnational turn"—besides that of "turns" in general.[23] The term "transnationalism" may refer to history or historiography. In the first case, it refers to a description of a historical phenomenon. I argue, along with others, that transnationalism, as a historical practice, is not new, contrary to what many more present-oriented globalists (usually in non-historical disciplines) have insisted. The "transnationalism" of people, goods, and ideas has clearly existed before our own globalizing times. The other use of the term "transnational" refers to its "discovery," or its current use as a new way of understanding and writing about the phenomenon. This historiographic turn, transnationalism as an academic perspective, on the other hand, *is* new. The problem, however, is that this latter use is sometimes elided with calls for other historiographic approaches: comparative history, connected or entangled history, *histoire croisée*, circulations, global or world history.[24] Each term means different things to different specialists while often being used ecumenically, in an undifferentiated manner, by other scholars.[25] Comparative history, a heuristic approach to phenomena occurring in different places (or periods), may or may not be transnational, particularly if "transnational" implies *interaction* among historical actors rather than just the comparative post hoc (albeit interesting) ruminations of historians. Nor is transnational history necessarily global history either, to the extent that the latter implies a truly worldwide scope, while the former can be limited to the study of the circulation of ideas, people, or goods across one or more borders. Transnationalism as a research agenda is thus both new and capacious, sometimes to a fault.

Yet despite, or because of, its multiple meanings and usages, transnationalism has caught on. It has even been enrolled by the European Union to describe its European integration project.[26] More importantly, for our purposes, transnationalism as an academic pursuit has spread among the social sciences and humanities and has been particularly fruitful in abetting historians' seek-and-find function. It has helped to stress earlier historical links, borrowings, and adaptations. It has helped to better emphasize the porousness of state and identity boundaries. The interconnectedness and interactions of the past have been (re) found. If the historic phenomenon of transnationalism is not exactly new, its historiographic conceptualization is.[27] And, in return, this new historiography has helped rediscover an older historical phenomenon.

As I will use it below, transnationalism, and more specifically, a transnational approach, does not merely extend geographic scope. It implies interrogating the relationships between regions—especially, but not only, as nations. And above all, it means questioning the impact of the circulation, mobility, and interactions on all individuals, parties, and things involved.

The Transnational Moment

Beyond problems inherent in defining a historic phenomenon and determining the best term to describe it, we can thus speak of a current "transnational moment" marked by a widespread use of the term. But then the question arises: why now?[28] Why has a transnational focus blossomed since the early 1990s? A series of explanations has been suggested, from the implosion of the Soviet Union to the expansion of Europe by law and geographic scope to renewed regional or multicultural identities. Many of the explanations are linked to a questioning of the nation-state, from without or from within. As a consequence, some have foreseen the withering of the nation-state along with its historians, a role that Pierre-Yves Saunier has described as "teeter[ing] on the edge of prescription and prophecy."[29] Is this a product of the 1990s itself? Has the enthusiasm for transnationalism characterized a specific period of writing from the increased free-trade globalization talk of the Reagan and Thatcher 1980s through the 1989 fall of the Berlin Wall, and on through the shock of September 11, 2001? Will the Trumpian era of walls be its final death knell?

The advent of the transnational agenda may be situated economically and politically. It must also be linked to the larger epistemological trends of the late twentieth century, notably poststructuralism, which emerged as a salutary critique of structuralism. Thanks to poststructuralism, focus has (re)turned to the subject and the individual and his or her agency. In recent years, scholars have insisted on multiple or hybrid identities and on movement itself in opposition to older notions of stasis linked to structures and structuralism. The notions of flexibility and mobility have been the logical corollary, which scholars, themselves sometimes frenetic conference and keynote travelers of a new sort, have eagerly embraced. They have also accompanied or encouraged such fruitful new fields of research as "borderland studies," an increased interest in elite multiple-passport holders, and new studies of international organizations or of missionaries.[30]

Furthermore, the transnational "moment" has been expressed differently, depending on the discipline. At least three genealogies of its emergence are evident. Political scientists, as we have seen, first used the term in recent times. Since the early 1990s, two other fields have most loudly claimed the use of the term: US history and migration studies.

In 1991, Ian Tyrrell (Australian scholar of the US) published an article in the *American Historical Review* entitled "American Exceptionalism in an Age of International History."[31] He argued for the necessity of transnationalism as a way of escaping an overly, if not overtly, nationalist interpretation of US history. In this context, "transnational" became a programmatic way of "internationalizing American history," a call that has been energetically undertaken, with impressive results, by Tyrrell, Akira Iriye, Thomas Bender, Carl Guarneri, David Thelen, Donna R. Gabaccia, and others.[32] These writings took place within a debate over American exceptionalism. Transnational history could be a way of overcoming a parochialism or isolationism in American history and historiography. With different emphases, Thelen questioned the national, and the eventual disappearance of the nation-state, in order to transcend it; Bender insisted on the importance of understanding the global context in order to understand a national American history; Iriye emphasized, among other things, the importance of using non-US archives whereas Guarneri encouraged comparative studies; and Gabaccia argued that US immigration history is thoroughly intertwined with foreign relations. Other US historians, such as Africanist Philip

Curtin, as well as China-scholar-turned-world-historian Adam McKeown, also innovated with global history before it became à la mode.[33] Tyrrell claimed paternity for "transnationalism,"[34] while, in another field and another discipline, a different genesis of transnational studies was occurring.

It is perhaps hardly surprising that "transnationalism" has caught on in migration studies. What better use of the term than in referring to the movement of people across borders? Three American anthropologists launched the term a year after Tyrrell's article in the *American Historical Review*—although they did not seem to know about Tyrrell's usage, nor he theirs—a mutual ignorance of different fields that persists. In 1992, Nina Glick Schiller, Linda Basch, and Cristina Blanc-Szanton published a now-classic introduction to their edited conference volume, *Towards a Transnational Perspective on Migration: Race, Class, Ethnicity, and Nationalism Reconsidered*, in which they proposed transnationalism as a new approach to migration studies, superseding the previous analytic models of either assimilation or ethnicity. The three authors may have exaggerated the traits of their epistemological adversaries—assimilation ("contributing both to a myth of social mobility . . . and to the construction of American nationalism") and ethnicity ("discrete, tightly bounded groups")—to make their point. But their emphasis on the circulation of money, goods, and people between countries of origin and countries of settlement struck a chord.[35] Their examples came from their own fields of research, from the money and goods sent home to the Philippines by Filipino immigrants in the United States; to the construction of a sports complex in Haiti thanks to prosperous Haitians and Haitian organizations in New York; along with the example of an import network of Grenadian products for Grenadians living in the United States.

The early articles and volumes on transnationalism in migration studies were explicitly programmatic, and they sought to overturn the previous paradigms of understanding migration: from the assimilation studies of the Chicago School of Sociology of the 1920s to research in the 1950s to 1960s that also focused largely on the integration of immigrants, to the late 1960s to 1980s reversals that brought to the fore the obverse, the immigrants' ethnicity. Thanks to Glick Schiller et al., the literature shifted decidedly to transnationalism in the 1990s. The "ethnic renaissance" that had swept away the idea of immigrants simply melting into an undifferentiated assimilatory pot and had spawned a vibrant series of community/ethnicity studies in the 1970s and 1980s was now superseded in the 1990s by the language of globalization and transnationalism in both the sociology and history of migration.[36] Fascination with new modes of transportation and communication—first the expansion of long-distance phoning, then satellite dishes, email, and ultimately Skype—seemed to point toward a new process of circulation, allowing effective and affective physical and virtual roundtrips between homeland and hostland in ways never known before. The newness of this mobility—or rather a renewed sense of a new mobility—called for a new methodology, according to its early proponents.

A decade after having launched transnationalism in migration studies, Glick Schiller and sociologist Andreas Wimmer argued subsequently and more explicitly that it was a needed response to "methodological nationalism."[37] They added that they were not blithe cosmopolitans and that scholars should not fall into the trap of methodological fluidism, either. Wimmer and Glick Schiller also included a cautionary statement against too great a technological determinism and against the tendancy to see the past in static terms, both arguments that are invoked to better underline the fluidity of the present. However, this cautionary part of their argument is rarely cited. It is their criticism of methodological nationalism, highlighted in the article's title, that is most often named. Sociologists enthusiastically embraced transnationalism, notably Alejandro Portes and Steven Vertovec, but not without some constructive criticism from other sociologists and anthropologists more interested in historic questions, such as Nancy Foner, Ewa Morawska, and Roger Waldinger.[38] A second wave of transnational studies has subsequently admitted that technology may be a difference in degree rather than in kind, that globalization is not completely new after all, and that the state continues to play an important role in different forms of "*long-distance nationalism*" and "*transborder citizenry*."[39]

The Newness Debate

Globalization itself is not new, although the widespread focus on its late-twentieth-century variant has most often ignored past precedents. Yet historians have patiently pointed out that its political, economic, or religious (a transnational phenomenon par excellence) manifestations have numerous predecessors, from the circulation of ancient relics to the Greek merchant diaspora, to the great eras of discovery to empires and colonization. (Indeed, the "barbarian" invasions have been reclassified as "migrations.") Closer to our time period, one has to look only at the more recent globalization of the late nineteenth/early twentieth century.[40]

A "newness debate" has emerged in migration studies with regard to transnationalism attributed to migrants. The interdisciplinarity of migration studies has led not only to appropriations but to tensions as well, notably with regard to this question. The first special issue devoted to transnationalism in the *Journal of American Ethnic History* (Winter–Spring 2006) stressed the interdisciplinary, as well as the international, perspective of the concept, while also insisting that the phenomenon was not new. Articles in the journal had already hailed the "transnational" activity of Italian workers, Chinese families, and Belgian glass workers. In the following issue, Matthew Frye Jacobson vigorously reiterated, "More 'Trans-,' less 'National,'" arguing that "Ours is a 'transnational' field by definition."[41]

A spirited discussion has emerged among the disciplines that could be summarized as Skype versus letters. For many historians, the anthropologists' and sociologists' "discovery" of transnational immigrants seems to ignore, deform, or, at the very least, flatten the past. Historians have objected that nineteenth- and twentieth-century immigrants have always been, in essence, transnationals. Modern migration is an inherently transnational activity that does not date solely to the late twentieth century. As such, it is a phenomenon that historians have been studying for decades, if somewhat like Molière's Monsieur Jourdain, speaking prose without knowing it: we have been doing transnational history without naming it as such. The reality is old even if the concept is new.

David Gerber, early historian of immigrant letters was one of the first to formulate a critique of the supposed novelty of transnationalism from the perspective of immigration history.[42] As he pointed out, during the mass migrations of the nineteenth century, transatlantic circulation was intense, in a way that today's jet setters have difficulty imagining. Immigrants remained attached to their homelands, all the while negotiating their transnational identities. As to the withering of the nation-state, he was even more explicit, declaring firmly, in 2000, "The nation-state . . . is hardly in its death throes."[43] Furthermore, the technological novelty argument also leaves most historians cold, resting, as José Moya has put it, "on a presentist and exaggerated estimation of the novelty and magnitude of late-twentieth century technological innovations in transportation and communications."[44]

The "newness debate" may thus be inherent to differences among disciplines. I suggest that the question is a temporally comparative one, with sociologists and anthropologists creating a temporal contrast in order to insist on a radical contemporary difference with the past, whereas most historians have taken a temporally comparative view that rather emphasizes similarities between past and present practices. Historians thus point out examples of continuity from the past, while anthropologists and sociologists insist more generally on the novelty of the present. Historians may then complain that contemporary social scientists ignore or minimize past examples. Anthropologists and sociologists may dismiss past examples that seem to pale in relation to their analyses of the present.[45] In sum, while most anthropologists and sociologists still largely hail transnationalism as a recent phenomenon (a disciplinary bias?), historians (and some of their social science allies) have claimed déjà vu (a disciplinary bias?): nineteenth- and twentieth-century migrants, as well as their twentieth-century historians, have always been transnationals, even if they might not have been recognized and named as such.

Historians of migration have thus been at pains to remind the disciplines-of-the-new that it is not just today's new technologies that have permitted cross-border connections.[46] Many nineteenth-century immigrants already practiced circular movement and remigration. The Gueydan family was not unusual in this respect. Other migrants remained actively involved in their home countries' politics from abroad, created homeland associations, returned home from time to time, and sent money and letters even more frequently.[47] Granted, contact was slower when letters were marked "ss.Champlain" and had to reach the boat on time. But people already sent money home (remittances are decidedly not new, although there was no centralized Western Union to track them in the past), and they were amazingly mobile even a century ago. The speed of transportation and communication is a relative concept. (Imagine the novelty of just ten days for a transatlantic crossing by steamship instead of a month by sail.) And mobility in the past was more frequent than the assimilatory imagination allows. The circulation of money, goods, and people between countries of origin and settlement has existed abundantly since the mass migrations of the nineteenth century.[48]

Yet, beyond arguing that the *historic phenomenon* is not particularly new, migration historians, too, have embraced a new transnational *perspective*. Consequently, the scholarly vocabulary itself has changed, and the prefixes have been dropped. "Immigrants" have become "migrants" as the term of choice. Dropping the "im-" allows for greater emphasis on mobility and multidirectionality instead of a one-way (assimilatory) process. Among other things, this has placed new emphasis on the countries of origin and a better integration of the history of emigration with that of immigration.[49]

The virtue of a new name for an old phenomenon must not be underestimated. "Transnational," as a concept, has brought new vigor to migration history. It has raised interesting comparative questions about present and past forms of movement and about the impact of new technologies (steamships then, Skype now) on transportation, communication, and connectedness; and it has accompanied the study of mobility per se. Although "transnationalism" has become so prevalent that it is often used as a simple, albeit redundant, equivalent for migrations past and present (as in the "transnational migrant"), the more interesting meaning of the term is related not just to the fact that migrants have crossed borders or may maintain some of their home identities. Transnationalism emphasizes the back-and-forth-ness of interconnected ties and how migrants have been and are actively able to keep in touch with their homelands via remittances, travel home, and so on. One could say that, thanks to the other disciplines, historians have reexamined sources and uncovered the long-term connections that many migrants always maintained with kith, kin, and places of origin. Yet while agreeing with the sociologists and anthropologists as to the heuristic value of analyzing transnational ties, historians have, by stressing the anteriority of the phenomenon, been uniquely situated to question the foundation of much of the other disciplines' "newness" argument. And, as I argue, historians are also well placed to question the seamlessness of transnationalism itself.

Transnationalism and Agency

One could argue, moreover, that transnationalism in migration studies has paradoxically led to two seemingly contradictory understandings of the term. On the one hand, transnationalism can be seen as a sort of *super-ethnicity*, although it is rarely declared as such.[50] Numerous studies have shown how transnational citizens may live in one place while remaining attached to another, visiting often and remaining tied to their homeland's people, places, identity, and networks. While helping migration studies become more global and emphasizing relations with the home countries, this transnationalism, in effect, reinforces an ethnic history that describes migrants maintaining contact with their cultures of origin.[51]

On the other hand, transnationalism has been heralded perhaps even more often as a sign of the end of fixed national ties. In this respect, it very often represents a supranational *super-agency* that implies the existence of an ultimately "anational" citizen of the world, someone who is attached to everywhere and nowhere. The celebratory transnationalism of this second usage has certainly been best expressed by the anthropologists and sociologists who introduced the term.[52] But it has led even historians of the national to ask whether the nation is still pertinent in a world of seemingly ever-frenetic mobility constrained only by body scans. Studies of dual nationality have blossomed, along with the notion of postnational membership.[53] In a related mode, the agency of early globetrotters has been fascinatingly resurrected, along with their translators and other key go-betweens in the early modern and modern transnational worlds.[54]

Transnationalism is thus perhaps the most recent avatar of agency. As Paul A. Kramer has pointed out more generally, "transnational works sometimes [convey] a breathless sense of freedom, while historians of the imperial [produce] grim accounts of domination."[55] Historians of migration, in a field that initially emerged out of labor history, have certainly never underestimated the difficulties of workers' movement and the often harsh conditions of readjustment. But migration history, too, has followed the more general poststructural move. Studies of the structural oppression of migration systems and grim secondary labor markets have given way to a celebration of migrants' own involvement. The historiography has thus shifted not just from assimilation to ethnicity to transnationalism, but, in other ways, from the lachrymose Oscar Handlin (1951) mode of describing alienated, "uprooted" immigrants to the more resilient "transplanted" image forged by John Bodnar (1987) to an emphasis on ethnicity as a shield from the emotional rift of displacement.

From there it was a short step from heralding immigrant strikers to emphasizing newcomers' agency as a welcome historiographic response to victimization.[56]

Yet this more general epistemological shift in the social sciences—from an emphasis on structures to a focus on agency—has had an ironic impact on migration historiography. I argue that poststructuralism and structuralism are still at odds in the migration literature, representing two approaches that do not always speak to one another. The turn to individual agency and fine-tuned anthropological and cultural studies of multiple and changing identities have captured the attention of many, while analyses of the state and its relationship to its immigrants has become a powerful focus of the new citizenship studies since the 1990s. On the one hand, the latter have fruitfully focused on the state and the ways in which its various meanings of citizenship have excluded large groups of people within the United States from "social citizenship": immigrants, women, blacks, Native Americans.[57] On the other hand, more socio-anthropological and cultural studies have argued explicitly or implicitly that the state is as irrelevant as the literal and metaphoric borders that are porous and easily crossable, allowing immigrants to stay in touch with their home folk and folkways. One set of studies thus points to the continued salience of the state, the other to its decline. One could argue that these two approaches—citizenship studies and agency-focused research—represent (important) variants on the old assimilation-versus-ethnicity debate: exploring the state and its citizenship (and assimilatory) concerns on the one hand; examining individuals' cultural retention, now aided by modern forms of telecommunication on the other. While the assimilation paradigm postulated a rupture between past and present for immigrants, the ethnicity paradigm and transnationalism theorists have argued for increasing levels of continuity in the migration experience. Today, while some social historians have forcefully "brought the state back in," others have turned to the anthropological subject. Some research has bridged the gap, focusing on individual responses (lawsuits) and state restrictions.[58] But by and large, these contrasting approaches—structure versus agency, states versus individuals, citizenship versus transnationalism—nonetheless have one thing in common. All of them have focused largely on *im*migration and questions of identity (both that of the individual and that of the nation-state) at the place of settlement.

Agency, like structure, has undoubtedly been with the field of migration history since the early uses of oral history and autobiographies, if not heralded as such. Today, such sources are read for the testimony of the courage and pluck of ocean crossers more than for the structural constraints surrounding their movement. Go-betweens and cultural brokers have become the focus of numerous fascinating studies, if not necessarily by migration historians per se, from Natalie Zemon Davis's sixteenth-century "trickster traveler," Leo Africanus, to Sanjay Subrahmanyam's early modern cast of characters in *Three Ways to be an Alien*, or Sarah Abrevaya Stein's itinerant feather merchants.[59] Nobody claims that the adventures of past voyagers were always smooth, and their new biographers have noted well the travails of their travels. Leo Africanus, after all, was captured by Spanish corsairs and did prison time in Rome, and Subrahmanyam's subtitle is explicit: *Travails and Encounters in the Early Modern World*. His heroes encountered wildly oscillating fortunes in their travels hither and yon, while Stein's merchants suffered when the ostrich fad faded.

Migration historians have taken up the gauntlet of transnationalism with fine studies that both decry older nation-based histories of *im*migration and celebrate the ingenuity and resourcefulness of migrants' agency. Matthew Frye Jacobson urged migration historians to work hard to scrape the stubbornly sticky nation-state gum off their shoes. Dirk Hoerder, after his 750-page history of a millennium of migration systems ranging from the Atlantic to the Mediterranean to the Pacific oceanic worlds, explicitly argued for the importance of agency and a better understanding of "transcultural" (the term he prefers to "transnational") lives. This, he argued, can furthermore help bridge the disciplinary divide between the social sciences and the humanities.[60] Adam McKeown pointed to the transnationalism inherent in Chinese migrant networks from Peru to Chicago to Hawaii, while Philip Kuhn stressed the merchant bridgeheads of overseas Chinese migrants, the niches and corridors they created, and more generally the ways in which they constantly adapted to changing historical contexts. Jesse Hoffnung-Garskof has shown quite well how the exchanges of people and popular culture between New York and Santo Domingo illustrate how migrants have been able to use adopted ideas from both places to understand themselves, just as Deborah Cohen has highlighted the importance of bracero agency in contrast to previous stories of structured oppression.[61] As Mae Ngai has summarized the new trend:

> Transnational history offers an opportunity to alter the master narratives of national histories. . . . By directing attention to the circuits and flows of social forces and discourses that span nations and cultures, we unfasten the blinders of national history. In a sense it is an indirect approach, which hopes by way of the broader context to deflate claims of national greatness and to gesture to histories that are more connected, more aware and of a piece with the modern world.[62]

Furthermore, biography has become a favored mode of expression, highlighting the courage and creativity of individual actors. Microhistory has been reaffirmed in this respect as an important scale of transnational history.[63]

The historiographic newness, without question, has had a salutary impact on research: a new concept has forced us to ask new questions of our (old) sources (and to discover new sources). The transnational moment has encouraged us to reread our documents, rethink the links that past immigrants maintained with their countries of origin, and question the quantitative and qualitative differences of communication by letter versus Facebook. If in the past we read the archives for information concerning different forms of assimilation or integration and then concerning elements of cultural maintenance and traces of ethnic identity, today we reread them to seek out transnational links and other forms of physical or virtual connection with the homeland.

The Limits

Yet if the transnational turn has largely taken the form of excitement at the depth and breadth of connections; and if, for the late twentieth century, it has become a heroic tale of multiple passports in which flexibility and movement are the watchwords of a poststructural emphasis on fluidity and agency; and if historians have shown that earlier individuals also fit the bill, a nagging question remains. Is transnationalism as easy as it looks, past or present?

We can also use historical sources to explore some of the drawbacks involved. No one has argued that life was easy for Chinese coolies, Italian masons, Dominican domestics, or Mexican fruit pickers, but the recent focus—by historians, sociologists and anthropologist alike—on the possibilities of interconnectedness has more often emphasized the agency of mobility while minimizing the obstacles. The problem, I argue, is that, along the way, we have lost explicit focus on the difficulties embedded in the lived practice of transnationalism.

One objection to the transnational lens has already been raised: a class bias inherent in many transnational studies. As sociologists Sallie Westwood and Annie Phizacklea have pointed out, not all transnational actors are rich, although the early literature has more often focused on the elite. Transnationals may be rich or poor, but the celebration of the legal and economic freedom to move has often focused more on transnational entrepreneurs than on sweatshop workers per se. Westwood and Phizacklea have questioned the term's limitations by looking at the different forms of mobility in relation to social class.[64] Sociologist Alain Tarrius has studied contemporary mobile merchants at both ends of the economic spectrum, from international businessmen circulating within Europe—analyzing their boredom and sense of rootlessness—to Mediterranean women criss-crossing the sea with more modest goods to sell at market, not to mention his more recent study of the globalization of criminality.[65] Historian Marie-Claude Blanc-Chaléard has suggested the term "poor man's transnationalism" to describe those constrained by colonial history.[66]

Doubts about a certain heroization of the transnational figure have also been expressed. In his prescient critique, Gerber criticized the early anthropologists for overemphasizing the agency of their subjects—their ruses, their passports—leading to an overly optimistic vision of their transnationalism. Anthropologist Aihwa Ong, who invented the term "flexible citizenship," criticized too great an insistence on the anthropological subject's power to oppose structures. Studying the Hong Kong cosmopolitan elite, globetrotters par excellence, she insisted on the fact that "[c]ultural politics [are] embedded in specific power contexts"; the state, the family, and economic regimes all have an impact on border-crossings and may even encourage or discourage them for their own ends. (States can themselves use flexible notions of citizenship and sovereignty.) As American studies scholar Simon Turner explained with regard to "the dilemmas and conflicts of transnational engagement," there is a fundamental tension: "It is important to avoid the illusion that flows are liberating while closure is restrictive." And, as historian Sanjay Subrahmanyam concluded in his otherwise upbeat discussion of early modern go-betweens, intermediaries themselves are frequently limited by "a bounded rationality," constrained "between a rock and a hard place."[67] Individuals "plot and maneuver"[68]—à la François Gueydan de Roussel—but transnational relations are anchored in power relations. And Gueydan de Roussel was decidedly unsuccessful.

Yet these reminders of limits have been insufficiently heeded. Historians can help rethink the complexities of transnationalisms past and the networks that arguably underpin them.[69] Even among the transnational elite, "forms of friction", as Subrahmanyam says, or "*frottements*," as socio-anthropologist Pierre Bouvier would have it, are part of the story.[70] After the excitement of its discovery, it is time to raise questions about the facility of transnationalism past or present.

Two major limits to transnationalism are well-known obstacles on the migration path, although they are rarely discussed as such: xenophobia and immigration policy. They have not been examined as the roadblocks that they are to transnational movement, but the abundance of literature on these subjects obviates a long discussion in this book. Suffice it to remind us here that both anti-immigrant sentiment and legal restrictions have been concomitant with human mobility itself. Both wax and wane historically. As John Higham argued in his classic analysis of American nativism, anti-immigrant attitudes increase especially when the host society itself is in existential crisis.[71] And when it takes on legislative and bureaucratic form, it becomes part and parcel of the material barrier to movement.[72] To the extent that water has been a metaphor of choice for migration movement (waves, flows, streams, osmosis), the faucet function is the pertinent metaphor here, particularly insofar as states can turn it off at will.

Scholarly literature on immigration restriction is an old and still burgeoning field of research. For the United States, numerous books have examined the ways in which the country succeedingly enacted xenophobic laws barring Chinese, and then Eastern and Southern Europeans, with thinly veiled racist exclusion and quota acts.[73] And the restrictions were not implemented only at the Ellis or Angel Island borders, but, as Aristide Zolberg pointed out, the United States, like other states, also effected "remote control" at consulates or other embarkation ports.[74] Scholarship on other countries, such as France, has also focused on the ways in which immigration policy has both fluctuated and been a way of defining the state and nation itself.[75] Comparative work on other countries of immigration has expanded along these lines. Political scientists have shown how immigration control in Europe has been structured (and also failed, although it does give immigrants access to certain rights), and legal scholars have emphasized how the immigration law itself creates and maintains sovereignty: "migration law is at its core a border construction site."[76] The comparative literature has increasingly become international, from studying numerous comparisons among European countries to comparisons among settler states.[77] However, as I will argue, the time is ripe to focus on the frictions of movement per se. Exciting new work has started to examine the difficulties of the *lieux de passage* or the route itself: shipping companies' structuring of the migration route, locked emigration trains, the trials of transit.[78] I propose to look at the difficulties of movement from two different perspectives that have been neglected in this context: the states of *em*igration, and the uses of citizenship by the mobile subject.

In the chapters that follow, I thus go beyond François Gueydan de Roussel's exclamatory prose to remind us of several salient aspects of the rust that still may impede the greased wheel of transnationalism. What about the stubborn state and the impediments it imposes? What about lost links in complex international networks? Brian Connolly has trenchantly asked, "If we turn to the transnational as a critical frame in order to expose the fragility of the nation, where do we turn to expose the fragility of the transnational?"[79] It is not just a matter of bringing the state back in. We can question the ease of transnationalism in two new and significant ways. First, we can reverse the focus of how transnationalism looks from the countries of settlement and reexamine how countries of origin have anxiously conceived of those who leave (chapters 3 and 4). At the same time, we can show how, when the departed try to connect to their homelands for aid from abroad, their success is far from simple (chapter 5). As we will see, transnational connections can form a far-from-seamless web.

3

Expatriation: The Obverse of Transnationalism

François Gueydan de Roussel was a transnational. Born of mixed Franco-American parentage, known as an upstanding American citizen to his fellows Texans before he moved to France, he transformed himself into a French winegrower. At the end of his life, he become a Swiss citizen, regaling his Lausanne grandson with stories of his inventions, which proved to his grandson how "American" his grandfather was. However, Gueydan de Roussel was a thwarted transnational, and his migrations were both voluntary (from the United States to France) and of the voluntarily-on-the-run variety. He left France for Switzerland one step ahead of French court/prison and his nemesis, the jealous and threatening French farmer Boyer. Both governments that defined his past—the US and France—had a role in his flight, namely because neither would protect him as he felt was his due. States matter.

During the period of Gueydan de Roussel's sojourn and settlement in France, the United States began scrutinizing its citizens abroad. One result was the 1907 Expatriation Act, which codified the possibilities for leaving the US and the limits of the state's protection thereafter. It is not surprising that the US government took a hard, if somewhat inconclusive, look into Gueydan's citizenship just in the period when the government was becoming somewhat alarmed by the growing numbers of Americans overseas.

For the better part of the twentieth century, transnationalism was framed by state laws that presumed one country equals one citizenship. While rules loosened everywhere by the end of the twentieth century—states themselves allowing and abetting individuals' transnationalism—it is worthwhile reviewing one country's view of the matter through the 1960s. And not just any country: the United States, which has symbolized open borders to the world.

Although with the twenty-first-century calls for greater border controls are back with a vengeance, it is important to remember their gatekeeping function vis-à-vis ordinary citizens on the move even during periods of relatively "free" migration. Expatriation in its legal sense means the involuntary loss of citizenship, revoked by the state. It has been a symbolic but legal reality since the nineteenth century. The number of people who have lost their American citizenship is small, but debates about it, I argue, mark the limits of transnationalism.

Expatriation in sum is the technical obverse of transnationalism. While transnationals can blithely flash more than one passport today, the cloud of suspicion, with its attendant name calling—"fifth column," "ex-patriots"—seems never far from the surface. Reviewing the century-long debate on expatriation in the United States through the lens of transnationalism allows us better to understand both changing attitudes toward citizenship and the ways in which the threat of expatriation was a hindrance to the as-yet-unnamed transnationalism.

Of the many expatriates, few have expatriated. That is because the term has two different meanings in the US. Living abroad—expatriates—is one thing. Losing one's citizenship—expatriation—is another. With the notable exception of Henry James in 1915, those well-known American expatriates who chose to live and write abroad rarely gave up or lost their citizenship in the process.[1] The terms "expatriate" and "expatriation" have a long and complex history, but until Patrick Weil's book on US denaturalization and Ben Herzog's recent *Revoking Citizenship*, they have been largely absent from recent studies of citizenship.[2] The use of the words ranges from simple residence abroad ("for a considerable amount of time") to the more definitive legal renunciation or destitution of allegiance, "denationalization" or "decitizenization."[3] Most often, the noun "expatriate" conjures up the interwar Lost Generation writers. The lives, essays and novels of the American expatriate writers in Paris in the 1920s have captured the imagination and framed an important debate on exile. The term "expatriate" has extended backwards to refer to Edith Wharton in the early twentieth century and beyond World War II to James Baldwin and Richard Wright. Encompassing everyone from the Henrys—James and Miller—to Gertrude Stein and Alice B. Toklas, from White Bostonians and New Yorkers to Black Harlemites, from those escaping sexual and social convention to those fleeing prejudice and discrimination, the expatriate writers, artists, and musicians have become a romanticized icon, haunting Parisian cafés where Hemingway's *Moveable Feast* can still be seen, clutched by earnest would-be Ernests.[4]

However, the writers and artists have eclipsed a broader understanding of expatriation both as a legal act and with regard to its meaning for changing notions of citizenship and the contours of transnationalism. The concept itself comprises somewhat contradictory elements. Ever since Roman times, the question of belonging has turned on the question of *patria* or *domus*. To which place does one belong and/or owe allegiance: to one's place of origin or to the place where one hangs one's hat, literally where one keeps one's *sedes*—seat?[5] Birthplace and domicile considerations have given way to the distinction between *jus sanguinis*, the right of blood or the acquisition of citizenship through parentage, and *jus soli*, the right of soil or citizenship by virtue of being born in a territory. Most contemporary democracies incorporate a mixture of both in their citizenship laws, which means that one country's citizen by *jus soli* may be another's by *jus sanguinis*. With ever increasing geographic mobility over the last two centuries, the uneasy relationship between birthplace and domicile and the multiple identities that they may engender have become ever more complex. The word "expatriation," loss of citizenship, is sometimes used as coterminous with "emigration," the physical change of domicile. Emigration and legal expatriation are often linked, but it is possible to move without losing one's citizenship of origin, just as it has been possible to lose one's citizenship without ever leaving home. The meaning of expatriation also varies depending on who is initiating the act, the state or the individual, and whether it is voluntary or not. The state banishes; the subject can choose to depart. As we will see, the valence given to assignment or consent has changed over time. Whereas exile used to be the first definition of the noun "expatriate," the *New Shorter Oxford* now lists voluntary leave taking as the primary definition, a sign of a transformation in the meaning of departure.[6]

The aim here is threefold. First, it is to argue for the importance of incorporating expatriation into our categories for understanding the state's relation to its citizens and their transnational activities. The important upsurge of citizenship studies since the 1990s has focused mainly on those *within* the state's boundaries. Long celebrated as a country of inclusion, the United States nonetheless has a long history of exclusion within its borders. This has been explored notably since T. H. Marshall advanced the idea of "social citizenship." Political citizenship alone does not define how members of the polity are included. Over the last two centuries, slaves and African Americans, women, Native Americans, and the poor have often had limited rights to participate in educational, welfare, and other social services. The domestic limitations of belonging have been reexamined in a broader understanding of these long-embedded exclusions within American social citizenship.[7] Much less attention, however, has been given to those who have left the country and/or lost their legal citizenship.[8] Only the expatriation of American women married to foreign nationals between 1907 and 1931 has received due attention in recent years.[9] Yet even this well-known case of involuntary expatriation needs to be situated within a two-centuries-long history of the term.

Migration studies, too, have largely ignored expatriation. Immigration history, largely written in the countries of arrival, has most often focused on the problematic policies and experiences of entry, acceptance, rejection, and/or settlement of newcomers. Yet emigration and expatriation provide reverse mirrors of immigration and are connected to it both in theory and practice.[10] Individuals are emigrants before they reach the other shore and become immigrants; their past and present cannot be so neatly severed, as transnational studies emphasize. For states, one country's emigrant is another's immigrant, embedding the transnational subject in a web of international relations. For historians, immigration studies need to integrate emigration and expatriation. We can reverse the usual immigration and citizenship questions by reflecting on how the state defines itself not only through those whom it incorporates (more or less well) within its boundaries but also with regard to those who cross beyond.

The second point argues that the concept of expatriation represents both a legal *and* a social construct. The American legal debates over citizenship rights and obligations have been grounded in the political and the social. The shifting image of the presumed expatriate has helped frame the legal issues tackled at each juncture. By laying the basis for an interactive history of the leave takers and the state's legislating of citizenship loss, I want to show how the "imagined expatriate" has helped construct the ways in which the possibilities of transnationalism have been conceived.

Third, then, I suggest that this sociolegal history of the last two centuries comprises four periods during which the meaning of expatriation has shifted from an inclusive view to an exclusionary notion to a new embracing of citizens abroad today (although suspicions about overseas activities persist). The first two periods, inclusive in nature, imagined expatriation as concerning someone coming *to* the United States. During the first, revolutionary and early national period, expatriation was tied to nation building. Separation from Britain depended upon defining the right of expatriation *from* Britain to the US, and the early nineteenth-century American debates were conceptualized with British seamen or landless Englishmen in mind. From the mid-nineteenth century on, with mass immigration from northern Europe, a second, equally inclusive, period expanded on the first. Legal thinking about expatriation became a corollary to immigration policy, reassuring the newcomers that their naturalization in the US was secure against competing claims from their birth countries. By the early twentieth century, however, a third period, marked by the Expatriation Law of 1907, reflected a new, more worrisome figure. The expatriate was now defined as someone *leaving* the US, whether for love (American women marrying foreign men), money (naturalized businessmen staying away too long), or just to write, although only the first two groups were legally excluded from citizenship. The list of potential acts that could incur citizenship loss was codified and lengthened. Naturalized citizens were a first concern.[11] US-born citizens with foreign parentage such as François ("Frank") Gueydan could be scrutinized. But, more generally, as twentieth-century US globalization led more and more Americans abroad, the concerns of the 1907 law, heightened during World War II, eventually abated. With a major leap in departures after World War II, a fourth period, from the 1960s on, has seen one more shift in the meaning of expatriation, leading to a more inclusive consideration of transnationalism. One could argue that the transnational business expat has had a role in whittling down the list of legal expatriating acts, as voting abroad and even dual citizenship have become increasingly accepted. From welcoming "expatriated" foreigners in the nineteenth century to becoming suspicious of those Americans who waded overseas throughout much of the twentieth century to easing laws on citizenship loss today, two centuries of American comings and goings have shifted the concept of expatriation from welcomed newcomer to traitor to emissary, with certain qualifications. In all cases, the law both reflects visions of transnationalism while it defines it.

Expatriation as Nation Building

Expatriation was, in the first instance, a form of nation building. For the US to justify its break from Britain, it had to legitimate the notion of leaving one's country of birth. Expatriation was thus initially seen as a form of inclusion in America, with former British subjects in mind. Like citizenship itself, expatriation was both a theoretical/rhetorical and a practical/legal issue for the young state. The Declaration of Independence, which complained that King George had impeded the peopling of the colonies ("He has endeavoured to prevent the population of these States; for that purpose obstructing the Laws for Naturalization of Foreigners; refusing to pass others to encourage their migrations hither, . . ."), was a declaration of the right of emigration. In the ensuing decades, to consolidate American independence and citizenship, expatriation from Britain had to be deemed a legal, indeed natural, right both for the state and the individual. The United States had to counter both politically and philosophically the competing British claim that birthright or perpetual allegiance bound those born under the crown everlastingly to it, a fundamental opposition to transnationalism. This essentially feudal notion of perpetual allegiance, most forcefully expounded by the famous jurist Sir Edward Coke in 1608, considered expatriation a moral travesty and a legal impossibility. The new nation needed several decades to impose its view that expatriation was a natural right. The right of exit was the necessary corollary to a right of entry, and a Lockean notion of free will underwrote the definition of the new American citizen. One could say that the United States, for its own purpose, was founded on the possibility of transnationalism, literally transcending one's birthright ties.

The founding fathers and early jurists did not fully agree on these matters, however, as political scientist I-Mien Tsiang well showed in *The Question of Expatriation in America Prior to 1907*

(1942), one of the most complete treatments of the first century of expatriation law. Hamilton, for example, still stressed the primacy of an organic, "natural" attachment to the state. When legislation was proposed in New York in 1784 to cancel the citizenship of those who had taken the British side during the Revolution, Hamilton objected:

> The idea, indeed, of citizens transforming themselves into aliens, by taking part against the State to which they belong, is altogether of new invention, unknown and unadmissible in law, and contrary to the nature of the social compact.[12]

In this view, the right of government superseded that of the individual (and the federal government that of the individual states). Jefferson, however, tended to emphasize a consensual notion of citizenship choice, defending expatriation as a natural individual right to justify American independence and the right of British citizens to become Americans.[13] Does this make Jefferson the first theorist of transnationalism?

The worry about American citizens voluntarily giving up their citizenship was raised in several early Supreme Court cases. In *Talbot v. Jansen* (1795), the question was whether the native Virginian William Talbot had committed treason when he had illegally outfitted a French privateer ship. When arrested, he claimed that since he had become a French citizen in Guadeloupe, he could not be tried for treason in the United States. Treason is a matter of citizenship; only a citizen can be a traitor.[14] Someone who had foresworn or lost his birthright citizenship could be an enemy, perhaps, but not a traitor. Talbot was found guilty as charged. However, while arguing that expatriation was a qualified right constrained by patriotism and the public good, Justice Iredell left one of the more memorable expressions of the principle of expatriation, still quoted today:

> That a man ought not to be a slave; that he should not be confined against his will to a particular spot because he happened to draw his first breath upon it; that he should not be compelled to continue in a society to which he is accidentally attached, when he can better his

> situation elsewhere, much less when he must starve in one country, and may live comfortably in another, are positions which I hold as strongly as any man, and they are such as most nations in the world appear clearly to recognize.[15]

Iredell thus turned the wily pirate into an oft-cited legal precedent; ironically, a native-born American trying to abandon the US became a touchstone for considering the right of others to abandon their birthplace to come to America.

By the early nineteenth century, focus turned less on the Talbots who might jump the American ship than on British seamen and others who opted for the newly created American citizenship. The War of 1812 unleashed a period of heated debate in the United States over the question of expatriation, considered to be one of the three great international issues of the time (along with the neutral flag and blockades). The war broke out, among other things, over the definition of expatriation and differing conceptions of citizenship. With a full panoply of family metaphors linked to the notion of perpetual allegiance and insistence that one could not alienate oneself from one's mother country, Britain continued to object to the upstart new nation's redefinition of those whom Britain still considered to be its subjects. Britain thus refused to recognize American naturalization and forcefully conscripted British-turned-American seamen as its own. This led American jurists and publicists of the period vigorously to condemn the notion of perpetual allegiance. Nonetheless, a spirited pamphlet debate broke out, which lasted throughout the three-year war, showing that the matter was not just a British-American dispute but an internal American discussion as well. Should the United States defend this revolutionary concept of expatriation to the point of war over who belonged to whom? Some argued that expatriation was a natural right to be defended at all costs. Others, while agreeing with the principle of expatriation, did not think it was worth fighting an extended war over it.

A "Gentleman of the City of New York," as one polemicist—transnationalist we would say today?—signed his pamphlet in

1813, argued passionately that it should be "no crime for a man to leave that country, where, by chance, he commenced his existence."[16] He strenuously made the case that emigration devolved from a (competing) natural right, that of departure, and that all laws to prevent it were unjust and highly tyrannical. Other treatises stressed that the young nation should welcome all those who came from abroad, a matter not just of liberty but of the pursuit of happiness, and Pennsylvania was the first state to inscribe the right of emigration in its constitution: "That all men have a natural, inherent right to emigrate from one State to another that will receive them, or to form a new State in vacant countries, or in such countries as they can purchase, whenever they think that thereby they may promote their own happiness." Vermont, Kentucky, Louisiana, Indiana, Mississippi, Alabama, and Missouri followed suit.[17]

The early nineteenth century debates show how the American expatriation *imaginaire* was constructed in three ways. First, the American perspective in favor of expatriation was constructed mostly to defend the ingress of British subjects becoming Americans, in contrast to the British refusal of expatriation based on fear of egress. Second, the philosophical justification for this change of status was based on the idea that individual consent—agency, as we would now say—with regard to citizenship was essential. Third, the legal debates were also construed with actual expatriates in mind. Subsequent imaginings of *who* was doing the leave taking would have an important impact on transformations in the social and legal notions of expatriation over the next two centuries, framing what we could today call the social experience of transnationalism.

Expatriation as Immigration

By the second half of the nineteenth century, expatriation had become immigration. The 1868 Expatriation Act, declaring "the right of expatriation to be a natural and inherent right of all people, indispensable to the enjoyment of the rights of life, liberty, and the pursuit of happiness," was another way of welcoming the new "expatriates" of the mass immigration—Germans, Irish, Scandinavians—to the demographically growing nation. The figure of expatriation had changed, from British seaman to northern European immigrants in general. This second period of American thought on the subject of expatriation reaffirmed the right of ingress in a double context, domestic and international. On the domestic front, the Expatriation Act of 1868 was passed one day before ratification of the Fourteenth Amendment, which reinforced birthright in order to overturn the Dred Scott decision and confirm African American rights to citizenship. For Peter Schuck and Rogers Smith, the 1868 act along with the Fourteenth Amendment represented a "marriage of convenience."[18] Together they allowed ascriptive *jus soli* citizenship to ensure the rights of African Americans born on American soil while permitting European immigrants to extricate themselves from the prescriptive citizenship of *their* birth lands. The contradiction was both necessary and, I would add, shows how nation building can be linked to sociological understandings of the citizens at stake. The inclusive nature of this early expatriation law was intended to allow trans(fer-of-)nationalism for those arriving.

Expatriation was also a domestic demographic issue. Chief Justice Oliver Ellsworth had invoked this matter in 1799, in his however disputed opinion against expatriation, when he argued that the little-populated country needed to keep its inhabitants, not lose them:

> In countries so crowded with inhabitants that the means of subsistence are difficult to be obtained, it is reason and policy to permit emigration. But our policy is different; for our country is but sparsely settled, and we have no inhabitants to spare.[19]

Concern for the peopling of the United States ultimately worked to the advantage of ideas favoring expatriation as the mass migrations beginning midcentury brought ever more inhabitants to the land. The passage of the Expatriation Act also came two years after a *cause célèbre* in which the US government had protested energetically against the 1866 arrest in Ireland of two Irish-born, naturalized American citizens who had returned to Ireland during the Fenian agitation.[20] The 1868 law was a way of reassuring European newcomers that expatriation *to* the US and acquisition of American citizenship were secure against demands of their native states.

The 1868 law was thus also a sign of new transnational times. As the mass of European migrations moved millions of people away from their places of birth in what Aristide Zolberg called "The Exit Revolution," the notion of perpetual allegiance declined throughout Europe by the 1870s, leading to an "entire change of doctrine" and a flurry of international treaties redefining who belonged to whom.[21] Other countries were declaring the right of emigration to be a natural right, albeit often with strings still attached (see chapter 4). Even Great Britain, one of the most articulate proponents of perpetual allegiance, revised its Nationality Law in 1870 to allow expatriation. The United States signed naturalization treaties with Belgium, Norway and Sweden, Great Britain, Austria-Hungary, Denmark, Mexico, and Ecuador, in essence recognizing that one country's expatriate was another's citizen, although momentum slowed as many European countries introduced obligatory military service that blocked legal emigration until satisfied. Refuting other states' claims to perpetual allegiance and emphasizing individual consent, the US courts and the 1868 act confirmed the proposition that new immigrants, like the revolutionaries before them, had the right to choose to change the legal ties that bind. As one legal scholar commented, the 1868 law formulated "a practical desire to secure international recognition for the view that naturalization in the United States effects complete expatriation from a former allegiance." "[D]ictated by expediency, though announced in terms of principle," the 1868 law still emphasized ingress and inclusion, defending those who wanted to become American citizens.[22]

Scrutinizing Those Who Leave

By the turn of the twentieth century, the figure of expatriation in the United States had changed radically, from a perspective of ingress to one of egress. Americans were now leaving as well as coming. In this third period, expatriation became conceptualized less as a welcoming inclusion of newcomers than as a discussion about excluding certain categories of American citizens. Whereas the 1868 law had reaffirmed the right of aliens to become Americans, a new law, in 1907—the year François Gueydan de Roussel gave up hope of help from the US government and fled France for Switzerland[23]—sought to define the contours of Americans who could become aliens.[24] On the one hand, the country no longer felt demographically challenged. Indeed, anti-immigration forces had gained the momentum that would ultimately culminate in the immigration quota laws of 1921 and 1924. Accepting other countries' expatriates was no longer a priority. Naturalizations themselves were now sometimes suspect in the face of increasing fraud and corruption; Presidents Cleveland, Harrison, and Roosevelt all made appeals to Congress to provide stricter controls on naturalization to rout out spurious citizenship, although they were ignored until a denaturalization law was passed in 1906.[25] On the other hand, a century of US globalization had begun, and American expansion overseas led more and more US citizens abroad. Yet the image of the departed citizen was complex, and those leaving were a mixed bunch.

By clearly delineating those acts that could lead to loss of citizenship, the 1907 law of expatriation in effect marked the shift from inclusion to exclusion. From 1907 to the 1960s, transnationalism would be potentially suspect and the limits as to what a citizen abroad could or should do increasingly codified. Between 1906 and 1944, 22,026 naturalized Americans were deprived of their citizenship.[26] From 1907 on, US-born citizens came under increasing scrutiny as well. Whereas the 1868 law had made explicit an abstract principle, it had not actually defined what constituted losing one's citizenship, and ever since *Talbot* there had been a sense of the need to codify the matter. This explains why, for Tsiang, the 1907 Expatriation Act was the satisfying resolution of "the long circuit of doubts" resulting from the founding fathers' reluctance to take a definitive stand on born or acquired allegiance. But Tsiang, focusing on a legal teleology leading to the 1907 law, did not focus on the exclusionary aspects of the law.

The three principal acts that could lead to citizenship loss were naturalization or an oath of allegiance pledged to a foreign state, extended residence abroad (of naturalized American citizens), and marriage of women to foreign citizens. The second provision reaffirmed the 1906 denaturalization law: naturalized American citizens, although still protected under the law no matter where they roamed, risked losing their new citizenship if they resided for two consecutive years in their country of origin or five consecutive years in any other foreign state. They could overcome this loss of American citizenship due to extended residence abroad only by providing satisfactory evidence that they never intended to relinquish their American citizenship. The image of the transnational traveler, picking up citizenships at will before going "home" or elsewhere was already beginning to develop, but not in a particularly positive way. Talk of "serious abuse" shadowed those naturalized citizens who took up US citizenship only to leave again.[27] Dual citizenship was theoretically inconceivable for much of the twentieth century.[28]

The image of the American abroad was complex. Former secretary of state Root hailed the brave new world of American businessmen forging into new markets in a notable 1910 address on "The Basis of Protection to Citizens Residing Abroad." Emphasizing the new importance of trade and commerce, Root spoke of the declining tariffs and the increasing facility of transportation and communication that had "set in motion vast armies of travelers who are making their way into the most remote corners of foreign countries to a degree never before known." In an early paean to globalization, Root spoke eloquently of the enormous shifting of population and the increased mobility of everyone and everything from (European) peasants to money to (American) businessmen. The generalized abandonment of the doctrine of inalienable allegiance, "so inconsistent with the natural course of development of the new world," had created "a new class of citizens traveling or residing abroad." This meant new concerns for states, as Edwin M. Borchard's *The Diplomatic Protection of Citizens Abroad*, published in 1915, also attested. "The drawing together of the world by increased facilities of travel and communication" justified the new attention to the matter.[29] Root and Borchard emphasized that citizenship was not just a domestic matter. It was enmeshed in international relations not only in the government's responsibility for its citizens abroad but due to the ways in which immigration and emigration necessarily implied treaties to respect one another's nationals. At the turn of the twentieth century, without using the term, there was already a sense that transnationalism was on the rise, but legists warned that it remained embedded in national laws.

While one vision hailed this new mobility, another raised questions of loyalties of those Americans dabbling with the foreign: naturalized citizens going back to their home states and American women married to foreigners. By setting clearer parameters regarding those who had overstepped the boundaries of belonging, the 1907 law more explicitly defined those who could be excluded as a result. Over the next half century, a widening circle of acts that could lead to the loss of citizenship was confirmed, leading to an increase in involuntary expatriation. The 1940 Nationality Act expanded the criteria of nationality loss by adding service in the armed forces of or employment by a foreign state, voting, desertion, or treason.[30] In 1952, the Immigration and Nationality ("McCarran-Walter") Act consolidated all previous nationality laws, and all of the expatriating criteria were maintained. Expatriation thus came to be reconceptualized over the first half of the twentieth century under a cloud of doubt. In contrast to one discourse admiring American entrepreneurs abroad, a competing, negative vision considered leave takers with misgiving. More than one government immigration expert questioned both a too-inclusive right of naturalization and the extension of protection to Americans abroad.[31] Subsequent to the reinforced 1940 Nationality Act, the total number of denationalized Americans, mostly native born, reached 120,770 between the years 1945 and 1977.[32] The image of expatriation had shifted from a friendly figure, welcomed to a sparsely populated continent, to a series of suspicious characters: from increasingly unwanted immigrants and suspect naturalized citizens to two very different groups of transnationals: women and writers.

Women Transnationals between Domicile and Citizenship

Expatriation was, furthermore, explicitly gendered. And both citizenship and domicile could come into play. Take the case of the Duchess of Mecklenburg. In 1931, the Duchess of Mecklenburg died in San Francisco.[33] Not every day does a duchess die in San Francisco, but this was not as surprising as it seems. She had been born Natalie—Lily—Oelrichs in Cheyenne, Wyoming, in 1880, and, in between birth and death in the American West, she married twice and lived in Germany and France. Her second husband was the Duke Heinrich Borwin von Mecklenburg-Schwerin, transforming her into a duchess in what was at the time a not unusual exchange of American female fortune for European male title. The *New York Times* had described the duke at the time of his first marriage (to another American, twenty-nine years his senior) as a prominent figure in German aristocratic circles who was "popular in society, but penniless" and who hobnobbed with rich Americans.[34] After Lily's first husband, an internationally known polo player, died, and after Mecklenburg divorced his first wife, the two married in 1915. They divorced in 1921.

Good democrats may sniff that Lily had what was coming to her social-climbing self/set. Yet her story, like François Gueydan de Roussel's, goes beyond the sui generis nature of her marital and posthumous legal woes. It is a vivid example of being caught in a transnational web. By marrying the duke, Lily had lost her US citizenship according to the Expatriation Law of

1907.[35] Having married a foreign national and thereby acquiring her husband's nationality, Lily was no longer a US citizen. Even after divorcing the duke, she was still a German national, unless she formally applied for naturalization in the US.

However, when the duchess died in San Francisco in 1931, it was less a question of citizenship than of domicile. After having lived in Germany and France and traveling under a German passport, the question was: where would her estate be adjudicated? The will would be probated in San Francisco as to property in California, but domicile would determine the general validity of the rest of the provisions. She had last lived in Paris and returned to California approximately a year before she died. But before Paris, she had lived in Germany, and she was formally German.

The main question was: could she disinherit her son? The problem was not just an international one—the adjudication between two or more states—but it was also a transnational one, speaking to the circulation of Lily and her entourage over the years. The Duchess of Mecklenburg's San Francisco will, favoring her sister, had been written with the intention of disinheriting her son, and he was contesting it. It is indeed possible under US law to completely disinherit a child since one can freely bequeath assets to anyone one chooses: relatives, institutions, or . . . a dog.[36] But not all countries look kindly on the severing of blood ties. Neither Germany nor France allows parents to completely disinherit their children. Thus, a first question raised by the lawyers was, where was she domiciled: in Germany, France, California? Can a hotel be a domicile? And what about intent? Had she meant to stay in France? Her lawyer in Paris commented that she had only lived in (however fancy, residential) hotels in Paris; a hotel could nonetheless constitute a domicile; but whenever he saw her, the duchess had been much too unhappy in Paris for him to believe that she meant to stay there. Another lawyer (who had a personal interest in the matter, his wife being Lily's sister) doubted that she had any fixed domicile. Was she thus the ultimate homeless cosmopolitan—a reminder that not all those adrift are down and out?

The second question was: how badly does a child have to behave to be disinherited under French or German law? As there seemed to be more proof of domicile in Germany, the question was pursued there. Indeed, the German Civil Code did permit a parent to disinherit a child—if the child had tried to kill the parent. Violence against a parent was grounds for disinheritance (although hitting a stepparent apparently was not). So too was a child's dishonorable or immoral life, unless the child had demonstrably reformed his or her behavior between the will's writing and the parent's death. Simply being ungrateful (Lily's son?) did not make the list. Last but not least, pardon was possible. In the end, Lily's sister and son reached a settlement, based on a partial reconciliation between Lily and her son during her last illness. Although, in the meantime, a poor Russian friend of the Duchess had shown up at the Paris law firm handling her affairs, wondering whether, as he had been led to believe, he and his wife, a good friend of the Duchess, had been named in the will. Cosmopolitan circles may potentially aggravate while they animate the transnational condition.

Lily's case is but one—if a particularly wealthy, entitled one—of many American women who lost their citizenship between 1907 and 1922 due to their loves, lives, and transnational conditions. One of the most egregious historical cases of involuntary expatriation in US history is that of American women married to alien men between the Expatriation Law of 1907 and even beyond the Cable Act of 1922, which putatively rectified the injustice. (Women married to aliens ineligible for citizenship [i.e., Chinese, Japanese, Filipinos] were still expatriated until 1931.[37]) Section 2 of the 1907 law stipulated that

> [a]ny American citizen shall be deemed to have expatriated himself when he has been naturalized in any foreign state in conformity with its laws, or when he has taken an oath of allegiance to any foreign state.[38]

The "he" was explicit because the subsequent section 3 dealt specifically with women, only to understand their expatriation as being effected through marriage. Section 3 specified that any American woman who married a foreigner would take the nationality of her husband. A circular instruction on April 19, 1907, clarified the evidence that would be considered as overturning the presumption of loss for naturalized citizens due to extended residence abroad, once again using a telling "he":

> (a) That his residence abroad is solely as a representative of American trade and commerce, and that he intends eventually to return to the United States permanently to reside; or
>
> (b) That his residence abroad is in good faith for reasons of health or for education. . . .[39]

Business, health, and education were all acceptable reasons for transnational activities—in that order. The enterprising American naturalized male was protected from citizenship loss as long as he could prove a worthy reason for absenting himself.[40] However, the American female expatriate was a woman who "followed" her husband's nationality, whether she left the United States or even continued to reside there. In the latter case, expatriation could occur even without emigration.[41]

As many scholars have shown, the American citizen had been conceptualized as a white male, who furthermore had the power, through marriage, to transform a foreign woman into an American citizen.[42] According to the Naturalization Act of 1855, American citizenship had been automatically granted to foreign women who married American men. There was no mention of the opposite category of mixed marriages, American women who married foreign men. This resulted in an anomalous situation that the 1907 law supposedly corrected, but it did so to the disadvantage of all married women, by making them all dependent on their husbands' status for their citizenship. Marriage, a voluntary act, was deemed to result in expatriation, voluntary or not. As one legal commentator concluded (in 1935), the law of 1907, "which indulged the fiction that by marrying an alien the lady consents to a result 'tantamount to expatriation,' caused the feminist revolution, whose echoes still reverberate at home and abroad."[43]

The expatriation of American-born women was not just a consequence of trying to equilibrate a previous law. It can also be linked to the bad press that many transnational marriages such as that of the Duchess of Mecklenburg had received. By the turn of the twentieth century, both men and women who married "out" came under nativist scrutiny.[44] Foreign men marrying American women were considered questionable if not conniving in their efforts to obtain American citizenship and usurp the vote. At the same time, rich American women "who 'play at being' aristocrats by marrying (allegedly) titled foreigners instead of 'men of their own race'" came in for their share of castigation.[45] There seemed to be an epidemic of American heiresses wedding European nobility at the turn of the century. In 1895, two high-profile matches, that of Anna Gould and Count Boniface de Castellane and that of Consuelo Vanderbilt and the Duke of Marlborough, brought envy and scorn and translated into images of pots of American gold leaving the country. A 1911 congressional debate criticized rich female legatees "who are suffering from chronic titleitis."[46] Beyond the financial arrangements, "snubbing that national icon, the citizen man, was a serious transgression."[47] Newspaper articles condemning the neo-duchesses were legion, considering such slavish chasing after European titles a particularly loathsome renunciation of American democratic ideals. "Countess Spaghettis" were mocked, and Franco-American marriages were criticized as "pathetic comedies of credulous inexperience."[48] In sum, these marriages represented transnationalism at its worse in the eyes of those in favor of patriotic endogamy.

Writing Abroad

Besides expatriation as a legal act defined by the state, the term "the expatriate" came into usage at the turn of the twentieth century as a worrisome noun, often deriding a suspect citizen. While American women were losing their citizenship involuntarily, an entirely different image was emerging. The transnational expatriate writer or artist loomed as another problematic category of citizens, although at little risk of actual involuntary citizenship loss. If American women could be expatriated without emigration, the 1920s writers were expatriates without expatriation. Indeed, the meaning of "expatriation" as a legal category of citizenship loss and of the "expatriate" as simply a citizen abroad increasingly diverged in the early twentieth century. By the 1920s, the concept of expatriation had shifted from a category of citizenship to one of residence.

The new word "expatriate," which the writers and artists ultimately adopted themselves, first emerged as a critical term castigating the title-seeking legatees. The earliest American use of the noun "expatriate" seems to be a 1900 novel entitled *The Expatriates*, by Lilian Bell. In it, she harshly mocked rich Americans in Paris who, to their financial and even physical peril, succumbed to the sirens of impoverished and scheming titled French men and women. "'Where do you live now?' she demanded. 'In Paris.' 'Expatriates—both of you!' she said, scornfully, turning her glasses on them." "Why did this man . . . deliberately live away from her dear country and tacitly repudiate the flag?"[49] One of the main characters in the novel dies as a result of her desperate attempt to marry a French marquis. The term continued to be used in the interwar period with negative undertones that questioned the relationship of citizens abroad to the nation. True, the American novelists, painters, poets, and musicians in interwar Paris who had opted for creativity on foreign soil had not relinquished or lost their citizenship, let alone their attachment to the United States. Indeed, who was more American than Gertrude Stein, who proclaimed the "American Century" a good decade before Henry Luce?[50] But their choice of living abroad and their explicit writings on exile raised important questions about the relationship of the citizen to home. Their cultural visibility and critical success, however appealing to like-minded intellectuals, was bound up with worries about the nature of the nation. All the more so insofar as many of them, including Stein, explicitly expressed their dismay with American modernity, its standardization, its mediocrity. The 1920s expatriates were thus often seen disapprovingly at the time as rootless, hedonistic, extravagant, hard-drinking individuals, and/or as homosexuals. In his 1968 book entitled *Expatriates and Patriots*, Ernest Earnest made the distinction between the 1920s "Lost Generation" and those who had come before them, clearly preferring the more refined Whartons and Jameses, the old Brahmins and other upper-middle class East Coasters, early transnationals who had crossed the Atlantic eastward between the Civil War and World War I.[51] Yet, while Hemingway and others embraced the life of the exile and its spur to creativity, even they acknowledged the ambiguity of the status. While justifying his stay abroad, yet insisting that he was very American, Harold Stearns wrote in his "Apologia of an Expatriate": "No one knows better than I the bitterness of being an expatriate or hates it more than I do."[52]

Furthermore, not all Americans living in Paris in the 1920s were café dwellers. The sociological makeup of Americans in Paris in the first half of the twentieth century extended far beyond the well-known Left Bank writers and artists. They included business entrepreneurs and former soldiers. Of the estimated 40,000 Americans in Paris in the 1920s, most of them did *not* write or draw.[53] And this generally well-heeled American community, living for the most part on the Right Bank of the Seine, did not want to be confused with the Left Bank writers and artists. Indeed, the vast majority of the interwar American colony in Paris took umbrage at the very term "expatriate," considering it to be a derogatory epithet and writing in to the *Paris Herald* to say so.[54] But although they sought to distance themselves from those Bohemian types, even this more posh set came in for its own portion of criticism. The American industrialist overseas, hailed for opening up new markets, was nonetheless suspected, along with the idle rich, of having left home to avoid paying taxes after the first income tax law was passed in 1913. Whether fleeing taxes or Prohibition, the transatlantic writers, drinkers, and tax evaders never lost their citizenship in the process. (Marrying a foreign man was apparently a much more serious sin.) But they contributed to an image of the expatriate that was often far from flattering. Into the 1960s, the term "expatriate" was still often used pejoratively. Those who left the United States during the Vietnam War era as draft evaders or conscientious objectors came in for their share of opprobrium.[55] And the critical implication of the term was summed up by a frequent misspelling: expatriot.

Yet a new explosion of historical writing in the 1960s and 1970s turned its focus on the 1920s writers and helped reinvigorate a fascination with the concept of expatriation even before the transnational turn. The 1920s Americans in Paris and their 1950s cousins became the center of attention of a new generation of historians who were critical of American politics or culture and captivated anew by the stories of those who had left the United States in the interwar years or after World War II. Whites and African Americans, men and women, the writers, artists, and musicians, straight and gay, were happily rediscovered and heralded for their intellectual vibrancy and critical spirit.[56] By the 1960s–1970s, the noun "expatriate," most often referring to a time and a place—1920s Paris—had clearly transformed the legal concept into a historical and metaphorical term. The romanticized interwar expatriates, symbols of voluntary self-exclusion, thus can also be seen as harbingers of the more inclusive late twentieth-century transition to expatriation without citizenship loss and transnational agency to which we may now turn.

Toward Transnationalism . . . and Its Limits

By the mid-1960s, a new figure of the leave taker had emerged: the globalized expat. In this fourth period of contemplating expatriation, increased mobility and transnationalism have given new meaning to the image of citizens abroad. US immigration law has become more inclusive since the 1965 Hart-Cellar Act finally eliminated nationality quotas and the new hemispheric-defined entry system ultimately changed the complexion of the United States. At the same time, expatriation case law has evolved to re-include categories of individuals formerly banished for bad behavior.

US citizens abroad, acclaimed as a novel phenomenon by Elihu Root at the beginning of the twentieth century, became ever more commonplace by the end of the century. "Expats" and most recently dual nationals have been conceptualized as potent proof in the new discourse on globalization, mobility, and transnationalism. The colloquial abbreviation "expat" seems to date to the 1960s, appearing as the title of a poem by British author D.J. Enright,[57] apparently in the British colonial context. But by the latter part of the twentieth century, it was frequently used in the United States and elsewhere to mean literally a new class of citizens abroad, clearly differentiated from the 1920s writers and artists. In business circles, the "expat" is most often used to designate someone sent abroad to represent a multinational firm. International companies and NGOs offer assistance, advice, and benefits to those they send overseas. The expat's status is generally a privileged one, replete with expense accounts and tax adjustments. It could not be further from a notion of "expatriation" as citizenship loss.

And, indeed, after half a century of effectively criticizing transnationalism by expanding the definition of expatriating acts (with the happy exception of the 1922/1931 reversals on marriage), case law defining citizenship loss took a new turn in the second half of the twentieth century. By restricting the list of actions that could lead to loss of nationality, the US government abetted the new sense of expanded opportunity for transnationalism. Voting abroad, for example, slowly disappeared as a potentially expatriating act. When an American citizen living in Greece voted in an election there in the 1950s, that act was not considered a cause for citizenship loss since the individual argued that he did so not with the intent of relinquishing his US citizenship but due to the duress of political circumstances: he had voted so as not to raise suspicion among his (hostile) neighbors that he was a Communist. However, in the early 1960s, when a dual national who voted in Japan defended himself against expatriation on the grounds that not doing so would have incurred the suspicions of *his* neighbors, the court found that he had otherwise good relations with his neighbors and that there was no independent proof that he was at risk. In that case, the fear-of-neighbors defense did not suffice, and he lost his American citizenship.[58]

However, the general tide was turning, in favor of allowing a wider range of activities on the part of American citizens abroad. In 1967, the US Supreme Court made a key ruling, in *Afroyim v. Rusk*, that turned the page on the 1907, 1940, and 1952 definitions of expatriating acts. The *Afroyim* decision emphasized that expatriation must be the clear result of the voluntary intent of the individual to relinquish citizenship, and that the party alleging expatriation (i.e., the government) had the burden of proof: "In our country the people are sovereign and the Government cannot sever its relationship to the people by taking away their citizenship."[59] After half a century of suspicion, transnationalism was given legal solidity. The renewed insistence on personal intent relocated the act of expatriation clearly with the individual rather than the state, in withdrawal rather than banishment. As voting and ultimately naturalization abroad have come to be viewed with greater equanimity, the risk of involuntarily losing one's American citizenship has decreased.

Acceptance of dual citizenship has been an important corollary to the limitation of involuntary expatriation and has accompanied greater acceptance of transnationalism.[60] The high era of the nation-state, from the late eighteenth to the late twentieth century, rested firmly on the notion that one could belong to one country only. Expatriation and naturalization were construed as antithetical to dual citizenship. The possibility of *changing* one's citizenship did not mean that one could belong simultaneously to two nations. The American view was that "naturalization invests the individual with a new and single allegiance, automatically absolving him from the obligations of the old."[61] Dual citizenship was characterized as everything from a "disagreeable dilemma" (*Talbot*, 1795) to "a self-evident absurdity" (Theodore

Roosevelt in 1915). Through the 1960s, international law considered that "every person should have a nationality and should have one nationality only."[62]

However, dual citizenship has grown recently as the result of two concomitant trends. First, major countries of emigration (e.g., Mexico, the Dominican Republic, the Philippines) have begun allowing it, forcing receiving countries to accept that those who naturalize do not necessarily shed their original identities, let alone passports. The United States has long since abandoned the pretense of enforcing its own naturalization precept that requires the abjuring of previous citizenship. But second, dual citizenship today not only refers to Mexicans in the United States but also to Americans abroad. As Gerald Neuman has emphasized, US citizenship has increasingly become disconnected from territorially limited rights, extending greater protection to citizens abroad along the lines of global due process. Growing acceptance of dual citizenship for Americans abroad also relates to the new figure of the transnational expat. The ever-increased travel of traders has brought new visibility to citizens abroad. As states are increasingly reluctant to lose their citizens, dual citizenship, and what some have called "external citizenship," is clearly no longer grounds for expatriation.[63]

Different terms have been used over the last two centuries—from "expatriation" to "expatriates" to "expats"—to imagine, condone, condemn, and again accept varying forms of transnationalism. A concept implying the severing of ties with one's place of origin has become a notion linking one to home while glorifying transnational connections. Yet the history of the terms shows how representations of transnational ties can change over time: both the state and individuals are involved in oscillating notions of favorable and unfavorable transnational connections. As long as expatriation was meant as welcoming newcomers to the United States, it was an inclusive concept. As Americans started moving abroad in the opposite direction from their ancestors and furthermore seemed to be criticizing the US through their marriage alliances or critical writings, the concept of the expatriate became more worrisome, and legislators increased the actions defined as leading to citizenship loss. However, by the late twentieth century, as the number of Americans abroad swelled, and businessmen continued largely to outnumber disgruntled writers or escapees from racism, the law followed its citizens—or their business. Even acts that once seemed obvious causes for citizenship loss, notably naturalization abroad, became redefined as unproblematic. Until very recently, the legal pendulum has swung back to expats and transnationals with a language of liberty, of movement, and of choice of belonging.

The declining valence of legal expatriation and the increasing acceptance of transnationalism in the late twentieth century—an important reversal of a one-wo/man, one-country norm—cannot mask, however, a longer history that shows the worries transnational figures may engender and the ways in which the United States tried to legislate their activities. While the figure of the expatriate has become transformed today, the romanticized figure of an international globetrotter still needs to be counterbalanced with past and present frictions in mind. The international business expat can be a contested figure, and recurrent congressional debates over tax law continue to raise the specter of new forms of voluntary expatriation to avoid the long arm of the IRS. The newsletters of the Association of Americans' Resident Overseas over the last few decades testify to competing tensions related to citizens abroad, sometimes seen as suspicious characters in hyperpatriotic times.[64]

Expatriation, dual citizenship, and the reconfiguration of the legal contours of citizenship remain challenges to state sovereignty, and sovereignty remains a challenge to transnationalism. This challenge has been true for the United States. It has also been true of other countries since the nineteenth century, as we will see next.

4

On States and Exit: Letting People Go . . . with Gritted Teeth

The emigrant is a human figure disliked by the masses; at the point of departure, he is often seen as a deserter, or at the least, an egotist; from the perspective of arrival, he is seen as a cumbersome competitor or as a pariah to exploit.[1]

States can be helpful to transnationalism—or not. The idea that today all countries are interested in their diasporas and are embracing their citizens abroad, as part of a two-way transnational street, makes the process seem inevitable. Yet there is a long history of countries of origin struggling with what to do about citizens who leave.[2] Should they see them as traitors, taking their soldierly potential or inherited wealth with them? Simply treat them with good riddance, representing fewer mouths to feed when local resources are insufficient? Or cheer them on as cultural ambassadors or sources of economic aid via remittances? Jean Bodin (1530–96), early modern French legal scholar worried about French depopulation, has oft been quoted for his pithy statement to the effect that neither the strength nor wealth of a nation could exist without an abundant population: "Only men create force and wealth." (*Il n'est force ni richesse que d'hommes.*[3])

We have seen that in 1813 a Gentleman of the City of New York argued vigorously that the right to emigration was a natural one and that measures against it were unwarranted and despotic. Nonetheless, in the imaginary dialogue he constructed between a king and a subject, the king saw things from another perspective: the prosperity of a kingdom depends upon its manufacture and commerce; emigration would interfere with this process, entailing the loss of skill to foreign nations. Above all, argued the king, departure must be considered not a natural right but a permission, subject to recall. Worse yet, if a subject took up arms against his home country, that would be "the heighth [*sic*] of enormity, and deserving death." In a *cri de coeur*, the king protested: "Does not every good man love his country?"[4]

To emigrate is to leave home and country. Although, as already pointed out, much focus has historically and historiographically concerned the barriers and difficulties pertaining to arrival—the oscillations of restrictive immigration policies—less attention has been focused on the obstacles surrounding departure. Certainly the twentieth-century regimes that prevented free departure have been studied and stigmatized. Indeed, the 1948 Universal Declaration of the Rights of Man stipulated in article 13 that "everyone has the right to leave any country, including his own, and to return to his country."[5] Yet states have been placing hurdles on emigration for two centuries—with more or less success. It is worthwhile reviewing some of these policies to understand how, beyond the changing US views on expatriation, emigration states' policies could in and of themselves hinder transnational movement and connections.

The king's concerns in the 1813 dialogue were no less real for the Western nation-states that came into being in the post-monarchical century following the French Revolution. We can look at how modern states have defined their body politic not just by those who arrive but with regard to those who leave. Exit, like entry, are nodal points for eventual limitations on transnational movement.

Reversing the Perspective

Migration has been studied through as many perspectives as there are disciplines and theories.[6] But one thing has characterized most of the historical and sociological literature in the major countries of *im*migration in the last few decades: it has been resolutely, if understandably, a literature mirroring itself, a history of immigration. The social sciences have paralleled public debate in their interest in the matter ever since the Chicago School of Sociology began studying immigration in the context of debates surrounding the 1920s quota legislation; John Higham wrote his important *Strangers in the Land* during the deliberations leading up to the 1952 McCarren-Walter Act;[7] the upsurge of immigrant community studies took off alongside the "ethnic renaissance" of the 1970s and 1980s. Similarly, in another immigration country such as France, the arrival of foreigners has repeatedly prompted social scientists to study the problem, from demographers worried about depopulation since the late nineteenth century and the numerous legal theses published at the turn of the twentieth century to the economists, sociologists, and historians of the 1970s.[8] The highly public politics of immigration, the places from which we write (the countries of immigration), the sources most readily available, and the languages we know fostered a rich new social and legal history of *im*migration from the 1970s on.

The historiographic shift from assimilation to ethnicity to transnationalism that we have seen (chapter 2) has largely taken place within this idiom of immigration studies: studying the adaptation or cultural resistance of new arrivals in the first and second stages and then questioning how immigrants stay in touch with home as transnational subjects. The sneaking suspicion that transnationalism may be difficult has started to join up with a literature that asks how emigration has an impact on home countries, for better and/or for worse.[9]

Looking at transnationalism from the perspective of the home state has several advantages beyond providing an important mirror image to the history of immigration. For the migrants themselves, the attitudes and constraints surrounding departure are an important framework for understanding subsequent arrival and settlement; later relations to "home" will in part be grounded in how the homeland conceives of its emigrants. For the state, looking at emigration is another way of understanding the expectations of nation building and its fears of loss; emigration even more so than immigration defines the outer boundaries of the state. Em/immigration is of a piece for those who move, but emigration and immigration policies are also interrelated aspects of transnationalism's possibilities.

By looking at emigration from the perspective of the home state beyond the US example of changing ideas about expatriation, we can focus here too on one of the ways in which home states affect the possibilities of mobility. If *im*migration has become a litmus test for how nations define themselves, attitudes toward those who leave have also helped conceptualize citizenship, not just through entry but also through exit. Nevertheless, surprisingly little attention has been given to the history of policies and attitudes of states and societies with regard to departure or to the ways in which this can have an impact on transnational ties.[10] Some countries have formally forbidden their citizens to leave; others have forced some of their citizens into exile.[11] The focus here, as with most of the transnational literature, is on free movement—neither forced nor forbidden—and the European emigration debates that took place during the mass migration from Europe during the nineteenth and first half of the twentieth centuries. The point is to rethink transnationalism from the point of departure.

The Historiography of Departure

To argue for a new focus on leave taking is not to suggest that the question has been entirely invisible. Irish ballads are powerful testimony (and an important source) for the heart-wrenching experience of departure. Irish wakes for emigrants were community send-offs for those undergoing a virtual death by going into exile. Italian priests provided benediction ceremonies for those undertaking the long voyage. Various visions of America—the golden mountain for the Chinese, the *goldene medine* for Yiddish speakers—were part of the predeparture imagination. However "the destination question"—the comparative representations of possible sites of emigration before leaving—still merits greater exploration.[12] Most notably, to what extent did or have leave takers taken into account the dangers and difficulties of the road (or sea) ahead?[13]

Three different disciplines have called for a more thorough analysis of the predeparture world in order to better understand the migration process. The sociologist Abdelmalek Sayad, himself a border-crosser, argued forcefully throughout his life for a more thorough analysis of home and for understanding the perspective from the place of origin in order to comprehend the "double absence" of the migration experience. Sayad emphasized how emigration and immigration are two dimensions of the same phenomenon, linked in a dialectical relationship.[14] Today we would call Sayad a transnational by biography and scholarship.

Economists have furnished the most important body of literature on the effects of emigration on the home country, especially through the study of remittances. Indeed, some of the earliest economic treatments of the late twentieth-century migrations were done by economists anxious to quantify the impact of the "push" as well as the "pull." In France, for example, the political economist Georges Tapinos set up an elaborate table on the costs and benefits of contemporary migration for the countries of immigration and emigration, only to conclude with a question mark, underlining the impossibility of determining an exact balance sheet of migration for either country. Remittances and the economic impact of eventual return have framed many other contemporary studies in which consumption versus investment have been debated.[15] Indeed, remittances, important ties that bind, have come to be seen as proof of transnationalism itself. However, while some sociologists have started to dare to ask about the dysfunctioning of remittances, the developmental literature has engaged the post facto consequences of emigration more than the attitudes and policies that may encourage or discourage leaving in the first place.[16]

But it is the historical literature concerning the nineteenth and early twentieth centuries that interests me here. The conditions and causes of departure have been a staple of the immigration literature following early admonishments by Frank Thistlethwaite, Brinkley Thomas, and Dirk Hoerder to integrate the countries of origin into the migration story.[17] Most contemporary scholars of immigration indeed begin with a chapter on the "old country." Demographic, economic, and political transformations have long been recognized as the causes of the great nineteenth- and twentieth-century migrations. And, not surprisingly, works written from the perspective of the countries of mass *em*igration have been more attentive to the structural reasons for departure, the questions of its control and surveillance, and some of the economic effects.[18]

The aim here is to look at the political and cultural attitudes about emigration to think about the ways in which they can have an impact on subsequent transnational behavior. We can confront the ways in which states and societies of origin have aided and abetted but also fretted about and even obstructed the emigration movement. A full history of emigration could range from the laws governing departure and the formal ties that bind (passports, consulates, military service) to research into attitudes on the part of those who stay home.[19] A social history of emigration could reexamine letters from home rather than to home and consider newspapers and novels from the perspective of an *em*igration literature. Even within the context of free movement alone, emigration may be encouraged or discouraged, seen as adventure or folly, hailed as the spread of civilization or feared as treason. The following arguments, for and against emigration, show how public policy debates have often questioned the emigrants' ultimate ties to home. While the rhetoric has shifted slowly over the last two centuries from a concern about rupture to an emphasis on connections, the concerns that states have historically expressed remain as understudied clouds on the transnational horizon.

The Importance of Vantage Point

The interrelationship of emigration and immigration does not mean that sending and receiving countries see eye to eye on transnational movement. On the contrary. One country's attitude toward emigration may collide with another's politics of immigration; one country's *jus soli* can conflict with another's *jus sanguinis*. Attitudes (and historical research) often depend upon positioning in space and time.[20] Sending and receiving countries can have distinct perspectives depending on their positioning at either end of the migration route. Individuals may be caught in between.[21]

Two examples from opposite ends of the nineteenth century illustrate the discomfort of in-betweenness. The Gentleman of New York's brochure, which can be taken as a general exposition of intellectual arguments for and against emigration, as we have seen, was also clearly a product of its time. In the aftermath of the War of 1812—a war that broke out over different notions of citizenship—Great Britain and the United States, as sending and receiving nations, still had different ways of looking at the same individuals. When the British royal navy took to impressing American sailors on their ships during the Napoleonic Wars, it did so under the common-law precept that those born under the crown owed perpetual allegiance to it—in spite of colonial birth, residence, and the colonies' declaration of independence. To counter this impressment, the US argued strongly in favor of expatriation, especially insofar as they were the new American citizens who had done it. On the one hand, the home country sought to discourage transnationalism/expatriation/emigration. On the other, the host country sought to favor transnationalism/immigration and ultimately exchange of citizenship. While the British maintained perpetual allegiance over its subjects, Americans countered with a notion of voluntary choice of removal and allegiance. The debate over what we would today call structure versus agency shows the two states grappling with the possibilities of transnational movement.[22]

In 1889, an international conference on the Intervention of Public Powers in Emigration and Immigration took place in Paris that reversed the problem. Now transnational—particularly transatlantic in this case—movement was assumed. The question was how to channel it.[23] Two things are striking about this conference. First, emigration and immigration were linked from the very conceptualization of the conference. Second, the possibility of state intervention was postulated from the outset. However, the international gathering showed the tensions generated on both of these issues and how attitudes toward migration and its free or constrained flow could depend upon vantage point.

Constellations of interests cut across national lines, and the arguments reveal a variety of positions not solely dependent upon place. Humanitarian concerns about protecting migrants conflicted with the business interests of those speaking for port towns and steamship companies.[24] Debate focused on the importance and inevitability of international migrations and what action, if any, the governments should take. Above all, the discussions reflected the larger political economy debate over laissez-faire, still at issue a century after the French Revolution. Once the free movement of goods had been postulated, that of men and women had been (grudgingly) accepted as its correlate.[25] Yet throughout the nineteenth century, in the face of repeated abuses by shipping companies and emigration agents, even the most dogmatic proponents of unfettered movement accepted the idea that some limits had to be enforced. Indeed, from the beginning of the nineteenth century, passenger laws had been voted to protect the migrant. Britain was the earliest to do so in 1803. Emigration agents were increasingly regulated from midcentury on. But the 1889 conference brought together the nations involved on both sides of the Atlantic to discuss what further could or should be done in the face of increased migration and worsening conditions.

What is apparent in the course of these debates is that there would also be different perspectives depending on position along the migration routes: East or West, countries of emigration or of immigration. By and large, the delegates from the New World—where demographic and economic growth proceeded apace—were the most fervent partisans of complete freedom of movement (i.e. to their shores). Those from the countries of emigration, loath to see their citizens leave, were the more avid proponents of intervention, couching their argument in terms of humanitarian reasons. Untrammeled movement was thus perceived as favorable to the former; it represented a literally and figuratively unsettling concern for the older countries of Europe.

The conference conclusions show the difficulties that states had, both theoretically and practically, with a movement that went beyond their borders, their laws, and their nineteenth-century laissez-faire beliefs. The final resolutions (like individual national legislation before them) explicitly reaffirmed the theoretical notion of nonintervention while calling for the practical establishment of a nongovernmental organization to regulate the anarchy of the migration flows. It was necessary to interfere with the freedom of movement to maintain it. But this intervention could be conceptualized only as an exception from the principle of unhindered activity.[26]

The debate over spontaneous versus organized emigration lasted well into the twentieth century, with some proponents of the latter arguing that one purpose of regulation should be to ensure a more even gender balance among those departing.[27] But even within the context of a free market language of the right of movement, principles and attitudes toward transnationalism were often situationally located. Like American or British commentators earlier in the century, late nineteenth-century authors often viewed migration in relation to their own countries' demographic or economic concerns. Nineteenth-century issues seemed to prefigure twentieth-century ones, with a twist. If the nineteenth-century debates showed some countries worried about losing population while others were happy to get new workers, in the twentieth century, we see some countries happy to send off excess population with others unwilling to take on newcomers.

The European-wide Debates

Transnationalism can thus represent a spatial conflict of interest between countries. Yet within any one country, attitudes about leave taking may be varied at any given moment and/or change over time. Concerns about a lack or an excess of population have led to a variety of negative and positive attitudes toward emigration. Torn between wanting to retain one's citizenry and seeing departures as a safety valve or a source of remittances, discourse and practice can be contradictory. The emigration debates have always expressed concerns over the health, welfare, and identity of individual nations as well as over the individual-as-citizen: as transnational ally or national traitor.

GREAT BRITAIN

In 1803, Great Britain passed the first Passenger Act, followed by those of 1828 and 1842. The 1803 act's stated purpose was to protect emigrants from the hardships and abuses of overseas travel. But it was also intended to limit the growing outflow of Scottish Highlanders.[28] At the same time, artisans were in principle prohibited from emigrating altogether, for fear of losing valuable workers to the New World. However, as fears of overpopulation grew, the strictures against leaving were eased, and even in the early part of the century, some departures to the colonies were assisted. The prohibition on the emigration of artisans was removed in 1824. And beyond the early dispute with the upstart American nation over who belonged to whom, political and popular debate over emigration in Britain was often couched in the context of the social question, itself largely seen as the "Irish question."

In many ways, the British debate frames the way in which nineteenth-century emigration has been conceptualized in general, thanks to that infelicitous phrase, "shoveling out paupers."[29] Two 1826 and 1827 reports of the House of Commons Select Committee on Emigration argued in favor of emigration as a solution to misery. Of course, if there should be emigration, most of its proponents argued, it should best be organized and directed toward the empire, which could be called a sort of intra-imperial transnationalism.[30] A Colonial Land and Emigration Commission was set up in 1840. While naysayers objected that subsidizing emigration was too costly, and radicals criticized emigration plans as a conspiracy against the poor, imperial enthusiasts formed a tacit alliance with those who thought removal would solve the problems of poverty and unrest. A gradual reconceptualization of exit postulated a link between domestic policy, overpopulation, poverty, and the encouragement of emigration, insofar as the latter was imagined as an extension of self, to the empire.

There is debate as to whether the "shoveling out" was ever truly implemented; levels of direct government aid remained low due to fiscal constraints.[31] While the 1834 Poor Law Amendment Act helped pay for a small portion of those who left for the British dominions, in the end, Australia was too far and too expensive, and more people opted to leave for a former colony, the US, than a current, less developed, one. Over the nineteenth century, the terms of the debate shifted dramatically, from perceptions of expatriation as treason to an understanding of emigration and thus transnationalism as an economic necessity from the perspective of the home state. Emigration came to be seen as a social fact if not social policy, with the citizenship issue implicitly downplayed. After Great Britain formally rescinded the feudal notion of perpetual allegiance to one's birthplace with the Nationality Act of 1870 (in itself recognition that most emigrants were heading to the United States and not to the empire), the Colonial Land and Emigration Commission was dissolved in 1878. Explicit aid was no longer offered, but implicit hindrance was finally abated.

FRANCE

France, as most accounts have it, could barely conceive of emigration, so convinced were state and society that there was no better place to be than the Hexagon. The word "emigration" does not appear until the fifth edition of the *Dictionnaire de l'Académie française* in 1798. Emigration was imagined before 1789 as only temporary—or only enacted with an "esprit de retour"—and even afterward, the term "émigré" has been largely reserved for a specific historical category, that of the nobility who fled during the Revolution.[32]

Yet even the French, notoriously disinclined to leave home, did so in greater numbers in the nineteenth century than has been previously understood, especially if certain regional areas of high out-migration are examined.[33] Yet attempts were made to discourage them. As prefects from various parts of France noticed increased levels of departures toward North and South America in the 1820s and 1830s, they alerted the minister of interior, who in turn became concerned about the loss of potential soldiers. Public debate took up the matter in other terms. Statisticians and economists, like policymakers, worried about emigration as a demographic issue. Some saw it as weakening the population; others considered it a sign of and a stimulus to a healthy state. In addition, transmigration (the travels of other countries' emigrants across France to the port towns), like the emigration of French subjects, was recognized as good business for French port towns. In 1854, a government commission published a lengthy report comparing port statistics and emigration legislation throughout Europe.[34] A year later, the first French legislation aimed at protecting emigrants was passed. Notably this was done by regulating emigration agents.

In France, too, emigration was seen as positive or desirable mostly in connection with the imagining of empire. But the latter was never construed as a peopling project to the same extent as in Great Britain. On the contrary, French worries about depopulation rather than overpopulation characterized the national dilemma, reigning in too great an encouragement of departure, without contravening the principle that emigration is a fundamental right. As in the British case, though, emigration from France without intent of return implied forsaking citizenship until the nationality law of 1889, which both expanded the rights of immigrants to become French and redefined citizens abroad as part of the nation.[35]

GERMANY

While the older nation-states of Europe grappled with the meaning of movement and departure in relation to their long-held and yet changing understandings of self, two states of more recent vintage, Germany and Italy, confronted the contradictory aim of inventing themselves just as large numbers of their subjects were leaving.[36] Not surprisingly, the nineteenth-century German states viewed emigration as a source of loss and more generally distrusted movement for the instability it implied. Their constitutions allowed for emigration under certain legal conditions, but dowry and inheritance laws were serious impediments to leaving while the necessary exit permits cost time and money.[37]

The 1848 National Assembly (like the 1791 French Constitution) included the right to emigrate without restrictions as one of its basic tenets, but it (like the 1791 Constitution) was short lived. Even after unification, "emigration policy still steered an uncertain course between paternalistic advice and bureaucratic hindrance."[38] Nonetheless, as elsewhere, opinion slowly shifted from a mercantilist opposition to emigration to a more opportunist approval of same with the hope of relieving resource scarcity (or ridding the Reich of unwanted social democrats). Like Le Havre, German port towns such as Bremen were amenable to municipal legislation to regulate the emigration trade to reassure and encourage the business that it brought. The first emigration law at the federal level, passed in 1897, was meant to organize and control emigration and hopefully steer emigrants toward the German colonies. (Indeed, the little success of the latter was sometimes attributed to a weakness in the emigration law itself.)

If emigration could thus come to be understood as a positive means of relieving poverty or building empire, it still, however, meant loss of citizenship. Throughout the nineteenth century and until the 1897 law, leaving without intent of return meant disenfranchisement, as in most of the nineteenth-century countries; emigrants had to reapply for citizenship if they did return. However, at the same time, the development of a strongly cultural notion of the nation was almost contradictory in this respect, for it sought to maintain close ties with those who had moved abroad. The 1913 German citizenship law would formally bind overseas citizens to the homeland through the codification of *jus sanguinis*, holding on to nationals even as they became transnationals.[39]

ITALY

Indifference, anxiety, embrace. The Italian case particularly shows how states have shifted in their attitudes to transnational movement since the nineteenth century, translating into attempts to control emigration while hanging on to those who leave.[40] If before the 1870s emigration from Italy was both limited in number and seen as a marginal phenomenon, as the outflow became a tidal wave by the end of the nineteenth century, the emigration question moved to center stage of public debate. A first emigration law of 1888, which reiterated the principle of free emigration, was in effect partially restrictive. More to the point, it was by and large ineffective in its larger purpose of preventing abuses. In 1901, another law was passed that has been called "the most important of [Italy's] social laws."[41] It sought again, somewhat more effectively, to aid and protect the credulous from fraud. At the same time, a Commissariato dell'Emigrazione was set up to investigate the best means of doing so.

Two important issues were at stake. On the one hand, while investigating and debating emigration was a way of delineating the contours of the nation, such discussions also implied imagining the emigrants themselves. And the latter were invariably seen as vulnerable individuals needing protection from unscrupulous predators: "These great currents of our workers who go abroad resemble the currents of birds and fishes; the fishes are pursued by sharks seeking to devour them, the birds by falcons."[42] On the other hand, the question then was: protection by whom? The Italian state sought to take over functions previously managed by private (Catholic or socialist) organizations. Bilateral labor treaties were signed with countries of destination to replace private labor *padroni* there and better regulate recruitment. Ultimately, it was in part due to the mass emigration that the Italian protective welfare state came into being; the government sought first to count and then to aid the emigrants, as a way of maintaining their transnational ties.[43]

In 1912, a new citizenship law was passed that codified *jus sanguinis* as well as *jus soli* as a way of defining belonging, again reinforcing the ties of emigrants to their homeland. If in Great Britain emigration was conceived as a partial solution to the Irish question, in Italy, mass departures were seen as both a southern problem and as its solution. Here, as elsewhere, the question of emigration was integral to internal debates about political economy and a way of imagining a solution to the problems of uneven development. Only in this way could the "outpouring of human tragedies," seen by some as God's will, be interpreted as helpful to the nation and its consolidation.[44] After ignoring and then fearing population loss, the Italian state turned to regulating it, to encouraging return at best or at least the maintenance of transnational ties to home.[45]

HUNGARY

While the Slovak bourgeoisie argued against emigration, believing it weakened the Slovak nation, Hungarian debates interpreted emigration variously depending on who was leaving the empire. In Hungary, emigration was part of the debate about local agriculture and developmental policies; but it was also (like the meaning of the Irish to the British or the southern Italians to northern Italians) a debate about the social and ethnic composition of the monarchy. [46]

County authorities in Hungary, like local prefects in France, wrote to the central government with their worries about mass emigration. They spoke of "blood-letting" and of military weakening as a result of the departures; many hoped that the parliament would simply bar emigration to remedy the situation. As elsewhere, smooth-talking emigration agents received the brunt of the blame, but the emigration question also revealed clear distinctions between political parties and differing (agricultural and industrial) economic interests.

An 1881 bill took up the issue to reiterate that emigration was free all the while beginning to put into place certain restrictions. Here, as elsewhere, an ideology of free movement went hand in hand with attempts to regulate the emigration business. The relative ineffectiveness of the 1881 bill was apparent, as in other countries, by the repetition of subsequent laws (1903, 1909) that attempted to strengthen the measures of control.

On the one hand, many were happy to see at least the non-Magyars go—emigration as defining the contours of the nation's ethnic identity. On the other hand, emigrants could be lamented as lost soldiers, misled by "resourceful peddlers of human beings, who annually deplete Hungary's armed forces by as much as two battles of Mohács would."[47] As in Germany, men of military age were particularly suspect and allowed to emigrate only if they left behind a substantial deposit. In general, as Julianna Puskás well showed, the issue was closely linked to debates about the necessity of social and economic reform at home.[48]

Politicians, poets, and pamphleteers across Europe all joined the emigration debates in the nineteenth century. The representations of departure ranged from tragedy to opportunity, from moral decay and economic loss to spreading riches and civilization. The arguments for and against were many and, as we have just seen, varied by place and over time. The arguments as a whole may be seen as fluctuating between the positive and the negative with regard to what we would today call transnationalism. The steamships helped it happen, while wary states implemented some brakes on the movement.

Taken collectively, the nineteenth- and early twentieth-century debates on emigration reveal two strikingly different attitudes from the perspective of the state of origin: fear of flight on the one hand; encouraging departure on the other.

Fear of Flight

Emigration is, after death from starvation, the worst of necessities.[49]

Emigration is a form of suicide because it separates a person from all that life gives except the material wants of simple animal existence.[50]

So not just monarchs were worried about losing subjects. The nineteenth-century republics were similarly troubled about the potential loss of population, soldiers, and economic resources. "Depopulation anxiety"[51] was not just a French obsession. It was an early modern concern that continued to frame much of Europe's apprehension as subjects and citizens increasingly took flight to the New World in the nineteenth century. Political and economic images were closely linked in this fear of manpower depletion. The idea of a weakened military force, not to mention the even scarier thought of former citizens taking up arms against their countries of birth, haunted some writers. At the worst, emigration was considered a national emergency, equated with war.[52] Desertion became the more general metaphor for emigration; abandoning one's polity was strongly associated with the moral and physical abandonment of home, family, and ancestral tombs.[53]

But if emigration were a political, demographic, and military issue for the state, it was also and, perhaps above all, an economic one. While states could be afraid of losing citizens, they could be just as concerned that citizen workers were going to enrich other lands. Mercantilism continued to undergird nineteenth-century concerns that it was in the state's best interest to harbor a large, economically active populace.

Yet post-Malthusian nineteenth-century authors understood that it was not a question of population alone but the relationship between the number of inhabitants and resources that determined the wealth of a nation. The nineteenth-century French political economist Jean-Baptiste Say (1767–1832), who is often quoted as being hostile to emigration (a "dead loss for the country," comparing it to a whole army leaving, with weapons and baggage[54]), was more measured in his overall evaluation. While he taught that "no loss is more detrimental to the abandoned fatherland," he also believed that you cannot restrain citizens by force.[55] But to the extent that population loss was seen as a potential drain of both capital and especially labor, the economics of emigration continued to be a concern. The king in the 1813 dialogue was explicit (and could have spoken for nonmonarchical regimes):

> Were we to permit mechanics and sailors to depart, our manufactories would be deserted, and our ships unnavigated; because, as some other nations might offer greater prices for their skill and labour, they would resort to that nation; and the consequences would, to us, be fatal.[56]

The export of capital was (already) worrisome, but it was the loss of hard-working peasants and skilled laborers that was uppermost in the emigration imagery of the nineteenth century, similar to worries about the brain drain in the twentieth. It was a specific form of economic treason that most nineteenth-century landowners, industrialists, and deputies had in mind.

While the negative representations of emigration were largely conceived of with relation to the good of the state, the arguments used against it were also often couched in terms of the good of the individual. Pamphlets and parliamentary debates stressed the necessity of protecting the migrants from duplicity and harm. Thus, for one critic, who described leaving home as "frightful and impracticable,"[57] moral dangers lurked. The deserter was not just a lost soldier but a lost soul. The imagined pathos of leaving seconded the practical difficulties involved. A language of natural bonding with home and hearth had difficulty conceiving of a voluntary leave taking. And widespread concern about the material misery that may have encouraged the "push" was aggravated by the forces of "pull" incarnated in the widespread stereotype of unsavory emigration recruiters.

The emigration agents and ship companies—transnationalism's intermediaries—thus became a frequent focus of opprobrium in much of the negative discourse on emigration. As Julianna Puskás argued, it was undoubtedly easier to legislate the intermediaries than to outlaw emigration itself.[58] After the passenger laws, legislation aimed at regulating the emigration business became one of the major ways in which states intervened to regulate transnational movement in the nineteenth century. Thus when Georges de Pardonnet published his practical guides aimed at Frenchmen thinking of moving to the Far West, he prefaced his remarks by distancing himself from the less scrupulous of his profession. He was a special emigration agent appointed first by Kansas and subsequently by Oregon, and a member of the Société de géographie commerciale de Paris, with undoubtedly close relations to the Agence générale maritime that printed one of his brochures. While reassuring his readers about Indians and the desert, he warned them against the even greater threat of unscrupulous compatriots along the migration trail.[59]

While emigrants were thus often depicted as hapless victims or voluntary traitors, those same individuals could also be described as the front line of the spread of national glory. While emigration naysayers sought to complicate the movement, others at home realized the growing reality of the undertaking, saw its benefits, and ultimately sought to aid transnational ties. Thus, while many anxious commentators in the nineteenth century depicted separation from home and country as fraught with danger and contrary to the well-being of the individual and the state, others conceived of emigration in a more favorable light, as a way of letting their people go.

Encouraging Departures

States found it easy to let dissenters go—or even to encourage them to leave. Dissidence has always been one powerful motive for governments to allow departures. Dissent may be expressed through voice or exit, as Albert Hirschman cogently analyzed.[60] It may indeed be in the state's own interest to shovel out protesters along with paupers. Clearly, in those cases, not only is emigration welcomed by the state, but the maintenance of transnational ties is not. Political émigrés are clearly the least desirable transnationals from the state's point of view, and few exiles want to turn to their consulate for help.[61] Another category of undesirable transnationals may be unwanted minorities, also shed without too much regret, nay encouraged by the state.

But, less polemically, the safety-valve function of emigration has been perhaps the most prevalent metaphor for envisaging a happy solution to the problem of excess population. Insofar as earlier fears of underpopulation gave way to worries about its opposite, emigration was seen for most of the nineteenth-century European countries as one way to solve both overpopulation and pauperism. In Great Britain, neo-Malthusians argued in this vein, while in France, mid-nineteenth-century Frederick Le Play and his followers understood emigration as a demographic stimulus, not a drain—good for the emigrants but also good for the state, motivating those left behind.[62]

Emigration was also recognized early on as good business. Although specific economic interests worried about the loss of peasants or factory workers, other sectors of the economy, notably the shipping industry and port towns, saw the movement of migrants with glee. Remittances, hardly new to the late twentieth century, were already seen in the nineteenth century as part of a transnational family economy. As one Slovak pithily summarized the economics of emigration as seen from home: "We could pay off our debts."[63] Parliamentary debates show that government officials and politicians also clearly understood that emigration carried within it the seeds of economic development at home at the least, a spread of customers and civilization abroad at best.

In one specific way, emigration was seen not just as a domestic issue—a mechanism for letting off political, demographic, and/or economic steam—but as a way of aggrandizing the nation itself through emigration to the empire. Many theorists, skeptical if not hostile to emigration per se, agreed that in fact it depended upon the direction it took. Emigration to one's own outpost was possible if not desirable, and it could solve several problems at once (including the evil of birth control!):

> Too large a population in too small a country. And when it is so, either men must conquer colonies or emigrate or must become neo-malthusians. But the last course is vile, emigration is servile, and only the conquest of colonies is worthy of a free and noble people.[64]

The term "colonizers" was often used to refer to the spreading of culture, wealth, or power while implying the maintenance of greater ties with the homeland. The term "emigrants" designated those who left permanently to go overseas, maintaining few links to home.[65] Insofar as empire was seen as combining a civilizing mission with the prospect of greater economic and political strength, it could be a solution for the "emigration problem." The empire could channel the emigration fever, just as emigration could aid the colonial project.

More often, however, the two terms were used interchangeably as functional equivalents. Calling upon a "spirit of fraternity" that should "fulfill a sublime mission, that of the civilizing mission,"[66] colonial enthusiasts combined economic and moral language in their imagining of imperial emigration. For many abolitionists, European emigration was the logical and necessary conclusion to the ending of the slave trade and slavery.[67] Francesco Crispi, one of the earliest proponents of Italian expansion, wrote that emigrants

> must be like arms which a country extends far away into foreign places to draw them into its orbit of labor and exchange relations; they must be like an enlargement of the boundaries of its actions and its economic power.[68]

The most enthusiastic and optimistic saw emigration as draining off excess population and creating consumers abroad while carrying, through *jus sanguinis*, the ethnicity/blood of the nation itself abroad. As cultural ambassadors, emigrants would spread civilization and, it was argued, further world peace.[69]

Emigration as Transnationalism

"The debate over emigration addressed almost every problem of the times"[70] in the nineteenth century. And a history of transnationalism encompasses every issue from the relation of the individual to the state to domestic policies, national identity, and imperial hopes. Both the chronology and the interpretation of the emigration story can be "unstable" in the postmodern sense. Depending on when they start (beginning, mid-, or late-nineteenth century) and how they are interpreted, tales of emigration may emphasize closure, transnational openness, or altruistic or ideological constraint. The French Revolutionary Constitution of 1791 is often hailed as the first proclamation of an Enlightenment principle of the freedom to leave. But the Constitution was short-lived, and its declaration may be situated between Louis XIV's confiscation of property and imprisonment for those who left the realm and the Revolution's own laws against the noble émigrés.[71] The 1803 British Passenger Law has been acclaimed as the first law to embody humanitarian concern for emigrants, but it has also been described as a cynical move to slow emigration by making the process itself more difficult.[72] Are emigration laws humanitarian or self-interested, for the good of the emigrant or that of the state? How do they affect transnational lives? Regulation constrains anarchy, but it also hinders free movement. Should we emphasize that Prussian law increasingly accepted emigration in the 1840s or that at the same time it restricted men of military age from leaving?[73]

We can even ask what is an "emigration law." Rules about emigration and citizenship are found in nationality law, military service rules, and property laws. How do we interpret them, and to what extent are they signs of state interference in transnationalism? Laws could be passed to defuse criticism rather than actually to implement barriers to emigration, as Julianna Puskás suggested for the Hungarian case.[74] Furthermore, leaving and losing one's citizenship are not coterminous, as we have seen. The right to emigrate is not the same as the right to expatriate, and losing one's citizenship in the process may or may not be a deterrent to leaving. The question of intent (of return) looms large in determining both the individual's and the state's attitude with regard to departures.[75]

Each country's debates about leave taking tell their own stories about demographic, social, economic, and political concerns as states seek to define the outer boundaries of belonging. Nineteenth-century proponents and detractors of emigration existed in every country and undoubtedly within every family. The same act could be seen differently from departing and receiving ends, and attitudes could and did change over time. Positive or negative attitudes toward the movement itself would have an impact on the possibilities or limitations of subsequent transnational ties.

At the international level, however, we can discern a general shift over the nineteenth century in the European discourse about departure, moving from the negative to the positive, just as the right of expatriation and the freedom to change one's citizenship became more firmly entrenched in international law by the end of the century. Aristide Zolberg described nineteenth-century transatlantic migration patterns as a revolution in exit. As feudal ties to the land were released, as structural changes in the European population created a surplus, as North and South America created places of massive recruitment, and as the transportation revolution measured in railway tracks and shipping companies eased the way, controls on exit declined while the burden of control shifted to places of entry.[76]

As mercantilism gave way to Malthusianism, the general European history of emigration corresponded to a more general shift: from wanting to hoard bodies to wanting to shovel them out.[77] Political economic theory evolved from a belief in population (like precious metals) as constituting the wealth of the nation (encouraging marriages, taxing bachelors, and rewarding large families) to a worry about overpopulation, all of which would have an impact on ideas about transnational movement. Suspicions about emigration gave way to its reconceptualization as favoring colonial empire and trade and commerce more generally. As "depopulation anxiety" thus gave way to fears of excess population and as migration fever took hold, even the most skeptical theorists realized you could not prevent it. Explicit arguments in favor of emigration came increasingly to the fore. The positive assessment of transnationalism, as we would call it today, combined two major tenets of nineteenth-century liberalism: freedom of trade and freedom of movement. Emigration was articulated as both a new concept (and an increasingly common practice), in contrast to feudal notions of being bound to the soil, but also as an age-old natural right that could not be contravened.

This European-wide story of a progressive march toward an expanded right to leave reverses some long-held characterizations about nineteenth- and twentieth-century migrations. The history of *im*migration has long drawn a dichotomy between a nineteenth century of unhindered movement and a twentieth century replete with passports, visas, and border controls. In contrast, the history of *em*igration tells a counter tale, from land-bound servitude based on a people-rich mercantilism to an increasingly open later nineteenth-century ideology of the right to departure. The two versions are complementary, of course, but the story of progressive closure—the history of *im*migration that is—has become the metonymy for all migration history of the last two centuries whereas the story of *em*igration—if taken as the generic narrative—would be one of expanding openness. The emigration perspective reverses the directionality of the supposed nineteenth-twentieth century open-shut dichotomy.

Just as research has questioned any absolute divide on the *im*migration history timeline,[78] so the mercantilism to Malthusianism teleology, from castigation of emigration to the acceptance of transnationalism, needs to be qualified. As we have seen, the shift in attitudes toward emigration was far from a smooth or linear process. Successively (and at times simultaneously), the language of emigration ranged from cries of treason to benign neglect to active aid. Over the nineteenth century, hostility most often gave way to indifference before emigration was fully accepted as a "natural" right. Policy and theory often seem to have followed social reality, while shaping it in turn; states have more often followed where emigrants tread. Paul Leroy-Beaulieu initially considered emigration to be no more than a nose bleed with regard to the health of the nation, inconsequential as a cure for overpopulation. But between 1874 and the second edition of his book in 1882, he admitted that emigration could be a useful demographic remedy for Germany, Belgium, and Italy, while he had also become a frank enthusiast of French colonization.[79]

As people voted with their feet, the right to leave was reiterated sporadically throughout the nineteenth century and ultimately came to be regarded as a new natural law within the Western democratic tradition (while its counterpart, immigration, has never been construed as such). However, this did not mean that administrative and legal hindrances to exit disappeared. As we have seen, regulations on everything from transportation to emigration agents grew with the movement itself. The language of protection that surrounded the new passenger laws emphasized humanitarian help but also created hindrances to unfettered movement. As abuses, anarchy, and desolation over mass departures confronted the limits of a theory of free movement, regulating emigration was easier than regulating emigrants per se. As states contemplated the massive loss of soldiers or workers, "free" emigration had its own limitations. Military service and inheritance laws continued to act as obstacles across Europe as the state put limits on transnational movement and ties.

While the twentieth century has seen a generally more inclusive attitude toward emigration, the debates of the nineteenth century are well worth pondering for the more general story of transnationalism. From today's perspective, we forget how the possibilities of mobility have been constrained, even during the period of the great migrations. And those earlier debates—and practices—have echoes in the twenty-first century: bureaucratic hindrances or "the 'work' in paperwork" as Julie Chu has described it more recently.[80] Although the right of exit (albeit without a concomitant right of entry) has expanded and there are fewer barriers to leave taking, nonetheless international relations over the twentieth century, and not just immigration laws, have repeatedly created obstacles to effective transnational ties. Gendered worries about military service or about taking wealth or labor power abroad have not disappeared. While as we have seen, for the United States and the twentieth century alone, the figure of the expatriate has shifted from a worrisome "traitor" to a more benign "expat," the long arm of Tax Form 1040 stretches to wherever US citizens roam.[81] Other countries, such as France, have recently encouraged expatriation for the greater good while also favoring return ("impatriation") and keeping an eye on earnings abroad. The general arguments for and against emigration, fearing or hailing departures, continue to lurk in the transnational *imaginaire* of states.

We can now turn back to individuals, to see how they slalom around the transnational landscape. Transnationalism is a question of individual choice. But it is also embedded within a series of constraints and regulations with which the individual must comply or—willfully—ignore or escape. We can take a closer look at some of the most privileged transnationals around—US citizens—to see how even they have been snagged in between competing jurisdictions of citizenship and domicile.

5

"Au secours": Individuals Betwixt and Between

Americans in Paris, the Ultimate Transnationals?

What better way to explore the vicissitudes of transnationalism than to look at individuals' lives, even elite individuals, those who could seem to embody the epitome of transnationalism, with the ability of moving where they wish, shuffling back and forth between country of citizenship and country of domicile, enjoying the benefits of being abroad while turning to their home country in time of need. I focus here on a group of US citizens less well known than the famous writers and artists who came to Paris in the 1920s, but numerous and important in their own right, those whom I call the "other" Americans in Paris.

Who indeed could be more breathlessly free than the iconic Americans in Paris—those symbols of the roaring twenties *à la française*, living it up in Parisian cafés, in a city where they had come to write, to paint, or to do business in the heady early days of the "American Century." Americans in Paris in the first half of the twentieth century, both cultural and business "workers," were what I call peripatetic settlers. They settled in while still traveling a lot. The term "transnationalism" could have been invented for them. A transatlantic flow eastward began in the nineteenth century and picked up with earnest after the Civil War. Paris was one of the prime destinations for those who went to Europe for work or play, and by the late nineteenth century, Americans had created a large resident "colony," as they called it, the largest group of Americans abroad.[1]

Yet while reading files on this particular set of elite migrants, focusing on the longer-term residents who settled in the City of Light to sell American modernity while enjoying the benefits of old-world charm, I became intrigued by all of their difficulties that were nonetheless missing in many of the usual academic tales of transnationalism. It was not just that "selling the American dream" (to use Emily Rosenberg's phrase) was hard work for sometimes stymied industrialists when American soft power was just getting under way.[2] It turns out that even for elite migrants, there is the possibility of being trapped not just in translation but in transnationalism. At the least, transnationals are limited by the legal systems in which they are living, a necessary reminder of the constraints of the state.

Even well-heeled transnationals can conjugate extreme movement with solitude and tensions. The advantage of mobility can come with anomie and a loss of centering rather than a heady freedom of movement.[3] And this is not just a contemporary malaise. The cosmopolitan elite past or present, to whom I now turn, may be symbols of the ultimate free agents, traversing borders encumbered only by their Vuitton trunks. Yet they too are constrained in their transnational lives. What does this suggest about transnationalism for the less fortunate?

To look at Americans as *em*igrants is both a striking departure from American *im*migration history (focused on those who arrive and become Americans) and an important addition to European immigration history, where the usual focus is on poor immigrant workers. It is also a necessary venture into transnationalism. Anthropologists and sociologists have recently begun to study "expats," often emphasizing their novelty in the late twentieth century, an addition to the "newness" literature analyzed above.[4]

Indeed, the numbers have grown. The US State Department estimated some 6.8 million Americans living abroad in 2013.[5] Yet migration historians can provide a potent reminder of elite migrants of the past, before the term "expat" or "transnational" came into vogue. More specifically here, we can look at Americans who ventured abroad in increasingly large numbers over the last century as missionaries and as merchants, to proselytize and to make profits, notoriously successful in taking their models and manners with them.[6] As we have seen, US citizens became emigrants themselves in increasing numbers from the late nineteenth century on, coming under government scrutiny with regard to their citizenship as they did so. Carrying American goods and ways with them, they created immigrant communities of their own abroad. The term "American colony" was frequent in the first half of the twentieth century, but the naming of their condition remains highly unstable to this day: emigrants? expats (a late twentieth-century term as we have seen)?[7] Rarely have American citizens living overseas accepted the moniker "immigrants" (due to its lower-class connotation); the most frequent term is simply "Americans abroad" or "overseas Americans." The term "transnational" fits as well.

Taking Paris as a site to study the transnationalism of Americans abroad may be cheating. Americans in Paris are seemingly well known, the source of never-ending stories of artists-in-awe at the Louvre, writers-in-residence at cafés, or jazzmen wowing troops during World War I and then the locals at Montmartre cabarets.[8] However, already during the first half of the "American Century," many more American businessmen and lawyers settled in Paris than writers and artists. Living in Paris's posh neighborhoods, founding and facilitating American commercialism rather than criticizing it, they created their own clubs, organizations, churches, library, and a major hospital, all initially good "immigrant" community organizations.[9]

It was through the study of these privileged migrants that the conundrum of transnationalism started becoming clear to me. Americans abroad have turned to their transnational home networks when in need. This strategy does not always work. Yet if some elite migrants could have so much trouble negotiating transnationalism, what cautionary tale does this offer other migrants? Knowing that even the relatively privileged sometimes find transnational practices trying should push us to reread the sources about everyone else with a more critical eye. As we have seen through Gueydan de Roussel's (chapter 1) and Lily the Duchess's (chapter 3) experiences, crossing borders is complex, and multiple networks do not always function. Mobile lives create their own problems, most notably at the crossroads of different legal systems. So what is a thwarted transnational to do? Two major options emerge from the archives: call your lawyer or head to the consulate.

The Vicissitudes of Transnationalism: Gertrude and Clara

A law firm archive and the "Protection of Interests" files of the US State Department may be particular concentrates of tales of woe, skewing the sample away from the happy multitude who settle in *sans soucis*.[10] But they allow a varied view of the troubles encountered by citizens abroad. While the most well-heeled turn to their lawyers, a broader cross-section of citizens turn to their consulates in despair or with entitlement in time of need, trying to marshal networks both at home and abroad to get them out of trouble. The wide-ranging problems run from custody cases to philandering spouses, but two types of issues show the complexity of the transnational situation: how wandering can be wearisome, and how transnational ties via the consulate show individuals turning to their home state and putting their citizenship to work.

In the first instance, we can ponder the joys but also the tiresome aspects of transnationalism. Mobility can be fatiguing. Two women who turned to their lawyers left a trail of letters speaking of worries and woes. A biased sample no doubt since that is what lawyers' ears, or in this case eyes, are for. But the tales of these two divorcees, one mostly gay (in the older sense of the term), the other considerably less so, are useful reminders of the limits of transnationalism.

Marriage can be risky, as we all know, although more than half of couples do live happily ever after—or at least do not divorce. Marriage abroad carries its own risk, and "international marriages" (mixed marriages—that is, mixed by nationality) have always combined the thrill of adventure with the reality of foreign customs and laws. Such marriages may be asymmetrically gendered by time period: more American heiresses marrying European noblemen in the first part of the twentieth century, more American soldiers marrying foreign women after each war. For women, the legal cost of an international marriage could be high, economically and citizenship-wise. Heiresses such as Lily the Duchess could trade their fortune for an aristocratic title, but, as we have seen, any American woman marrying a foreigner after 1907 (and until 1922) lost her US citizenship, having to "follow" the nationality of her husband.[11] Furthermore, gendered laws in the spouse's country could also be considerably different than at home; for example, a foreign woman marrying a Frenchman (before 1965) would find out that she could not open her own checking account in France without her husband's signature.

Yet even Americans married to other Americans living abroad could find themselves in the crosshairs of not just different legal systems but of exchange rates and other complications related to living overseas. On the one hand, all divorces may be messy, but they may be compounded in a transnational setting. On the other hand, the transnational setting may contribute to the circumstances surrounding the divorce. We can take the example of two American divorcees, one ultimately exuberant at her newfound freedom, the other forlorn, both of whom, after years of married life in France, ended up crisscrossing Europe in the interwar years.

In 1929, Gertrude Moulton, who had been living in Europe for two decades, separated from her husband, Arthur Moulton. As she headed to the Hôtel Princess, a posh hotel in the fancy sixteenth arrondissement of Paris, she left behind their Parisian apartment and their suburban chateau, as well as her precious porcelain collection. She was a wealthy woman who had inherited wealth and had married into wealth (twice in fact; Moulton was her second husband). When she and Moulton divorced, they each turned to North American lawyers practicing in Paris. There were no particular Franco-American legal problems, but the divorce negotiations were underpinned by political and economic events on both sides of the Atlantic, and the divorce seems to have made Gertrude into a particularly peripatetic transnational.

Her abundant correspondence with her lawyer, often focusing on long lists of disputed possessions, reflects the transatlantic and intra-European mobility and concerns of a wealthy elite.[12] She and her ex-husband had different assessments of the future of American and European economics and politics in the fraught 1930s. Exchange rates, bond values, and European politics took on central roles in the divorce and alimony negotiations. In 1936, her ex-husband feared that if "soak-the-rich" Franklin Roosevelt were reelected, the US investments that formed the basis of both his income and her monthly alimony payments would tank. With greater faith in the British Empire, Arthur Moulton therefore argued that the investments should be transferred to British insurance annuities (purchased in Canada). The exasperated Gertrude wrote to her lawyer from Salzburg to protest. She had greater faith in the American dollar and did not agree to the change in investment strategy. At the same time, she was cautiously optimistic about the situation in Europe as she traveled to Austria and Italy to marshal support for an international music project.

Gertrude was undoubtedly an energetic woman from the outset, but her divorce seems to have invigorated her and not just to fight the terms of the divorce settlement and get back her porcelain collection. The divorce increased her mobility and also strengthened her resolve to bring to fruition her project for an International Center of Music. She had already drawn up plans for the project in 1928, and French authorities had offered a site in the Parc de St. Cloud. But with her divorce, the crash, and the depression, the St. Cloud proposal disappeared, and the now traveling transnational took her project to Salzburg. There she presented it to Federal Chancellor Dollfuss and met Mussolini, writing back exultantly to her lawyer that her project had been well received and that she planned on seeing Mussolini in Rome the following year—if only Arthur Moulton could see her now. Ultimately, war arrived, and the novella-worthy law firm file ends. We don't know whether Gertrude got her porcelain back, and it seems that her music project was never implemented.

Gertrude Moulton's story may describe transnationalism at its best: the freedom of a determined woman with wealth and connections traversing Europe, even in the troubled 1930s, with access to cosmopolitan salons and political palaces. But in the meantime, Gertrude left hints that the euphoria of her transnational life had its down side. She complained to her lawyer about "drifting about in hotels," from Vienna to Salzburg to Paris. Only the Chase Bank in Paris gave her some stability as she used it as her permanent mailing address.[13]

Gertrude was not alone in expressing the weariness of the transnational condition. The jealous and hurt first wife of Edward Steichen also found herself a traveling transatlantic woman in the interwar years, even more frustrated with her divorce settlement and her wandering life.[14] Clara Smith had met Edward Steichen in Paris, and although they married in New York, they returned to settle outside of Paris in 1906. There Steichen was building his career, first as a (failed) painter, then as a very successful photographer (and ultimately famed curator of the "Family of Man" exhibit). They were friends with the Rodins and other French and American artists in Paris. They had two daughters and seemed destined to live happily ever after as Steichen's fame grew. However, Clara suspected Edward of having an affair with a friend of hers, another American woman in Paris. (There were also rumors about Isadora Duncan.) Exasperatingly, however, the (French) domestic help, whom she thought were on her side, refused to make any formal depositions in the matter. In any case, Clara's jealousy was getting the better of her, the Steichens were drifting apart, and in 1915 Clara returned to Missouri. But she missed Europe and Paris in particular.

After World War I and after her divorce, Clara oscillated between Missouri and Europe. She ended up in Spain in the 1930s, largely it seems because Spain was cheaper than France. But she was not happy there and complained about other Americans in Majorca: "[With] all deference to its scenery I loathe [this hole], a very second-rate, pseudo-artistic colony of my own compatriots. . . . I am fed up on scenery and olive oil and such atmosphere."[15] She longed to be within reach of libraries and streets passable in the winter. She would have preferred Paris but could not afford it. She hoped that Steichen's fame and presumed new wealth could lead to a reevaluation of her alimony, with little success apparently. (But archives do not necessarily include final chapters.)

Clara's story, like Gertrude's, can be told in two ways. One would emphasize the two women's freedom of movement and the agency of their travelling lives. Their mobility was real and had its advantages. But there were limits that were physical as well as emotional. Their transnational lives and the relative impoverishment of divorce were aggravated by the fluctuating politics and exchange rates of the interwar period. Even long-term upscale residential hotels were not the same as a fixed domicile, and the uncertainties of exchange rates were aggravating factors for both of them. There were days when they were fed up with the movement itself. We may legitimately ask—as for any historical study—how much weight we should give to the complaints in the sources versus competing tales of triumphant transnationalism. Gertrude, after all, was very proud of her accomplishments, and Spain was still more interesting for Clara than Missouri. Were the grumblings but that of disaffected divorcees otherwise profiting from living abroad? The uncertainty of currency exchange may be a small price to pay for a freedom of mobility. But the disappointments and difficulties are part of the story.

In their own ways, Lily the Duchess of Mecklenburg, Gertrude, and Clara were caught between domicile and citizenship, maneuvering despondently (Clara), exultantly (Gertrude, for the most part), or in death (Lily and her will) between different cultural, legal, and symbolic regimes, while they all turned to their lawyers for help. Other Americans-in-distress turned to the consulate. Consulates—those legal and symbolic representations of home—are indeed another hub for examining transnationalism. The "Protection of Interests" files in particular provide a fascinating glimpse at the intersection of individuals and their government, or how citizens abroad draw upon their connections to home.

Protection of Citizens Abroad

Allegiance is reciprocal. While we have looked at the ways in which states relate to their citizens abroad, we can also ask about the ways in which citizens overseas turn to their home countries both in times of war as in times of peace.

Citizenship rights can be mustered, demanded, and used by those who have left home. As for other countries, Americans abroad have been seen at times as functional ambassadors, carrying cultural models or goods to outlying markets. They have also, as we have seen, been perceived as ungrateful ex-patriots for having left the homeland behind. In either case, citizens abroad provide a test case on the limits of what the state can do for them. They furnish a particularly interesting example of how "thin" ties of citizenship can become "thick" when a problem is at hand.[16]

We can look at how demanding Americans outside of the United States, fully convinced of their rights, could draw upon their citizenship vociferously. Most were motivated by personal problems, but many argued that their individual case implied a defense of the value of American citizenship as a whole. When e.e. cummings was arrested in France during World War I, his father—a well-connected Harvard professor—beseeched Woodrow Wilson to "do something to make American citizenship as sacred in the eyes of Frenchmen as Roman citizenship was in the eyes of the ancient world."[17]

By shifting the focus from the state to the individual to look at the social uses of citizenship by transnational individuals, we can examine what I call the quotidian use of citizenship. While scholars have often made the distinction between functional and affective citizenship, the first describing the tie to the state and the second to a sense of nation, I prefer what legal scholar Kim Barry called a practiced identity as distinct from legal status.[18] This use of citizenship raises more general questions about emigrants' transnational relationships not just to home and family but to government. Passport-wielding individuals can be found in consulates around the world demanding a variety of services, from helping them do business to safeguarding their possessions to getting out of town during wartime or keeping out of prison at other times. By focusing on the US consulate in Paris in the first half of the twentieth century, we can see more concretely how transnationals may use their citizenship to help get them out of a variety of scrapes.

Consulates are an externalized borderland where foreigners seek admittance, but they are also places where overseas citizens seek protection. For the latter, consulates are the institutional intersection point between the individual and the state, between their domicile and their citizenship. They should also be at the historiographic crossroads of citizenship and migration studies.[19] We have ignored consulates undoubtedly due to a more general emphasis on immigration than on emigration but also due to the assumption that citizens abroad steer clear of them. Many undoubtedly do. Most im/emigrants do not go to their consulates unless necessary. Political refugees avoid or fear their embassies altogether. The celebrated interwar fugitive from the Teapot Dome Scandal, Harry Blackmer, who spent twenty-five years in exile overseas ("lightened by a second marriage and some high living in France"), spent much of his time avoiding the US consulate in Paris. So much so that the famous US Supreme Court case *Blackmer v. United States* reiterated the power of consulates to subpoena citizens abroad.[20] The social contract of citizenship was supposed to work both ways. What interests me here, however, are not those individuals summoned to their consulates but those who went voluntarily to mobilize them as flag-bearers of identity and strategic sites of help.

Consulates predate embassies as a form of representation abroad, and the young United States continued this custom by first appointing unpaid consuls in foreign lands. The main function of consulates in the early days of the Republic was to protect American shipping and commerce along with American citizens. They were instituted to generate "a sense of security and confidence conducive to foreign trade, travel and residence in foreign lands. . . ."[21] Seamen and shipping disputes were a major focus of their early activities. At the same time, the link between consulates and the promotion and protection of trade was clear from the outset. Consular posts were initially given to merchants residing abroad who continued their own businesses. Throughout the nineteenth century, various attempts were made to reform the system. Two acts of 1855 and 1856 regulating the service stipulated that consuls were to be salaried and that they were to turn fees over to the US Treasury. A consular convention was signed between the United States and France in 1853, giving US consuls the right to act informally on behalf of American citizens vis-à-vis the French authorities, a convention still in force during the interwar period.[22]

In spite of the 1855 and 1856 acts, the organization of the consular service was still often criticized, and other attempts at reform were engaged from the early twentieth century on to professionalize the function and to raise salaries. (Among other things, reformers wanted consuls to know at least one other modern language besides English.) The rank of ambassador was created in 1893 and, after the Spanish-American War, the expansion of the Diplomatic Service and its professionalization increased in line with the growing presence of American foreign trade and investment worldwide. The consular reform bill of 1906, but especially the Rogers Act of 1924 emphasizing merit rather than politics as a prerequisite for the job, led to the Diplomatic and Consular Services being combined into a unified Foreign Service, creating a permanent and professional corps of career officers.[23] The US Consular Regulations are explicit about the ways in which consular officers may promote the national economic interest:

creating a situation favorable for the importation of American goods; submitting frequent economic and commercial reports to assess market opportunities; and lending aid and advising American citizens with regard to commercial and industrial matters.[24] They are also the sites where citizens in good standing may demand that the other part of the citizenship bargain be enforced: protection.

"Among the most varied and interesting functions of a consular officer," "frequently arduous and unnoticed," includes the protection of citizens.[25] Initially envisaged to help stranded seamen or to retrieve deserters, the protective function grew along with the number of US civilians abroad over the nineteenth century. Besides looking out for US business interests, consular officials came to take care of everyone from the impecunious and stranded to the mentally deranged, and they helped those who had accidents, handled funerals, and even performed marriages in some locales. But, already in 1877, John Russell Young commented on "the tendency of the American mind to seek his minister [consular representative] upon all occasions when he is overcharged for candles, when he has lost his baggage, when he is homesick, and . . . when the right gloves have not come home from the bazaar." Young theorized that, as taxpayers, Americans had a "sense of possession in dealing with ministers and consuls," so much so that it was just as well, he thought, that the legation be not too convenient of access.[26]

At the turn of the twentieth century, as rising numbers of Americans went overseas, the protection of civilians abroad increasingly interested individual states and international law. As we have seen, in an early paean to globalization, former secretary of state Elihu Root turned to the importance of expanding trade and commerce in his 1910 address on "The Basis of Protection to Citizens Residing Abroad," while Edwin M. Borchard devoted an entire volume to *The Diplomatic Protection of Citizens Abroad* in 1915.[27] Early twentieth-century US policy generally deemed the consul duty-bound to accord protection once citizenship was unquestionably established.[28] Help, however, was always constrained by limited funds and three provisos: proof of citizenship; no intervention in purely private matters (a list of American lawyers was always ready to be passed on, with the caveat that the consulate assumed no responsibility for their services); and use of all available local legal remedies first.

Throughout the first half of the twentieth century, American citizens abroad and worried families at home turned to the State Department and the Paris consulate for everything from investigating the whereabouts of wandering Americans to retrieving forgotten purses or lost luggage. ("Americans are notably careless about their luggage."[29]) Not all requests were treated with perfect equanimity. The category of "ridiculous requests" encompassed pleas not always from transnationals, such as a California writer sending in a lengthy, detailed list of questions for a book he was writing on France.[30] The consuls' patience could be sorely tried, but the consular correspondence reveals the numerous problems encountered by overseas citizens as well as both their number and their variety, not to mention the fact that their families at home also turned to the consulate for help. The level of help that the consular officers of the time were willing and able to give is impressive to the jaded twenty-first-century eye. But the limits on their time and tolerance are also in abundant evidence.

Help in Time of War

Wartime requests by people overseas are undoubtedly the most obvious moments for transnational citizens to appeal to their home government for aid. At the beginning of the Franco-Prussian War, the US Legation in Paris issued passports to some 3,300 American residents and tourists and provided "protection papers" for Americans to post on their property in the hope that American belongings could be safeguarded from the invader's grasp.[31] (At the time, Americans did not otherwise need passports to leave the United States or to enter France.[32]) Similarly, at the outbreak of World War I, thousands of Americans abroad converged on their embassies. As the ambassador in London described it, "crazy men and weeping women were imploring and cursing and demanding—God knows it was bedlam turned loose."[33] At the US embassy in Paris, there was even a distraught retired major trying to leave with his pet bird.[34] Ambassador Myron T. Herrick stayed on in Paris even after the French government left for Bordeaux, and the embassy's tasks quadrupled with the need to issue emergency passports and help arrange letters of credit and transportation. Approximately 5,000 Americans registered with the embassy, either by letter or in person. The embassy set up a committee of private citizens to assist it, which in turn created five subcommittees—on transportation, credit, registration, relief, and protection. The relief subcommittee advanced cash for passage as long as individuals provided proper identification and gave promissory notes or other security. Leaflets were prepared in both French and German, and American flags were distributed, all to be placed on American property as protection. But, as the ambassador reported, "Fortunately the situation never became so serious [i.e., Paris was not occupied by the Germans (this time)] as to warrant the posting of these notices except in one or two châteaux in outlying districts."[35] They in effect became a trial run for placards that would be used in 1940.

The two major concerns during World War I were lost people and lost possessions. Worried Americans at home scrawled handwritten or typed letters to the secretary of state looking for relatives who had moved abroad and not kept in touch. Alice B. Toklas's father in San Francisco traced her through the State Department, which relayed the information to the consulate in Paris, which found her. The consulate made inquiries at 27 rue de Fleurus, where Toklas lived with Gertrude Stein, and found that they had left for Palma de Mallorca the previous April. As Stein recounted it, she and Toklas had gone to the embassy to get passports before leaving for Spain, but two embassy clerks said they did not need them unless they were going to the US; their French identification papers were sufficient. When Stein insisted, saying that a friend of hers had received one, the embarrassed official said that that was a very special case, to which she replied severely that there could be "no privilege extended to one American citizen which is not to be, given similar circumstances, accorded to any other American citizen."[36]

While people turned to the government to track family members, they also sought to protect possessions. Individuals who had settled in France but had fled back to the United States wrote worriedly to the State Department about their property in France. One American woman, caught in Connecticut at the outbreak of the hostilities, turned desperately to the government: "I am an American. . . . Everything I own in the world is there, relics, furniture, clothes, furs, everything. . . . Could you not advise the embassy there to help me?"[37] A man wrote from Cleveland in 1915 enclosing a pawn ticket and money. He wondered if the embassy could please redeem a diamond ring that he had left in Paris. And the embassy did, sending it back to its owner, even specifying that the unaccompanied ring should be exempt from duty.[38] In many other cases, the State Department told the consular officers to keep American property under observation.[39] One did not have to own furs or diamonds to be helped, but perhaps those who did felt a greater level of entitlement and had the wherewithal (nerve?) to ask the government for help.

Individuals mustered a variety of arguments to prove their US citizenship, first to the American consulate but ultimately with the final destination being the French government. Gustav Adolph Trube, head of Westinghouse Air Brake's French company, had lived in France since 1912, but he was expelled during World War I as a supposed enemy national due to his German-sounding name. He explained to the embassy that his father had been born in Germany only because his grandfather, an American citizen, had been traveling there; his father became naturalized in the United States upon coming of age; his mother was American born; and, he added, her ancestors had fought in the American Revolutionary War. Trube's employer and his friends at the exclusive Noonday Club, who, on behalf of the "Colonie Américaine à Paris," signed a petition in his support, all vouched for him to the embassy, which in turn vouched for him to the French government. (The expulsion order was suspended, but he was told not to return to France before the end of the war, and, in spite of repeated efforts to clear his name in France, he [and the embassy] was unsuccessful.) Trube ended up staying in Pittsburgh after the war.[40] Mr. Emil/Emile Supper, a German-born naturalized US citizen, had worse luck. He had lived for twenty years in Lyon and was "known and considered" as an American citizen there, although the consul was somewhat miffed that he had never contacted the office before. In his case, he was turned down by the State Department for help. He had overstayed the 1907 Expatriation Law's presumption of a five-year limit of residence abroad for naturalized citizens. He reverted to being German in both American and French eyes with disastrous consequences: his private and business goods were confiscated, and Supper was interned in a French concentration camp.[41]

While professional jealousies may have brought businessmen to the attention of the French authorities, other forms of denunciation could lead American civilians to turn to the US government for help with their identification during the war. One woman had been denounced as German by a discharged French cook who, "in her ignarance has not known the difference between a Holland Lady and a German Woman!!" Mrs. Haeften-Hatch wrote heatedly to the secretary of state from Cannes in 1916, arguing stridently that the US government should protect "American innocent citizens from the callomnious statements of infurated servants" and more generally the "infuriated lower classes." She brought all of her ancestry and connections to bear on the matter, from the fact that, born in Holland, she was well known by Queen Wilhelmina and the Dutch minister currently in Washington, to her more important US citizenship connection, her husband, Mr. Charles P. Hatch, a Rough Rider known to "Mr. Rooseveldt" himself.[42]

Later, with the outbreak of World War II, thousands of Americans flocked again to the US Consulate in Paris. Some sought help leaving. Others, who planned to stay, requested embassy certificates to post on their doors. By identifying the inhabitants as US citizens, these protective talismans were intended to keep the enemy at bay and prevent the Germans from appropriating the belongings of neutral (for the moment) individuals. After 1941 and the US entry into the war, it behooved those Americans still left in France to take the certificates down quickly. But in the meantime, Americans abroad, full of fear (of Germans) and trust (in the US government), contacted the embassy and filled out detailed descriptions of the contents of their apartments, houses, or châteaux down to the last asparagus tong.[43]

Questions of citizenship and its proof were paramount, but both American-born and naturalized Americans drew upon a variety of logics as they requested or demanded protection. Genealogies, friends, connections, and public reputation all became definitions of one's US credentials and networks to exercise the transnational citizen's right to protection. This was true in time of peace as in time of war.

Help in Time of Peace

Missing-persons inquiries persisted throughout the interwar period. At the same time, citizens overseas turned to the government for more mundane matters, requesting help in recovering everything from missing hats to lost handbags. To locate wandering Americans, the consulate acted as a veritable detective agency, checking records, sending circulars to all of the French prefects, writing to local mayors, visiting addresses in Paris, talking to concierges while also inquiring at the American Red Cross and the American Express Company or putting advertisements in the American papers in Paris: "letter waiting at the consulate-general." Whereabouts inquiries could begin with a handwritten letter from a woman in Kansas addressed directly to the secretary of state that would be transferred from the State Department in Washington to the embassy in Paris and to the consulate-general there or to one of the consulates in the provinces, which made inquiries and responded via the embassy to the State Department back to Kansas reassuring her that her son was safe and sound, just not much of a correspondent.

The "missing" in France could simply be laggard letter writers; and some Americans, once found, were happy to answer their home folks, via the consulate: please send money, I've been too embarrassed to ask. But a good number of Americans settled abroad did not want to be found and did not want to be known to the US officials. A company carrying a life insurance policy on a former employee tried to find him via the State Department; his wife thought him dead and presumably wanted to collect. The consulate found Mr. Jones all right; however, he was apparently reluctant to go home.[44] When eighteen-year-old Miss Gladys F. Brown fled toward France in 1913, she had no intention of calling in at the consulate. She had run off with Mr. George H. Dutting, approximately forty years old, and it was her parents who used the government to track her down. Once the SS *Kaiserin Auguste Victoria* arrived in Cherbourg, consular agent Osborne went on board and "made an earnest appeal to her sense of propriety, decency, filial affection, and expediency." Gladys absolutely refused to debark, and Dutting swore that he was not married, as her parents assumed, and that he intended to marry Miss Brown. In the end, a letter from the father thanked the State Department for its help, and reported: "As the persons connected in this case are now married, everything has turned out for the best."[45] Once ferreted out, some Americans abroad requested that no further action be taken or that their address be withheld. The reverse was also true. Sometimes Americans in France asked the consulate to find their nearest of kin in the US; yet families who had bid good riddance to troublesome relatives did not necessarily want to be reached either or simply had no funds to help. Some transnationals (and some of their families) sought to cut off ties, not maintain them. If states could sometimes engage in good-riddance policies, so could individuals.

However, in all of these cases that came to the State Department's attention, the initial assumption was that the homeland government could be mobilized for aid. Sometimes timidly, often with temerity, Americans turned to the consulate for everything from custody cases to lost jewelry. In one case, Mr. Fulton, an upstanding resident of the American community in Paris, asked for help in contacting the US Consulate in Florence, where his divorced wife had taken his four children. She had apparently abandoned them with a governess but no rent money, while she left for the United States with a "young Italian Prince." The children and the governess were returned to Paris. In another case, it was the mother who, after having initially left her three small children with family in Paris, had been able to have two of them join her in London, but she asked the consulate to help her find the third child who had been "spirited away by its uncle."[46]

The extent of consular help to worried parents and citizens in distress may have depended on the temperament, energy, and resources of the men on the job. If Vice Consul John R. Wood's 1925 report is any indication, it was a record year for visits.[47] Of the thirty-nine cases on which Wood reported, there were several cases of true duress due to accident or arrest. The Misses Moy and Connors of Boston had been in a serious car accident on their way to visit the battlefields; the consulate helped arrange their hospitalization, transportation, and negotiations for their insurance claims. Americans accused of smuggling also turned to Wood's office. They generally protested that they did not know enough French to understand the limitations on importing tobacco or exporting cash. Consular officials parleyed lesser fines and the return of impounded goods.

Asking the US government for help in dealing with dire health issues, custody cases, or customs officials seems, from an early twenty-first century perspective, logical arenas for state intervention. More surprising is how transnational individuals called upon the powers of their US citizenship to help them with travel arrangements, missing luggage, shopkeepers, and difficult dressmakers. Yet Wood reported with equanimity, indeed with satisfaction, how the consulate helped find and forward luggage, settle refunds, get reimbursements, or even recover a lost pocketbook from a taxi or a forgotten tie stickpin from a hotel room—not to mention the book manuscript recovered for a Mr. Smith from a literary agent who was no longer answering Smith's letters. When Miss Perkins, after a "gay and expensive life," pawned her jewelry to pay her way home, the consulate helped her recover the jewelry by finding the gentleman who held the pawn ticket. But above all, since Americans (already) came to Paris to shop, a surprising number of Americans turned to the consulate for help with dressmakers. The vice consul himself described one couple's dispute with the clothing establishment "A La Reine d'Angleterre" as "a very interesting and deserving case" in which he helped the Banghofs get justice for a defective lambskin coat. And when the stout Mrs. Beardslee, disappointed with a specially made coat, accused the dressmaker of fraud, a consular official personally accompanied her to the shop, and a new coat was made.

As transnational Americans turned to the consulate for help in tracking people and protecting possessions, the early twentieth-century consular officer seems to have played the role of chivalrous savior, charging off to right wrongs for the citizens in his care, negotiating first in a friendly manner then firmly when necessary. Apparently, as many citizens hoped, the official muscle of Uncle Sam helped convince foreign hotel owners and coat makers to reimburse sums or articles due. Not one case reported by Wood was unsuccessful. Indeed, the vice consul's report is full of pride as he detailed his efforts to his bosses at the State Department, including excerpts from thankful notes from grateful citizens abroad.[48]

Proving Citizenship

Proving citizenship, of course, is a prerequisite for getting help from one's home government. The US government had to ask: was the transnational individual still a US citizen? US-born Americans and foreign-born naturalized citizens alike came explicitly under the protective cloak of US citizenship. However, some categories of citizens were at particular risk abroad. During

World War I, the government advised young American men of French heritage that it behooved them not to travel to France lest the French government claim them for conscription.[49] As we have seen, naturalized citizens could lose their US citizenship if they stayed abroad too long (two years in their country of origin or five years in any other foreign state), and American-born women who married foreigners lost their citizenship between 1907 and 1922.[50]

Yet for those who felt firm in their citizenship status, or even some who brazenly tried to use a right they did not have, a double level of proof was necessary. People first had to convince the US government; when in doubt, the consulate checked out an individual's status before giving help. But often the ultimate purpose of that proof was to help Americans verify their credentials to the French authorities. The consulate and the State Department certified or helped produce birth certificates, passports, or affidavits. Passports have been studied as part of the means by which states exercise both sovereignty and surveillance. But they are not just controls on movement. They also function as protective devices, as proof of individuals' presumed right to aid, both vis-à-vis their home country and in facing foreign governments. In this regard, even passports are two-faced, identifying citizens to their home state but also identifying them to other governments. Yet, in the interwar years, while the format of passports was becoming more standardized, they were not an absolute necessity for leaving the United States or for entering France. Indeed, throughout much of the 1920s and 1930s, they were considered a nuisance or even an affront to the respectability of the "better classes," who considered such ID should be necessary only for criminals.[51] Furthermore, although a 1907 Registration Law (itself a sign of the growing number of Americans overseas) put into place the procedures for registration of American citizens abroad, then, as now, the vast majority never signed in at the consulate.

Americans abroad thus used a variety of papers and arguments to prove their citizenship and their Americanness to the ambassador or the secretary of state. They referred to their passport number when they had one but also to their ancestry—"my ancestors were among the founders of the Dutch Colony in America"[52]—and they garnered supporting letters from American friends to attest to their bona fide Americanness and general reputation. Frank/François Gueydan/de Roussel had seven Texas friends submit an affidavit on his behalf.[53] Another man stressed his American credentials by pointing out that not only was he a native-born citizen, but that he kept almost all of his fortune in the US, where he traveled frequently and where his bankers and business partners were located. He concluded by arguing that his particular problem had consequences for all American citizens doing business in France and thus for all American interests there.[54]

The fact is that many Americans living in France were illegal aliens. And they turned to the US government for help in regularizing their situation. Many had simply never bothered to register with the French authorities, but, especially as job opportunities for foreigners dried up due to anti-immigrant labor laws in the 1930s, Americans who had worked off the books began turning to American lawyers and the consulate for help in getting or renewing their French residence or work permits. The French government was not giving work permits to foreigners unless they had resided in France for ten years. The consulate could help provide proof of that residence.[55] Miss Grace V. Carpenter, who had lived in France since 1924, had let her French residence permit lapse since 1927 before turning to the US government in 1938 with an eight-page handwritten hard-luck story. She found she could no longer work without French papers, and in asking the State Department for help in getting them renewed, she added that she had been hospitalized for anemia—railing against both the French woman at her apartment and the consulate for not helping her—and that she was now without money, was without luggage (it had been sent on ahead), and had not bought a new dress in fifteen years.[56] Other Americans drew upon their connections, and one woman wrote directly to the White House when her French identity card was refused in July 1939. Mildred Arden Blandy sent a telegram to an old friend there, asking that he "act at once for AULD LANG SYNE." Edwin Watson in turn wrote to "Dear Summy," George T. Summerlin, Chief of Protocol, explaining that Mildred Arden, daughter of a very famous American actor, had married his roommate from West Point. The Department of State sent a telegram to the embassy, which looked into the matter and responded that her French ID card had been withheld because of a disputed 1933 hotel bill; she was now liable for about $125 in fines and possible imprisonment and expulsion for having failed to regularize her situation.[57] As restrictive laws tightened, a soldier turned chauffeur, a manufacturer's representative, but also musicians, actors, and dancers asked the US consulate for help to renew or get French working papers.[58] But there were also those Americans who asked the consulate to write to the Service de la main-d'oeuvre étrangère to help them get working permits for their Italian chauffeur, Yugoslavian valet, or Japanese domestic.[59]

In other cases, the proof was not sufficient, and indeed some transnationals may have tried to use an American citizenship they did not have. The US government was vigilant, questioning life stories and accents and whether the claimant had indeed been born in San Francisco: blaming the San Francisco fire for lost birth certificates seems to have been a common tactic. One individual, perhaps a legitimate manufacturers' representative but perhaps a crook or a spy, was imprisoned by the French and then, after his release, headed off, like Gueydan de Roussel, to Switzerland. He seemed to use distinctly German idioms when he spoke English, according to the US Legation officer in Switzerland (not those phrases "ordinarily used by native Americans, no matter how long they may have resided abroad"). Raymond Swoboda defended himself by saying that he spoke four languages, all with a slight accent. This did not prevent the US government from taking away his passport and his being arrested again, in Switzerland in 1917, for espionage.[60]

Protection of citizens is contingent on citizenship, and Americans abroad learned at their peril that letting proof lapse could be dangerous. The State Department found it "a very vexatious task" in having to determine whom to protect.[61] Some government officials were more suspicious than others in determining good faith. Consular officials could question the veracity of belonging, comment on accents, or criticize life styles. Yet the importance of American citizenship while abroad could have very tangible benefits when the homeland connection worked: help with the recovery of mislaid jewelry, a source of succor to find a job, or aid in warding off expulsion.

Irate Citizens and the Limits of Help

Citizens abroad and their concerned families at home were very grateful when they got help from the government and wrote to say so:

> My dear Mr. Hull, . . . I can not begin to tell you how deeply I appreciate the effort you made and the interest you and your Department showed in locating my son. . . . You not only relieved a worried mother but you have given me and many others, a new, deep respect and confidence in our country and in your Department.[62]

Or, as one of Mr. Wood's protégées wrote, "It makes one truly proud of being an American citizen to receive such help as you rendered."[63] Citizens in transnational contexts had their patriotism renewed when their home ties functioned and when the protective aid worked thanks to the "splendid attention and sympathetic care" rendered by consular officers:

> It is a matter of pride to be able to let our people know that in the event one of them is found in a distressful condition in foreign lands, there is one of their own who can and will cheerfully and competently lend the aid of this strong arm of our national government.[64]

Others, however, railed with irate disappointment when homeland relations did not work. The government's protective function was limited, as we have seen, by available funds, proof of citizenship, and first recourse to local remedies. When any of these reasons prevented individuals from getting help, their indignation and anger against the government was often as great as the (dashed) expectations of the flag's help. One man, brushed off by the US consulate in Bordeaux in 1918, complained bitterly about lèse-citizenship:

> The consul sent word out to me that he could not help me, and also that he did not have time to talk to me.
>
> It certainly was a surprise as well as an insult to me to be treated like this in a foreign country, especially an allied country, and when I had papers proving my birth and sailing under an American flag.[65]

Other Americans hounded the US consulates and every French official possible. Even the amiable Consul General Frank Mason could be exasperated at insistent demands by self-righteous and bona fide citizens:

> [C. seems] to have been under the very common delusion that "as an American citizen" he had some peculiar rights and privileges and should have been tried by American rather than by French laws. Men of this class are also apt to suppose that when under arrest in this country it is within the power of the Embassy or Consulate, by simply making a formal demand, to secure their immediate release. The fact is, however, that . . . any injudicious interference in [*sic*] behalf of an American citizen on trial or under sentence for crime committed in this country may be resented and aggravate rather than ameliorate the case of the accused.[66]

Americans could be unruly, insulting, irate, and downright difficult in their demands, insisting "that the Consul shall wave the starry flag" to settle local disputes.[67] Trying to use the symbolic force of their citizenship and the actual intervention of the consulate to escape prison or debt, Americans abroad addressed US officials with a mixture of gratitude, insistence, insouciance, or outright fraud.

For unhappy Americans whose citizenship was not sufficient to extricate them from their troubles in a foreign land, rhetoric escalated quickly, making a wronged individual a standard bearer for all Americans abroad. After Mrs. Blanche M. Turner was jailed in France for two months in 1934 for kidnapping her granddaughter, she was taken into custody again for passport tampering. Her passport had been altered in several places, including her birth date. And every time she had applied for a passport, she had given different dates as to her two marriages. She was furious when the consulate did not provide the help she expected. She wrote indignantly to Secretary of State Cordell Hull complaining that "pathetic and frantic appeals from prison brought no aid from the U.S. Consulate." "Will you kindly have the consulate refrain from writing me annoying letters. I am ill from this imprisonment through their negligence and their shameful after-math in trying to make an issue of the Passport of a trivial date of marriage twenty-three years ago." But, above all, Mrs. Turner argued on behalf of all "innocent American citizens in Paris" who might come to such "tragic circumstances" and be "at the mercy of consular services and American attorneys."[68]

There were clearly limits to the consulate's largesse and to its patience in dealing with demanding citizens overseas. Elihu Root had already noted in 1910 that "citizens abroad are too apt to complain" and commented on the greediness of some of their requests. [69] Although he was referring specifically to when they were beaten in litigation overseas, the comment bears generalization. At times the consulate turned a deaf ear to appeals for help: "Writer seems insane. May we not simply file this?"[70] Supplicants' demands were sometimes unreasonable. And the State Department had limited funds for helping Americans overseas. It was willing to make regular mail inquiries concerning whereabouts at no charge, but it drew the line at incurring telegraphic costs, which had to be reimbursed.[71] Furthermore, the consulate itself had no funds for stranded Americans. After World War I, the consulate most often referred relief requests to the American Legion Paris Post (set up in 1919), which had its own Welfare Committee for veterans, or the American Aid Society of Paris (1922), the latter still helping stranded Americans today.

Furthermore, while citizens turned to their country for help, they did not always return the favor. The treasurer of the United

States and the embassy carried on considerable correspondence in the months following the 1914 exodus to recover loans, ranging from $7 to $250, which had been extended by the wartime relief commission. After trying to hunt people down, all the way to Shanghai in one case, all too often the embassy had to write back to the Treasury that the debtor could not be found. In July 1916, some seventy-three people had still not repaid their loans, some of "whose manner of living presupposes a present ability to make payment." "All possible pressure" was to be brought on them, including tagging their files for the next time they sought to extend or amend their passports.[72]

"Dear Secretary of State": A Peculiarly American Practice?

The basic conundrum of citizens abroad has to do with the ways in which ordinary citizens, after leaving their homeland, may turn to it in times of need. Citizenship may be a gift handed out or limited by the home state. But it can also be a resource or a strategy, mobilized by mobile citizens to deal with the state where they have settled. The stories from the State Department in the first half of the century are testimony to the expectations of citizens with respect to their home ties. The "Dear Secretary of State" letter may be but a transnational variation on the American belief in the power of writing to one's legislator. Is this then a practice specific to US citizens, to the time period, or to social class?

It may be that the example of Americans in Paris is unique due to the symbolic power of the United States and the presumption of its rather elite migrants that they can draw upon that power and use their official homeland ties. Are US citizens particularly prone to pester their government officials, with the hubris of the strong arm of Uncle Sam behind them? Or do not all immigrants turn to their consulates for help, assuming that a state has greater power than an individual? Among Americans in Paris alone, there was a diversity of practices undoubtedly true for any immigrant group. A multitude of US citizens in Paris never had the need or the desire to call upon their government representative. The Left Bank crowd who went abroad to escape America apparently crossed the river to the embassy on the Right Bank of the Seine only under duress, or as Samuel Putnam put it: "At times . . . we would find ourselves alarmingly low in funds and faced with the bleak prospect of having to throw ourselves on the nearest American consul."[73] The quotidian use of citizenship in a transnational context is complex and may be uneven.

First, is there a class bias to the sample of those who even dare ask for help? Are elite migrants, with a greater sense of entitlement, particular in trying to exercise transnational networks through their consulate? More research needs to be done on consulates around the world. We only know about those people who showed up at the gate, and we can speculate that there were those who, due to class or race, did not feel that they could exercise their citizenship rights in this manner. There are few explicit traces in the US consular files of protection cases relating to African Americans, although names are no indication.[74] However, just as African Americans' relationship to America was fraught with trouble in the United States itself, it seems plausible that their relationship with officialdom abroad could be more complex than Gertrude Stein's insistence on her democratic right to a passport.

Like Stein, more than one petitioner admonished the government that what was good for one American had to be good for all. This could be a simple rhetorical device. But the democratization of travel and the increased variety of Americans living abroad after World War I, when many soldiers stayed on, means that a good number of supplicants were apparently ordinary folks. The hard-luck stories related in many of the letters attest that not only the rich turned to the consulate for help. This reiterates the question as to the extent to which other immigrants, from other countries, at other consulates, in the United States or elsewhere, have also turned to their home countries for help in matters ranging from the petty to the serious.

Nevertheless, the many privileged among the Americans abroad seem to account for the more surprising part of the sample concerning shopping complaints and other seemingly frivolous uses of citizenship in a transnational context. We may assume that certain categories of problems—with dressmakers, for example—were the province of a particularly self-entitled white American woman. The use of networks is telling. The written requests of ordinary citizens were sometimes mediated by friends, lawyers, prominent local citizens at home, or local companies there with connections abroad. Well-connected citizens drew upon an even fuller panoply of pull, like Gueydan de Roussel's US congressmen cousins. When a mother and daughter were arrested for shoplifting at a Parisian department store, they had affidavits sent on their behalf from the governor, a judge, a senator and a House representative, all attesting to the honesty, integrity, and moral qualities of the family ("highest type of American citizenship") and their "highest standing in banking and social circles" in Oklahoma City.[75] When, in 1927, one American woman got into a dispute with her American landlord in Paris—over storage space in the basement and the emptying of garbage bins—she sent a telegram to her brother in New York, who was the New York state comptroller. She asked him to get the governor, Alfred Smith, to write a letter to the prefect of Paris asking for protection; and indeed the New York governor's office wrote to the State Department, which forwarded the information to the consulate in Paris, which promised to help. Eight years later, Mrs. Benjamin (now living several blocks away in the same posh neighborhood) turned again to the New York governor, this time for help with her French taxes. Again he sent a query to the State Department that relayed the request to the embassy. Ambassador Jesse Isidor Straus wrote directly to "Dear Herbert" (Lehman) "with kindest regards" and wrote a formal letter to Pierre Laval, Prime Minister and Minister of Foreign Affairs. But he confided to Lehman that he doubted there would be a French ruling in Mrs. Benjamin's favor since she had failed to file the proper income tax declaration in France.[76] Not everyone suffered François Gueydan de Roussel's frustrations. The most elite of "elite emigrants" continued to draw upon their social connections to strengthen the bonds of their citizenship claims and to use them as shields overseas. Their troubles testify to the trials of transnationalism. Their networks often worked. But not always.

Citizenship abroad can be used as a mantle, cloak, or shield—the most frequent metaphors for its protective function. What is striking is the petitioners' tone of expectation and belief in the right to call upon their government from abroad. The assumption is that the homeland network will work and the government will protect all citizens no matter where they are or how obstreperously they behave. For some Americans domiciled abroad who may not have frequented any other American institution in town, the consulate was "theirs" by virtue of birth or naturalization, and their citizenship remained the ultimate source of help in disputes with the natives.

Yet their requests were sometimes ignored or turned down. And their strategies may not be unique. My hunch is that this is not, after all, a solely American practice.[77] Certainly, the symbolic power of the United States already in the first half of the twentieth century—at a time when consular officers seem to have had more time for petty complaints due to the ratio of US officers to citizens abroad, undoubtedly much greater than today—and the privilege of class may all mean that the experience of Americans at the Paris consulate during the interwar years represent a peculiarly American use of citizenship from afar. Nonetheless, comparison with other consulates in other places and other periods is needed, from the great transatlantic migrations of the nineteenth century through the great mobility of the twentieth. The uses of citizenship by transnational individuals can be asked of any emigrant/immigrant group. As countries of origin today step up their outreach to their citizens abroad, the consular hub is ever the place where the interaction of transnational individuals and their home states take place. Consular files hold a key to understanding transnationalism's networks, possibilities, and limits.

Conclusion

It's Not as Easy as It Looks

Should we just dismiss Gertrude, Clara, Lily, and Frank as idiosyncratic individuals trying to make the best of two (and more) worlds and sometimes failing? Is it simply that some international settlers of yore were transnationals before their time? The many lessons go well beyond the most elite of transnationals. Transnationalism in migration and mobility studies has been conceptualized at two ends of the spectrum: elite, multiple passport holders; ordinary migrants shuffling back and forth or staying put where they have settled but sending money back home. In both cases, the celebratory image of poststructural connectedness and agency, I argue, is overdrawn. The point is not to dismiss the activities of the active subject but to remind us of the obstacles he or she has faced. It is not just that border crossing itself oscillates from questioned exit to limited entry. Historically, both outgoing and incoming states have erected different types of barriers to mobility. If we have studied mostly the blockages of ingress, I argue here for a new look at egress—how states worry about those who have left and then help them, or not, depending on the case. At the same time, transnational individuals do not just send packages and money home. They turn to their home state *for help in being transnational.* And while most states are willing to consider help and today seem to be going out of their way to embrace citizens abroad, this does not mean that the process is a smooth one.

Transnationalism remains anchored in a fundamental paradox. For some, it means going beyond the nation-state, thanks to mobile migrants implicated in more than one country at once. For others, transnationalism fundamentally allows a reinforcement of connections with the homeland. Do we need to choose: a transnationalism whose agency flies above ethnicity or one that reinforces it? The varied uses of transnationalism in themselves show its methodological limits, and not just for migration studies.

Today, proof seems abundant of transnationalism triumphant, from dual citizenship to frequent flier miles. Many, particularly anthropologists and sociologists, have heralded this transnationalism as a powerful symbol of a new age of global ties. Historians (along with some anthropologists and sociologists) have pointed out that it is not just a late twentieth-century phenomenon. "The 'pushes' and 'pulls' of transatlantic migration have been studied in detail, but the 'intervening barriers' less so," as Drew Keeling pointed out in his analysis of the turn-of-the-twentieth century shipping industry.[1] We need to add the limitations to the study of transnationalism, particularly by understanding the practices of transnationalism past and present. Modes of circulation, connected histories, and other forms of entanglement need to be studied in conjunction with the power relations in which they are embedded and the frictions that can occur. States continue to test the agency of social actors, and not just with walls and immigration agents. The emigration perspective is equally important in understanding eventual brakes on unlimited mobility.

The plea here is to reflect on the "transnational moment" to historicize the scholarly literature and to caution against an overinterpretation of a fluidity of the present. The praise of mobility, of which transnationalism is a part, is still limited by power relations inherent in its forms and facets. "Transnational" as a concept is stimulating; as a practice it may be liberating—or frustrating. It is not always easy.[2] Past examples are telling and help point to constraints that persist. Transnationalism means first of all living between different sets of competing jurisdictions that may be "fighting" over individuals, bothering them bureaucratically, or, sometimes worse, remaining indifferent to their plight. Transnational practices may mean the agency of literally choosing one's court. But agency does not ensure success. As Donna Gabaccia has pithily put it, "the transnational life is doubly plagued by states rather than transcending their power."[3]

Citizenship may be a resource to be drawn upon by energetic appeals to embassies or consulates. But if citizenship papers matter, so does domicile. We may return to the old Roman distinction between birthplace and domicile.[4] With all of the attention to citizenship today, we have neglected the legal implications of domicile. Domicile trumps citizenship in many domains, notably for marriage, divorce, and death. Living abroad aggravated presumptions against women marrying foreigners between 1907 and 1922. Domicile mattered for the duchess's will. It mattered for Gueydan de Roussel, who felt forced to flee. Today's notions of fluidity ignore the constraints of both citizenship and domicile. Neither alone defines the individual. Multiple jurisdictions may allow creative use of same, but they are no panacea. Transnational networks may allow individual agency to bloom across borders, or not. They may also leave individuals metaphorically mid-ocean, or literally as veritable refugees in Switzerland.

In 1990, Barry Goldberg was the sole historian at Glick Schiller, Basch, and Blanc-Szanton's "founding" conference on transnationalism. He began his comments by confessing his worry "about being a historical interloper on anthropological turf." He argued for the importance of looking to the past (particularly in arguing about the changing meanings of race and ethnicity in the US) and concluded his paper:

> Of one thing we can be certain. If transnationalism *does* gain wider scholarly and popular currency as a medium of political exchange, its meaning will be contested. Already the reality of our new situation has been reduced to a series of advertising vignettes of materially, if not as yet emotionally, comfortable immigrants dialing family and friends in the old country.[5]

Yes, only twenty-five years ago, the rotary telephone represented transnationalism. Transnationalism-as-concept has been successful perhaps beyond its founders' dreams. And, in practice, thanks to smartphones, home has never been so close at hand no matter where one roams. The ease of identity and border crossings has been heralded as the new modernity. Scholars themselves do it; many of us study it. But the doubter has to note that transnationalism can also be hard work for the individuals—and even their historians. Archive-hopping proposals are both literally and figuratively costly; they take languages and money; scholars at resource-poor institutions may be at an unfair disadvantage; research may have to sacrifice depth for breadth; and how many multi-sited country visits will the Fulbright commission support?[6]

Transnationalism is neither as new nor as easy as it may look. Historians are perhaps best suited not just to (re-)examine transnationalisms past but, in doing so, to remind the more celebratory accounts of the present that border-crossing migrants do not live by Skype alone. Perhaps transnationalism as a concept has been but the product of a particular time period, emerging out of the seemingly halcyon period of 1989 to 2001, between the breakup of the Soviet Union and September 11th.[7] The historic record itself shows how the agency of individuals has been embedded in legal labyrinths of citizenship and domicile. The state is not giving up that easily.[8] While mobility, by ship then or by plane now, has extended geographical horizons and potential networks, the "web" may indeed be a good metaphor for our transnational times. But webs, we must remember, are sticky and also catch flies.

Like all historiographic "turns," the point is perhaps less the history itself than the questions the turns ask about the history. The newer emphasis on reinterrogating power relations—from below—and on historical actors' eventual transnational agency *adds* to our knowledge rather than necessarily *displacing* all older forms of inquiry. If only the turn-ers weren't so triumphalistically teleological. Can we ignore the "insistently flashing turn signals" as David Bell has called them?[9] Or is it a question of measure? As Lynn Hunt has remarked: "Let us not exaggerate . . . transnational history is not the only game in town. Things are hopping, everywhere."[10] And, after a vibrant plea for understanding *historical* globalizations past and furthermore global *historiographies* that were written from Persia to China long before our twenty-first-century hubris "invented" the latest turn, Sanjay Subrahmanyam, in his inaugural lesson at the Collège de France, "Histoire globale de la première modernité," ended diplomatically with a conciliatory call for methodological ecumenism: global history, yes, but it does not mean that one cannot still do local or national history.[11] By the same token, transnational history is undoubtedly here to stay. Another *very* interesting perspective. Among others. And with its limits.

Acknowledgments

I cite Molière's *Bourgeois gentilhomme* above but must admit that I felt like Monsieur Jourdain myself while writing this book: looking at work that I have done over the last decade, I realized that I have been thinking about transnationalism and its limits for a long time, if not in those words. The term "transnationalism" has caught up with us all, and I hope this book can serve as a convincing reminder of the never-ending malleable shifts of our own métier.

This book is thus greatly beholden to both my unpublished and previously published work, which I have thoroughly reframed here to make a sustained argument about the limits of transnationalism. My earlier thoughts on the matter have appeared, in chronological order, in the following works.

"The Politics of Exit: Reversing the Immigration Paradigm," *Journal of Modern History* 77, no. 2 (2005): 263–89.

"Expatriation, Expatriates, and Expats: The American Transformation of a Concept," *American Historical Review* 114, no. 2 (2009): 307–28.

"Le transnationalisme et ses limites: Le champ de l'histoire des migrations," in *Pratiques du transnational: Terrains, preuves, limites*, ed. Jean-Paul Zuñiga (Paris: La Bibliothèque du Centre de recherches historiques, 2011), 197–208.

"Americans Abroad and the Uses of Citizenship: Paris, 1914–1940," *Journal of American Ethnic History* 31, no. 3 (2012): 5–32.

The Other Americans in Paris: Businessmen, Countesses, Wayward Youth, 1880–1941 (Chicago: University of Chicago Press, 2014), esp. chap. 2.

"The Trials of Transnationalism: It's Not as Easy as it Looks," *Journal of Modern History*, 89, no. 4 (2017): 851–74.

I thank previous editors for their encouragement and the publishers for the right to reuse portions of this material.

I have happily been in dialogue about these issues over many, many years with David Abraham, Donna Gabaccia, Gary Gerstle, Jan Goldstein, Dirk Hoerder, Alice Kaplan, Leslie Page Moch, José Moya, Roger Waldinger, and François Weil, not to mention the discussions at the collective seminar of the École des Hautes Études en Sciences Sociales, "Histoires et historiographies transnationales," where, since 2005, Yves Cohen, Cecilia D'Ercole, Kapil Raj, Michael Werner, and I have repeatedly hashed out these questions. The students in my two seminars, "Histoire comparée et les migrations contemporaines" (especially our discussion on May 3, 2016) and "Immigration et sciences sociales" (January 29, 2018) provided fresh feedback at crucial moments, as did co-speakers and audiences at the Centre de Recherches Historiques conference on "Pratiques du transnational" on December 3, 2009, and those at two American Historical Association meetings, on January 6, 2012, and January 5, 2018.

Although they may have forgotten by now, special thanks go also to Marian L. Smith, for long-ago discussions on expatriation; to Yann Scioldo-Zürcher for helping me find articles on François Gueydan de Roussel (before newspaper collections were digitized!); and to Patricia Saltzman Heard, historian of Gueydan, Louisana. Her amiable correspondence urged me on as I became obsessed with the Gueydan family.

Finally, the book would not be what it is today without Readers 1 and 2. The well-read and keen-eyed José Moya and the encyclopedic Dirk Hoerder have both admitted their input. Many thanks to them both along with Doug Mitchell and Kyle Wagner. How fortunate can one be in having the wise, witty, and enthusiastic Doug Mitchell as an editor?! Hearty thanks, Doug! (even if you must professionally frown on the overuse of exclamatory punctuation).

Notes

INTRODUCTION

1. Letter (to unknown correspondent), dated November 28, 1768, *The Papers of Benjamin Franklin*, ed. William B. Willcox (New Haven, CT: Yale University Press, 1972), 15:272–73 (also quoted in Dolis, *Transnational Na(rra)tion*, 2, and it can be found at http://franklinpapers.org/framedVolumes.jsp). Franklin has been enrolled in the transnational cause. Cf. Suri, "Transnational Influences on American Politics."

2. Iriye and Saunier, *Palgrave Dictionary of Transnational History*; Saunier, "Transnationalism," 1047–55; Sewell, "Marc Bloch"; Cohen and Connor, *Comparison and History*; Green, "Forms of Comparison"; Green, *Repenser les migrations*, chaps. 1 and 2; Haupt and Kocka, *Comparative and Transnational History*; Gruzinski, *Les Quatre parties du monde*; Werner and Zimmermann, *De la comparaison à l'histoire croisée*; Lang, "Globalization and Its History"; Subrahmanyam, "Connected Histories"; Y. Cohen, "Circulatory Localities"; Raj, *Relocating Modern Science*. "Global history" and "world history" each have their own journal: *Journal of Global History* and *Journal of World History*, respectively.

3. Iriye and Saunier, *Palgrave Dictionary of Transnational History*; Khagram and Levitt, *Transnationalism Studies Reader*; *Diaspora: A Journal of Transnational Studies* (since 1991); *Global Networks, A Journal of Transnational Affairs* (since 2001); *Journal of Transnational American Studies* (since 2008); *European Journal of Transnational Studies* (since 2009). See, however, Thiel, *The Limits of Transnationalism*. For the debate

in the US, see "AHR Conversation: On Transnational History." For France, see, e.g., Zuñiga, *Pratiques du transnational*; Green, "French History and the Transnational Turn." Elsewhere in Europe, see, e.g., Faist, "Transnationalization in International Migration"; Bauböck and Faist, *Diaspora and Transnationalism*; Dahinden, "Dynamics of Migrants' Transnational Formations"; Vertovec and Cohen, *Migration, Diasporas, and Transnationalism*; Vertovec, *Transnationalism*. See also Gabaccia, "Thoughts"; Moya and McKeown, "World Migration"; and Hoerder, "Transnational—Transregional—Translocal: Transcultural"; Green and Waldinger, *Century of Transnationalism*.

4. See, however, e.g., Alain Tarrius, and Sallie Westwood and Annie Phizacklea, who have explicitly sought to study the transnationalism of both the rich and the poor. Tarrius, *Les fourmis d'Europe*; Tarrius, *Les nouveaux cosmopolitismes*; Westwood and Phizacklea, *Trans-Nationalism*; Smith and Guarnizo, *Transnationalism from Below*. However, over the last decade, as the term "transnationalism" has become omnipresent, it has appeared in titles of books on everything from organized crime to punk rock; e.g., Reichel et al., *Handbook of Transnational Crime and Justice*; Marciniak, *Transnational Punk Communities in Poland*; with an early use by the CIA: Milbank, *International and Transnational Terrorism*; Heine and Thakur, *Dark Side of Globalization*; Williams and Savona, *United Nations and Transnational Organized Crime*; Ackerman and Furman, *Sex Crimes*.

5. Particularly as a rejection of jingoism and nationalism. Saunier, "Learning by Doing," 170.

6. Westwood and Phizacklea, *Trans-Nationalism*, 15.

CHAPTER ONE

1. "La Justice en France n'existe pas pour un Citoyen Américain." Gueydan de Roussel to Estopinal, January 26, 1911, 351.112G93, General Records of the Department of State, Decimal Files, Record Group 59, 1910–29 [sic, even though there is some correspondence before 1910], National Archives at College Park, Md. (the complete reference hereafter referred to as "NACP"). A compendium of Gueydan de Roussel's pleadings, via petition and letters to his US backers, is held in this file along with his book, *La magistrature gangrenée* (n.p., n.d. [1910]). Not only did he send the book to the US secretary of state, but he also sent it to all of the French congressmen and to the president of the French Republic. There is, however, no copy at the Bibliothèque nationale de France.

2. Gueydan de Roussel, *La magistrature gangrenée*, 172.

3. Alfred Dreyfus was a Jewish army captain wrongly accused of treason. His arrest in 1894 and subsequent trials became a well-known "Affair" in France and beyond. E.g. of references to Dreyfus in Gueydan's correspondence include: Gueydan de Roussel to Henry Gueydan, February 10, 1910; Gueydan de Roussel to Alfred Westphal, August 31, and September 1, 1910, NACP.

4. Lachance, "Foreign French," 115; Bourdelais, "Les immigrants français"; F. Weil, "Les migrants de France."

5. Population 1,400 in 2014, one-third French ancestry. "Gueydan, Louisiana," City-Data.com, accessed June 2, 2016, http://www.city-data.com/city/Gueydan-Louisiana.html. On the duck-hunting festival, see Gueydan Duck Hunting Association, accessed June 2, 2016, http://www.duckfestival.org/index.html.

6. Patricia Saltzman Heard, *Gueydan Centennial*, http://www.gueydan.org/History.html. This link is no longer active; cf. Town of Gueydan, "The History of the Town of Gueydan and Its Founder," accessed September 27, 2018, https://gueydan.org/?page_id=15; Patricia Saltzman Heard, "Jean-Pierre Gueydan: One Man's Legacy," accessed September 27, 2018, http://www.vermilionhistorical.com/features/biographies/jean_pierre_gueydan.htm#_edn52. I thank Pat Heard for her amiable correspondence with me concerning the Gueydan family.

7. *The French and American Claims Commission, 1880–1884*, vol. 21, *Records of Claims from No. 181 to No. 190 Inclusive* (Washington, DC: Gibson Bros., [1884]), 32. François Gueydan's claim is no. 181; Jean-Pierre's claim is no. 226, in volume 26.

8. *Records of Claims*, vol. 21, 32.

9. Bredin, *Joseph Caillaux*, 69; Berenson, *Trial of Madame Caillaux*, 137. Patricia Heard writes that François Gueydan *père* returned in 1885 to retire at age sixty-seven (but he would have been only fifty-four). François Gueydan de Roussel said his father returned to France in 1895 at age sixty-eight (but he would have been sixty-four) "par suite de sa ruine complète au Texas." Gueydan de Roussel to Henry Gueydan, October 20, 1910, NACP.

10. [Isabelle] Couturier de Chefdubois, "Offertoire et Réparation: Souvenirs et témoignages," typescript dated November 2, 1957, Box 10, Émile Roche-Joseph Caillaux Archives, Archives d'histoire contemporaine, Fondation Nationale des Sciences Politiques, Paris, 45.

11. Chefdubois, "Offertoire," 57.

12. BB^{18} 6030 (par dérogation), Centre Historique des Archives nationales, Paris (hereafter "CHAN").

13. BB^{18} 6030, CHAN.

14. Gueydan de Roussel, *La magistrature gangrenée.*

15. BB^{18} 6030, CHAN.

16. Pech, *Entreprise viticole et capitalisme*, 520.

17. Diderot et D'Alembert, *Encyclopédie*, 17:293.

18. J. H. Smith, "La crise d'une économie régionale"; J. H. Smith, "Agricultural Workers"; Warner, *Winegrowers of France*; Paul, *Science, Vine, and Wine*, esp. 91, 261.

19. "Vive le vin naturel!" "Guerre aux fraudeurs." Bechtel, *1907*; Pech, *Entreprise viticole*; Stanziani, *Histoire de la qualité alimentaire*, 77–91.

20. Marcellin-Albert was a small winegrower, café owner, and director of a traveling theater troupe. "Rapport d'ensemble sur la crise viticole (mars-juin 1907)," 2, F^{7} 12794, CHAN.

21. Frader, *Peasants and Protest*, 141, and chap. 7.

22. Ultimately, the farmers' revolt had a long-term impact on Socialist politics in the south of France. See Frader, *Peasants and Protests.*

23. Gueydan de Roussel, *La magistrature gangrenée*, 173.

24. "Je réclame mes juges!! . . . Il [le gouvernement français] me refuse MES juges!" Gueydan de Roussel to Albert Estopinal, February 2, 1911, NACP.

25. BB^{18} 6030, CHAN.

26. Gueydan de Roussel to Westphal, August 31 and September 1, 1910, NACP.

27. *La Libre Parole*, articles throughout June 1907 and November 15, 1907.

28. Georges Thiébaud to Gueydan de Roussel, December 8, 1910; Gueydan de Roussel to Eugene [Gueydan], December 24, 1910, recounting the December 20 visit; Gueydan de Roussel to Albert Estopinal, February 2, 1911, NACP.

29. Allain, *Joseph Caillaux*, 1:79–82; Bredin, *Joseph Caillaux*, 69–70, 116–19; Berenson, *Trial of Madame Caillaux*, 133–50; *Le Figaro*, March 17, 1914.

30. Berenson, *Trial of Madame Caillaux.*

31. Couturier de Chefdubois, "Offertoire," esp. 47–48, 85–111.

32. Caillaux, *Mes mémoires*, 1:228–29.

33. Couturier de Chefdubois, "Offertoire," 86.

34. "Papillons autour de la flamme, des femmes aussi viendront tourbillonner autour de sa puissance." B. E. Gueydan, *Les rois de la République*, 1:115.

35. Couturier de Chefdubois, "Offertoire," 107; Berenson, *Trial of Madame Caillaux*, 133–50.

36. "Quand ton frère est venu me voir au Ministère, ai-je pu obtenir de lui des aveux nets, un exposé de sa situation ? Complet. Non n'est-ce pas ? Tu le sais et tu l'as reconnu. MAINTENANT, IL EST BIEN CERTAIN QU'IL Y A EU UN VIOLENT PARTI-PRIS CONTRE LUI, QUE LES PASSIONS LOCALES S'EN SONT MÊLÉES ET QU'IL A ÉTÉ BEAUCOUP TROP DUREMENT CONDAMNÉ." Letter, "Ton Joe" [Caillaux] to "Ma chère petite Berthe," August 21, 1909, hand-marked "Confidential" and "Not for our Paris Embassy," NACP.

37. Gueydan de Roussel to Eugene [Gueydan], December 24, 1910, recounting the December 20 visit, NACP.

38. "American Involved in Caillaux Case," *New York Times*, April 17, 1914.

39. George Bodet to James L. Slayden, House of Representatives, April 20, 1911, NACP.

40. Gueydan de Roussel to Albert Estopinal, December 15, 1910, NACP.

41. Gueydan de Roussel to Henry Gueydan, October 20, 1910, NACP.

42. Gueydan de Roussel to Arthur Bailly-Blanchard, March 29, 1911, NACP.

43. Gueydan de Roussel to Henry Gueydan, March 28, 1911, NACP.

44. There Bailly-Blanchard remained until 1912, when he went to the Tokyo embassy. He then served as ambassador to Haiti from 1914 until his resignation in 1921. After a final stint on special duty at the State Department, he died at age seventy in Montreal in 1925, of an apparent suicide. Glenn R. Conrad, ed., *A Dictionary of Louisiana Biography*, vol. 1 (New Orleans: Louisiana Historical Association, 1988).

45. Gueydan de Roussel to Henry Gueydan, February 10, 1910, NACP. Although Bailly-Blanchard is listed as an officer of the Legion of Honor and an officer of public instruction in the *Who's Who in Paris: Anglo-American Colony of 1905*, the Grande Chancellerie of the Legion

of Honor confirms that his decoration was awarded in 1912, for his activity as advisor to the American ambassador in Paris. Gueydan de Roussel to Albert Estopinal, April 6, 1911; and Bodet to Slayden, April 20, 1911, NACP. William H. Ingram, ed., *Who's Who in Paris: Anglo-American Colony* (Paris: American Register, 1905), 25; letter, American Society of the French Legion of Honor to author, August 24, 2007; telephone conversation with the Grande Chancellerie de la Légion d'Honneur, September 5, 2007.

46. Gueydan de Roussel to Albert Estopinal, April 6, 1911, NACP.

47. Gueydan de Roussel to Albert Estopinal, April 6, 1911, NACP. On the Coudert opinion, see below.

48. Pech, *Entreprise viticole*, 117. See also Stanziani, *Histoire de la qualité alimentaire*, 93–111.

49. Thanks to Yann Scioldo-Zürcher for hunting down the French newspapers, pre-Gallica.

50. Bodet to James L. Slayden, February 18, 1911, NACP.

51. Gueydan de Roussel to Albert Estopinal, December 15, 1910. See also Gueydan de Roussel to Henry Gueydan, February 10, 1910, NACP.

52. See December 15, 1910, letter and "rube" letter by friend, NACP. Kelly was the founder of what became the law firm of S. G. Archibald. See Green, *Other Americans in Paris*, 129–32, 230.

53. Gueydan de Roussel to P. Knox, Chief Department of State, December 15, 1910, transmitted via Estopinal, NACP. Note the French mistakes in the English text: "Frenchman" is not capitalized; "emprisonment" is written instead of "imprisonment."

54. "You'll tell me:" Gueydan de Roussel to Henry Gueydan, February 10, 1910, NACP.

55. Affidavit, February 25, 1908, NACP.

56. Veenswijk, *Coudert Brothers.*

57. They also opined that if Gueydan had really been treated unfairly, surely his very influential brother-in-law would have protected him. Since no such thing happened, they implied, perhaps he was guilty after all. Messrs. Coudert Brothers to Mr. Robert Bacon, American Ambassador, Paris, October 1, 1910, NACP. NB. All of the US documents (in this footnote and the next two) refer to him by his American birth name, "Gueydan" (without the "de Roussel"), Americanizing him.Cf. note 76 below.

58. Memorandum, Bureau of Citizenship (Department of State) to the Solicitor, November 9, 1910 (penned by RWF i.e. Flournoy, as

the second memo specifies), NACP. See Flournoy, "Naturalization and Expatriation," 702–19, 848–68; and chap. 3 below.

59. Office of the Solicitor (Department of State) to Mr. Clark, November 11, 1910; cf. Office of the Solicitor to Western European Division, March 7, 1911, NACP.

60. "ethniquement et juridiquement"; "la conception de la légalité [et] de l'incapacité de prendre une décision propre à l'ancienne bureaucratie française." He also fought to prove the legitimacy of the particle in his last name. Sabah, *Journal de Gueydan*, 126–27n98.

61. "qui ne voulait pas qu'il soit dit qu'il soit allié à des Américains!" Gueydan de Roussel to Henry Gueydan, October 20, 1910, NACP.

62. Gueydan de Roussel to Henry Gueydan, October 20, 1910, NACP.

63. Olivier Gueydan, telephone interview, August 16, 2007.

64. Cf. Stanziani, *Histoire de la qualité alimentaire*, 93, 102–3. Gueydan's file at the US National Archives does not corroborate Stanziani's point about varying economic functions. NACP.

65. Gueydan de Roussel, *La magistrature gangrenée*, 6, 20, 123.

66. "J'AFFIRME
que les Juges EN ONT MENTI,
et qu'ils en ont menti SCIEMMENT ! . . .
J'AFFIRME
que [le Juge d'Instruction] a, lui aussi, MENTI,
et qu'il en a menti SCIEMMENT ! . . .
J'AFFIRME
que [le Procureur de la République] a commis une
'lacheté' en ordonnant contre moi les poursuites en
Février 1907."

Gueydan de Roussel to Ministre de la Justice, August 20, 1910, NACP.

67. Both from August 31, 1910, letter, NACP.

68. Gueydan de Roussel to Albert Estopinal, February 2, 1911, NACP.

69. Gueydan de Roussel to Henry Gueydan, March 22, 1911, NACP.

70. Gueydan de Roussel to Henry Gueydan, March 22, 1911, NACP.

71. Estopinal to Knox, April 15, 1911, NACP.

72. B. E. Gueydan, *Les Rois de la République*.

73. Sabah, *Journal de Gueydan*, 128n99.

74. Sabah, 128n99.

75. Gueydan de Roussel to Henry Gueydan, February 10, 1910, NACP. His niece Isabelle Couturier de Chefdubois elevated it to a general principle: "these hatreds of malcontent farmers" ("ces haines de fermiers mécontents"). Couturier de Chefdubois, "Offertoire," 61. Boyer leaflet entitled "Les esprits de famille de Mr. Joseph Caillaux et autres que je mets en accusation sur les procédés suivants," under cover letter dated May 28, 1911, NACP.

76. First card, September 15, 1909, NACP. November 3, 1909, ibid: "Je viendrai à Lausanne pour te faire sauter la cervelle, non pas au beurre, mais avec une seule balle." Photocopies of the postcards are under cover letter of May 28, 1911, NACP; see also BB^{18} 6030, CHAN; and Gueydan de Roussel, *La magistrature gangrenée*, 149–51. On the leaflets Boyer said he circulated, see ibid., 73, 104, 149. N.B. Boyer referred to Gueydan as American (like the US government—see note 57 above—but in a demeaning tone). He referred to Gueydan's American citizenship and addressed his postcards to him in Lausanne as "François Gueydan, réfugié," not deigning to use "de Roussel." Postcard, October 1, 1909: "À te lire futur cadavre." Under cover letter of May 28, 1911, NACP. Gueydan de Roussel responded in kind. In an August 23, 1910, letter to the French minister of justice, he warned that if he did not get justice, he would be obliged to kill Boyer himself—out of legitimate defense, on his honor as an American, and in order to protect his family. *La magistrature gangrenée*, 92–94.

77. Couturier de Chefdubois, "Offertoire," 63.

78. Couturier de Chefdubois, 62–64.

79. Sabah, 128n99.

CHAPTER TWO

1. E.g., Mark Trepionok, *In the Land of Thieves*, subtitled "The 'Odyssée' of an American Merchant who while losing his Fortune in Paris lost his Citizenship." "Dogged by Detectives, snubbed by the French Judges and seconded by Representatives of his own Country," discussed in Green, *Other Americans in Paris*, 65–66.

2. Bourne, "Trans-national America." For two very useful overviews of the use of the term, see Saunier, "Transnationalism"; and Clavin, "Introduction: Defining Transnationalism." See also Vertovec and Cohen, *Migration, Diasporas and Transnationalism*; and Vertovec, *Transnationalism*.

3. Keohane and Nye, "Transnational Relations and World Politics"; Nye and Keohane, "Introduction," 330. This was republished the next year as a book.

4. Keohane and Nye, "Preface," 1971.

5. Field, "Transnationalism and the New Tribe," 356, 367.

6. Katzenstein, Keohane, and Krasner, "International Organizations."

7. Gilpin, "Politics.

8. Katzenstein, Keohane, and Krasner, 657 (citing Krasner, "State Power," 317).

9. Katzenstein, Keohane, and Krasner.

10. Camilleri, *Civilization in Crisis*, 112. See also, e.g., Cowling and Sugden, *Transnational Monopoly Capitalism*, who use the term "transnational corporations."

11. VanDaele, "Engineering Social Peace"; Tyrrell, *Reforming the World*; Saunier, *Transnational History*.

12. Brubaker, *Trans*. The book, however, does not discuss transnational identities.

13. Michael Werner, "Histoire et historiographies transnationales" (seminar, École des Hautes Études en Sciences Sociales, Michael Werner, Cecilia D'Ercole, Nancy L. Green, Kapil Raj), February 5, 2018. Cf. Kastoryano, "Vers un nationalisme transnational."

14. On translocality: Appadurai, "Production of Locality"; Levitt, *Transnational Villagers*; Hoerder, "Transnational—Transregional—Translocal: Transcultural"; Pereira, "Portuguese Migrants and Portugal." On pre-nation-state examples: Johnson et al., *Transregional and Transnational Families*; Howard, *Transnationalism in Ancient and Medieval Societies*; "Poena aut venia? Emigration in Rome, Byzantium and Beyond" (conference, American Academy in Rome, June 23, 2017); and notably Peter Heather, who has helped turn "barbarians" into "migrants." Heather, *Fall of the Roman Empire*.

15. Iriye, "Transnational History." See also Iriye, "Internationalization of History"; Iriye, "Transnational Turn."

16. Appadurai, "Global Ethnoscapes," chap. 3; Gilroy, *Black Atlantic*.

17. Glick Schiller, Basch, and Blanc-Szanton, *Towards a Transnational Perspective*.

18. Tyrrell, "American Exceptionalism"; Tyrrell, "Reflections."

19. Full disclosure: This is where I teach and the "lab" to which I belong. I, of course, was in favor of the project.

20. Reporting on the suspicion that globalizers and transnationalists are the latest henchmen of American imperialism, see Hunt, "Les Cultural Studies," 199; and Douki and Minard, "Histoire globale, histoires connectées." Cf. Chartier, "La conscience de la globalité (commentaire)."

21. Zuñiga, *Pratiques du transnational.* For the minority report, see Cavaillé et al., "Production locale du supralocal," 145–46, protesting against an increasing move toward generalizing in history that is accompanied by a depreciation of local knowledge. "Transnational, transrégional, transcontinental, transcommunal ou trans-ce-qu'on-voudra ne doivent pas constituer en entités transhistoriques des objets qui n'existent que d'avoir été construits en leur temps ou par des historiens qui les ont inventés comme objets du passé" (p. 146). (Transnational, transregional, transcontinental, transcommunal, or trans-whatever must not construct transhistorical entities out of objects that have been constructed in the past [in their specific contexts] or have been invented by historians as objects of the past.)

22. Revel, *Jeux d'échelles.*

23. "AHR Forum: Historiographic 'Turns' in Critical Perspective." See also Frader, "French History"; Green, "French History"; Fishkin, "Crossroads of Cultures"; "AHR Conversation: On Transnational History."

24. The literature on comparative history is abundant. The classic article is by Bloch, "Pour une histoire comparée." In addition to Introduction, note 2, see also Lepenies, *Entangled Histories and Negotiated Universals*; Gould, "Entangled Histories, Entangled Worlds"; "AHR Exchange"; Zuñiga, "L'histoire impériale"; Yun-Casalilla, "'Localism.'"

25. For a disentanglement of some of the terms, see Gabaccia, "Thoughts."

26. *European Journal of Transnational Studies*: "EJOTS would like to contribute to the steadily continuing process of European integration and is therefore actively committed to its intensification. Our aim is to promote a common European identity, based on the pluralistic traditions of Europe." EJOTS, accessed February 23, 2016, http://transnational-journal.eu/.

27. Although, as José Moya has pointed out, it is ironic that the new interest in transnationalism in its beyond-the-state meaning comes

after four waves of collapsing empires that created only more and more nation-states: from the Spanish empire to the Austro-Hungarian and Ottoman empires, to the British and French empires, and most recently, the USSR. Moya, "Historical Emergence." See also Siegelbaum and Moch, "Transnationalism in One Country?"

28. Cf. Struck, Ferris, and Revel, "Introduction."

29. Saunier, "Learning by Doing," 166.

30. E.g., White, *Middle Ground*; Sahlins, *Boundaries*; Nordman, *Frontières de France*; Rosental, *Les sentiers invisibles*; Ong, *Flexible Citizenship*.

31. Tyrrell, "American Exceptionalism." Tyrrell situated the new historiography in a triple context: the need to go beyond a fragmented social history; a renewal of US diplomatic history; and the collapse of the Soviet Union.

32. Tyrrell, *Transnational Nation*; Iriye, *Cultural Internationalism*, esp. chap. 3; Bender, *Rethinking American History*; Bender, *Nation among Nations*; Guarneri, *America Compared*; Guarneri, *America in the World*; Thelen, "Nation and Beyond"; Gabaccia, *Foreign Relations*. See also Paul Kramer's recent call for a "geopolitics of mobility." Kramer, "Geopolitics of Mobility." A sign of the success of this new trend in US history may be the right-wing backlash described in Hartman, "Internationalization." Some historians "did" transnational history before it was called such, e.g., Rodgers, *Atlantic Crossings*, not to mention Braudel, *Mediterranean and the Mediterranean World*.

33. Curtin, *Cross-Cultural Trade*; McKeown, *Chinese Migrant Networks*; McKeown, "Global Migration 1846–1940"; McKeown, *Melancholy Order*. For two early and impressive global histories of migration, see Hoerder, *Cultures in Contact*; and Manning, *Migration in World History*.

34. Tyrrell, "What Is Transnational History?"; Tyrrell, *Transnational Nation*.

35. Glick Schiller et al., *Towards a Transnational Perspective*, 16. Another important early study was by Levitt, *Transnational Villagers*. See also Clavin, "Introduction."

36. See the debate over what we can retrospectively call the "ethnic turn" in migration history in Conzen et al., "Invention of Ethnicity." Yet there has also been a return to assimilation for some scholars. Kazal, "Revisiting Assimilation"; Brubaker, "Return of Assimilation?";

Morawska, "In Defense"; Alba and Nee, "Rethinking Assimilation Theory"; Lucassen, "Gulf"; Alba and Foner, *Strangers No More.*

37. Wimmer and Glick Schiller, "Methodological Nationalism and Beyond." The article was republished in a special issue of *International Migration Review* 37, no. 3 (October 2003); see also the other articles in this special issue entitled "Transnational Migration: International Perspectives."

38. Portes, Guarnizo and Landolt, "Study of Transnationalism"; Vertovec, *Transnationalism*; Foner, "Transnationalism Old and New," chap. 3; Morawska, "Disciplinary Agendas and Analytic Strategies"; Morawska, "Immigrants, Transnationalism, and Ethnicization"; Waldinger and FitzGerald, "Transnationalism in Question"; Waldinger, *Cross-Border Connection.* Early transnational sociologists in France were Tarrius, *Les fourmis de l'Europe*; and Peraldi, *Cabas et containers.*

39. Glick Schiller and Fouron, *Georges Woke up Laughing*; Anderson, *Long-Distance Nationalism.*

40. See, e.g., Heather, *Fall of the Roman Empire*; Gruzinski, *Les Quatre parties du monde*; O'Rourke and Williamson, *Globalization and History*; Belich, *Prospect of Global History.*

41. "Immigration, Incorporation, Integration, and Transnationalism"; Topp, "Transnationalism of the Italian-American Left"; McKeown, "Transnational Chinese Families"; Fones-Wolf, "Immigrants, Labor and Capital"; Jacobson, "More 'Trans-' Less 'National.'" See also Gabaccia, *Italy's Many Diasporas*; Gabaccia, *Foreign Relations*; Liu, *Transnational History.*

42. Gerber, "Theories and Lives." See also Hoerder, "Historians and their Data"; and Gjerde, "Scandinavian Migration." On the emphasis on new technologies, see, e.g., Panagakos and Horst, "Return to Cyberia"; Diminescu, "Connected Migrant." Some of the early sociologist skeptics of the newness argument have been Morawska, "Disciplinary Agendas"; Morawska, "Immigrants, Transnationalism, and Ethnicization"; Foner, *From Ellis Island to JFK*; Waldinger and FitzGerald, "Transnationalism in Question."

43. Gerber, "Theories and Lives," 41.

44. José Moya, "Diaspora Studies: New Concepts, Approaches, and Realities" (Social Science History Association Annual Meeting, Chicago, November 18–21, 2004) (published in Spanish in *Diásporas,*

Reflexiones teóricas, ed. Nattie Golubov (Mexico City: UNAM, 2011), p. 18 of English typescript.

45. "We further postulate that the generality and parsimony of theories should be given primacy over their accuracy. In other words social science theories, rather than explaining phenomena as accurately as possible in terms relative to specific historical circumstances, should attempt to explain phenomena wherever and whenever they occur." Przeworski and Teune, *Logic of Comparative Social Inquiry*, 17; cf. Vertovec, *Transnationalism*, 14–17, 94. For a historian's methodological response, see Gabaccia, "Time and Temporality," esp. 43–44, 54–55.

46. On the current information technological turn in general, see Castells, *Rise of the Network Society*. For a sociologist's explicitly historic refutation, see, e.g., FitzGerald, "150 Years of Transborder Politics." See also Durand, "Mexican Policy."

47. On return migration, see notably Wyman, *Round-Trip to America*; Harper, *Emigrant Homecomings*; and Douki, "'Return Politics.'"

48. Green and Waldinger, *Century of Transnationalism*.

49. Abdelmalek Sayad, for one, urged taking emigration into consideration well before the transnational turn. "Les trois âges de l'émigration algérienne"; Sayad, *La double absence*.

50. As Christian Joppke has put it, increasing ties to emigrants have meant a "re-ethnicization" of citizenship even in an increasingly transnational world, although, for the receiving state, it means a shift from an ethnic to a territorial view ("de-ethnicization"). Joppke, "Citizenship."

51. Adam McKeown pointed to the problem of essentializing global links and networks in diaspora studies in *Chinese Migrant Networks*, 13.

52. Appadurai, "Global Ethnoscapes"; Glick Schiller et al., *Towards a Transnational Perspective*; Levitt, *Transnational Villagers*, etc.

53. E.g., Hammar, "Dual Citizenship and Political Integration"; Hammar, *Democracy and the Nation State*; Soysal, *Limits of Citizenship*; Aleinikoff and Klusmeyer, *Citizenship Today*; Aleinikoff and Klusmeyer, *From Migrants to Citizens*; Hansen and Weil, *Dual Nationality*; Sassen, *Territory, Authority, Rights*, esp. chap. 6 on postnational and denationalized citizenship; "Symposium: A Tribute to the Work of Kim Barry"; Barry, "Home and Away"; Faist and Kivisto, *Dual Citizenship in Global Perspective*; Cook-Martín, *Scramble for Citizens*; Spiro, *At Home in Two Countries*.

54. E.g., "AHR Forum: Transnational Lives in the Twentieth Century"; Davis, *Trickster Travels*; Deacon, Russell, and Woollacott, *Transnational Lives*; Raj, "Go-Betweens"; Schaffer et al., *Brokered World*; Subrahmanyam, *Three Ways to be Alien*.

55. Kramer, "Power and Connection," 1380, 1357. He adds that "transnational scholarship often unconsciously partakes in a language of post-sovereignty," using the "ideological language of emancipatory capitalist borderlessness," with accounts of "liberated and liberating flows of peoples, goods, discourses, practices, and institutions" (1352–53). Similarly, Patricia Clavin points out that transnational networks "appear to float free from the nation-state." "Introduction," 436. Sociologist Luis Eduardo Guarnizo already warned, in an interesting reflection on the macroeconomics of migration flows, that "transnational relations are neither free nor are they necessarily liberatory." "Despite hopeful prescriptive writings about the alleged autonomous and stateless character of transnational practices, there is no evidence that migrants are escaping either a capitalist or a nation-centered logic." Guarnizo, "Economics of Transnational Living," 690.

56. Handlin, *Uprooted*; Vecoli, "'Contadini'"; Bodnar, *Transplanted*; Hoerder, "Historians and Their Data"; cf. "Forum on the Legacy of Oscar Handlin." "[T]he diasporan subject is now vested with the agency formerly sought in the working class and more recently in the subaltern subject." Ong, *Flexible Citizenship*, 15.

57. Marshall, *Citizenship and Social Class*; Kettner, *Development of American Citizenship*; Shklar, *American Citizenship*; Neuman, *Strangers to the Constitution*; Kerber, "Meanings of Citizenship"; R. M. Smith, *Civic Ideals*; Keyssar, *Right to Vote*; Zolberg, *Nation by Design*; P. Weil, *Sovereign Citizen*; Herzog, *Revoking Citizenship*. As for immigrants protesting their exclusion, see, e.g., Salyer, *Laws Harsh as Tigers*; Motomura, *Americans in Waiting*; Parker, *Making Foreigners*.

58. E.g., Salyer, *Laws Harsh as Tigers*.

59. Davis, *Trickster Travels*; Subrahmanyam, *Three Ways to be Alien*; S. A. Stein, *Plumes*. See also Trivellato, *Sephardic Diaspora*; Schaffer et al., *Brokered World*.

60. Jacobson, "More 'Trans-' Less 'National,'"; Hoerder, "Historians and Their Data"; and Hoerder, *Cultures in Contact*.

61. McKeown, *Chinese Migrant Networks*; Kuhn, *Chinese Among Others*; Hoffnung-Garskof, *Tale of Two Cities*; Cohen, *Braceros*.

62. Ngai, "Promises and Perils."

63. Davis, *Trickster Travels*; Subrahmanyam, *Three Ways to be Alien*; S. A. Stein, *Plumes*; "AHR Forum: Transnational Lives"; Deacon, Russell and Woollacott, *Transnational Lives*; Raj, "Go-Betweens"; Lindsay and Sweet, *Biography and the Black Atlantic*; Scott and Hébrard, *Freedom Papers*; and Struck, Ferris, and Revel, "Space and Scale."

64. Westwood and Phizacklea, *Trans-Nationalism*, 1–3, 14–16, pt. 2. See also Potot, "Les mutations européennes au prisme des migrations." "[L]e transnationalisme dépolitise la recherche sur les migrations. . . . De là à considérer que le transnationalisme est la version néolibérale des travaux sur l'immigration, il n'y a qu'un pas . . . que je ne franchirai pas" (69).

65. Tarrius, *Les fourmis d'Europe*; Tarrius, *Les nouveaux cosmopolitismes*; Tarrius, *La mondialisation criminelle*. Cf. Wagner, *Les nouvelles élites de la mondialisation*.

66. Blanc-Chaléard, "Transnationalism and Migration," 253–55. More recently, Paul Kramer has spoken of "transnational hierarchies" and "transnational inequalities" with regard not to individuals but to state immigration policies. Kramer, "Geopolitics of Mobility."

67. Gerber, "Theories and Lives," 36, 38; Ong, *Flexible Citizenship*, 11, criticizes Arjun Appadurai's notion of "cultural globalization" (cf. Appadurai, *Modernity at Large*), "which gives the misleading impression that everyone can take equal advantage of mobility and modern communication and that transnationality has been liberatory, in both a spatial and a political sense, for all peoples"; she also criticizes both Western and subaltern approaches. Ong, *Flexible Citizenship*, 15; Turner, "Diasporic Tension," 1051; Subrahmanyam, "Between a Rock and a Hard Place," 440.

68. Ong, *Flexible Citizenship*, 6.

69. The classic work on networks in migration initially came from John S. MacDonald and Leatrice D. MacDonald, "Chain Migration." The more elaborate Actor-Network Theory developed by the Centre de sociologie de l'innovation in Paris in the 1980s has had a more general impact. Recent work on the migration industry has suggested a powerful critique of the notion that all networks are benign. E.g., Gammeltoft-Hansen and Sørensen, *Migration Industry*.

70. Subrahmanyam, "Between a Rock and a Hard Place," 430; Bouvier, *De la socioanthropologie*, 15–19.

71. Higham, *Strangers in the Land.*

72. See, e.g., Julie Y. Chu's fine ethnography on the difficulties of exit and entrance for Chinese villagers wanting to migrate to the US, *Cosmologies of Credit.*

73. E.g., R. M. Smith, *Civic Ideals*; Gerstle, *American Crucible*; Ngai, *Impossible Subjects*; Zolberg, *Nation by Design*; P. Weil, *Sovereign Citizen*; FitzGerald and Cook-Martín, *Culling the Masses.* For a recent treatment reminding us that the exclusion of many immigrant groups has run parallel to the welcoming of others, see Kramer, "Geopolitics of Mobility."

74. Zolberg, "Archaeology of 'Remote Control'"; Schneider, "United States Government."

75. Noiriel, *La tyrannie du national*; P. Weil, *La France et ses étrangers*; Viet, *La France immigrée.*

76. Dauvergne, *Making People Illegal*, 7; Guiraudon, *Les politiques d'immigration*; Schain, *Politics of Immigration.* See also Brubaker, *Citizenship and Nationhood*; Cornelius, Martin, and Hollifield, *Controlling Immigration*; Brochmann and Hammar, *Mechanisms of Immigration Control.*

77. Dauvergne, *New Politics of Immigration.*

78. Boyden, Krabbendam, and Vandenbussche, *Tales of Transit*; Brinkmann, *Points of Passage*; Gammeltoft-Hansen and Sørensen, *Migration Industry*; Green, "Trans-frontières"; Keeling, *Business of Transatlantic Migration*; Vidal and Musset, *Les territoires de l'attente.*

79. Connolly, "Intimate Atlantics." Connolly participated in a January 9, 2016, panel at the American Historical Association meeting entitled "Yet Another Effort, Historians, If You Would Become Transnational: Critical Perspectives from within Transnational History." A panel at the 2016 European Social Science History Conference in Valencia was entitled "Conceptualizing Global History: A Critical Look at Some of the Field's Central Terms."

CHAPTER THREE

1. A. James (no relation), "Memorable Naturalization." In 1915, upset that the US was not joining the Allied cause, Henry James took a public moral stance by becoming a British subject and thereby automatically losing his US citizenship under the 1907 Expatriation Law, discussed below.

2. P. Weil, *Sovereign Citizen*; Herzog, *Revoking Citizenship*. See also Aleinikoff, "Loss of Citizenship."

3. Earnest, *Expatriates and Patriots*, viii; Aleinikoff, "Loss of Citizenship," 1473; Flournoy, "Naturalization and Expatriation," 866.

4. Earnest, *Expatriates and Patriots*, 251, called the 1920s a period of "mass expatriation"; cf. McCarthy, *Expatriate Perspective*. The literature on James and Wharton and on the Lost Generation is too extensive to do it justice here. Two classic starting points for the interwar period by those who were there are Cowley, *Exile's Return*, and Flanner, *Paris Was Yesterday*. But see also Cott, "Revisiting the Transatlantic 1920s." A spurt of new literature beginning in the 1970s started to include more focus on women and African Americans, e.g., Benstock, *Women of the Left Bank*; Dunbar, *Black Expatriates*; Fabre, *From Harlem to Paris*; Lentz-Smith, *Freedom Struggles*; Stovall, *Paris Noir*. Stovall, however, has pointed out that the notion of African American expatriates in particular took some getting used to since the term had been so linked to the white writers in Paris. Stovall, xiii, 180–81. James Baldwin insisted that the term "expatriate" was a misnomer: "I am in 'exile' and was; one can never be an expatriate, really. One cannot possibly leave where he came from. You always carry home with you." Fabre, *From Harlem to Paris*, 210.

5. Y. Thomas, *"Origine" et "commune patrie."* Thomas argued, contrary to the usual interpretation that sees the Roman recognition of territoriality or domicile as innovative, that a hereditary link to one's place of origin persisted.

6. *New Shorter Oxford* (1993): Expatriate-n. "Orig., an exile. Now, a person who lives from choice in a foreign country"; Schuck and R. M. Smith, *Citizenship Without Consent*. Without agreeing with their conclusion (for a more restrictive notion of *jus soli* today, from which Smith himself has backed away), one can read this book for a useful intellectual history of competing tensions between consent and ascription with regard to citizenship. For a critique of Schuck's and Smith's conclusions, see Neuman, "Back to Dred Scott," 485; cf. Neuman, *Strangers to the Constitution*. See also Daniel, "Automatic Birthright Citizenship."

7. On social citizenship and exclusions, see chapter 2, note 57. For a contrasting, more optimistic view of the American egalitarian ideal, see, e.g., Karst, *Belonging to America*.

8. Yet see, notably, R. M. Smith, *Civic Ideals*; and Kerber, "Stateless as the Citizen's Other"; P. Weil, *Sovereign Citizen*; Herzog, *Revoking Citizenship*.

9. Bredbenner, *Nationality of Her Own*; Cott, "Marriage and Women's Citizenship"; Cott, *Public Vows*; Kerber, "Meanings of Citizenship"; Cott, *No Constitutional Right*; Gardner, *Qualities of a Citizen*; R. M. Smith, *Civic Ideals*; M. L. Smith, "'Any Woman . . .'". For the texts of the laws, see "American Citizenship Rights of Women," accessed June 3, 2017, http://www.loc.gov/law/find/hearings/pdf/0014160126A.pdf. For an earlier treatment: Borchard, "Citizenship of Native-Born American Women."

10. "Expatriation and repatriation represent nothing new in the history of this country; it is new only to those who are unfamiliar with its history." Theodore Saloutos, "Expatriates and Repatriates: A Neglected Chapter in United States History," unpublished paper (Rock Island, Ill., 1972), 18. Although political economists have studied the impact of the "brain drain" on the economies of origin, a more general history of exit and the relationship of countries to their citizens who leave is just beginning to be studied. E.g., Green and Weil, *Citizenship and Those Who Leave*; Scully, *Bargaining with the State*, 52–59; R. C. Smith, "Diasporic Memberships"; "Symposium: A Tribute to the Work of Kim Barry."

11. P. Weil, *Sovereign Citizen*.

12. Cited in Tsiang, *Question of Expatriation*, 28.

13. Tsiang, *Question of Expatriation*. On Jefferson, see also Whelan, "Citizenship and the Right to Leave"; R. M. Smith, *Civic Ideals*, 155–59.

14. Treason is also a matter of dates, as Talleyrand once said. "Sire, c'est là [ceux qui ont trahi la cause de l'Europe] une question de date." Talleyrand-Périgord, *Mémoires 1754-1815*, 723. To be faithful to Napoleon, for example, was no longer a good idea after Waterloo.

15. *Talbot v. Jansen*, 3 U.S. 133, 162 (1795). The judges spoke both in terms of allegiance and citizenship. At the same time, Iredell stressed that a citizen cannot dissolve one's duties to the state unilaterally. The Constitution did not specify that one must be a citizen to be a traitor; this silence created the "roots of ambiguity" that Rogers Smith examines in *Civic Ideals*, chap. 5.

16. A Gentleman of the City of New York [S. Johnson], *An Inquiry into the Natural Rights of Man as Regards the Exercise of Expatriation, Dedicated to All the Adopted Citizens of the United States* (New York: Pelsue and Gould, 1813), 5.

17. Tsiang, *Question of Expatriation*, 41n55; R. M. Smith, *Civic Ideals*, 156. See also Hay, *Treatise on Expatriation*; and A Massachusetts Lawyer [John Lowell], *Review of a Treatise on Expatriation by George Hay, Esq.* (Boston: Russell and Cutler, 1814), 16–17; cf. 5.

18. Schuck and Smith, *Citizenship without Consent*, 87.

19. *United States v. Isaac William*, cited in Tsiang, *Question of Expatriation*, 33. Ellsworth was castigated by the anti-Federalists as anti-Republican and pro-monarchical for his stand on perpetual allegiance.

20. Borchard, *Diplomatic Protection*, 675–76; Salyer, *Under the Starry Flag*.

21. "Opinions of the Heads of the Executive Departments, and Other Papers, Relating to Expatriation, Naturalization, and Change of Allegiance" in United States, Department of State, *Foreign Relations of the United States*, 1873, pt. 2, 1188; Borchard, "Citizenship of Native-Born American Women," 399, on the figure of the expatriate in these treaties: "it was primarily to citizens of foreign countries emigrating to the United States, and not to American citizens emigrating to foreign countries, that the treaties were deemed to have their practical application"; Zolberg, "Exit Revolution." On expatriation law as linked to immigration flows, see also Moore, "Doctrine of Expatriation"; and Flournoy, "Naturalization and Expatriation."

22. Both quotes come from Borchard, "Decadence," 313.

23. The Bureau of Citizenship was still investigating his citizenship in 1910. See chapter 1 above.

24. In relation to this point, see John P. Roche's virulent critique of ahistorical legal interpretations. Roche, "Expatriation Decisions."

25. Tsiang, *Question of Expatriation*, 100. Flournoy, "Naturalization and Expatriation," 848–49, was particularly suspicious of fraud and questioned the good faith of immigrants, suspecting them of taking on US citizenship solely to avoid military service in their country of origin. See also P. Weil, *Sovereign Citizen*, on fraudulent naturalizations.

26. P. Weil, *Sovereign Citizen*, 197.

27. Root, "Basis of Protection." His examples were Turkey, Morocco, and Mexico. On the issue of return in general, see Wyman, *Round-Trip to America*.

28. Although in practice it could exist for children of the foreign-born. See discussion of dual citizenship below.

29. Root, "Basis of Protection," 517, 518; Borchard, *Diplomatic Protection*, v. Root, no longer secretary of state, was president of the American Society of International Law, to which this paper was presented.

30. Sec. 401. Treason was explicitly included for the first time, turning Talbot's reasoning on its head. Whereas he had tried to argue that expatriation would invalidate an accusation of treason, in 1940 treason became cause for expatriation.

31. Flournoy, "Naturalization and Expatriation"; James, "Expatriation in the United States," 855, 875.

32. P. Weil, *Sovereign Citizen*, 198–99.

33. VD5, Archives 256, Mecklembourg [*sic*] Estate, Law Offices of S.G. Archibald Archives, Paris.

34. "Weds German Duke, Her Children Sue," *New York Times*, October 12, 1912, http://query.nytimes.com/mem/archive-free/pdf?_r=1&res=9904E6DD133CE633A25751C1A9669D946396D6CF (accessed June 1, 2015).

35. See below.

36. "Helmsley's Dog Gets $12 Million in Will," *Washington Post*, August 29, 2007.

37. Even after 1922, those who had lost their citizenship had to apply for naturalization to recover it. Completely equal nationality rights for American-born women were not reestablished until the 1940s. See note 9 above.

38. Importantly, however, military service abroad was *not* (yet) considered an expatriating act at this juncture, undoubtedly due to historical memory of the early British-turned-American sailors.

39. Cited in Tsiang, *Question of Expatriation*, 106. An 1873 opinion had included "amusement" in the list of legitimate reasons that an American citizen may reside abroad for an indefinite period: "for purposes of health, of education, of amusement, or business." Tsiang, 108.

40. This did not always work. See the Memorandum on the Citizenship of Mr. Emile Supper, July 27, 1915, from the American Consulate in Lyon to the Secretary of State, Washington, 351.11/890, General Records of the Department of State, Decimal Files, Record Group 59, 1910–1929, National Archives at College Park, Md. (Files on Supper continue in 351.11/1105 and 351.11/1227.) Having lived in France for twenty years, the German-born, US-naturalized Supper claimed that he did not know of the 1907 Expatriation Act.

41. The first case brought to the Supreme Court was that of a woman in California who lost her citizenship after marrying a Scottish man living there. She became expatriated without leaving the US. *MacKenzie v. Hare*, 239 U.S. 299 17, 20, 22 (1915).

42. See note 9 above.

43. Borchard, "Citizenship of Native-Born American Women," 403; Tsiang, *Question of Expatriation*, 110, 94. Borchard chided Tsiang for ignoring the issue of expatriated American women. Borchard, "Question of Expatriation." See also R. M. Smith, *Civic Ideals*, for whom the 1907 law is another example of the "multiple traditions" of the constant tension in American citizenship debates between exclusionary ascriptive inequality (of women, African Americans, and Native Americans) and more liberal Lockean consent. Cf. Bredbenner, *Nationality of Her Own*, 42, 19; and M. L. Smith, "'Any Woman . . .'".

44. There were in fact four different types of mixed marriage situations, depending on gender and domicile: native-born women married to foreign-born men living in the US (approximately 8.9 percent according to birth statistics of white children born in 1920); the more numerous foreign-born women married to American men also living in the United States (about 14 percent)—Bredbenner, *Nationality of Her Own*, 4n3—and both categories living abroad.

45. Cited in R. M. Smith, *Civic Ideals*, 457.

46. Montgomery, *"Gilded Prostitution,"* 166; A. Stuart, *Consuelo and Alva Vanderbilt*; Balsan, *Glitter and the Gold.*

47. Bredbenner, *Nationality of Her Own*, 74, 63.

48. Dodd, "Expatriates," 262. Cf. Montgomery, *"Gilded Prostitution."*

49. L. L. Bell, *Expatriates*, 69, 121; *Oxford English Dictionary*, 2nd ed. (1989).

50. "America created the twentieth century." G. Stein, *Autobiography of Alice B. Toklas*, 78. Henry Luce's famous "The American Century" article appeared in *Life Magazine*, February 17, 1941.

51. Earnest, *Expatriates and Patriots.* On two centuries of an increasing democratization of travel to France, see Levenstein, *Seductive Journey*; Levenstein, *We'll Always Have Paris*; Endy, *Cold War Holidays.*

52. Stearns, "Apologia of an Expatriate," 339, for both quotes. The "Apologia" is a letter Stearns had written to F. Scott Fitzgerald.

53. Green, *Other Americans in Paris*, 18; Susman, "Pilgrimage to Paris," 165, citing the *Chicago Tribune European Edition.*

54. Laney, *Paris "Herald,"* 144.

55. R. N. Williams, *New Exiles*; Hagan, *Northern Passage.*

56. See note 4 above.

57. The shortened term, "expat," is used only in the title. The poem uses the full term, "expatriates," in a self-mocking way: they "speak in

loud voices," are "in it for gain"; "One is neither one thing nor the other./So one is loved by no one." Enright, "Expat." Cf. *Oxford English Dictionary*, 2nd ed. (1989). The *Random House Dictionary*, 2nd edition unabr. (1983), dates the origin of the term to 1960–65, and indeed it is absent from *Webster's Third New International Dictionary* begun in 1961. The 2000 *American Heritage Dictionary* considers the term "chiefly British."

58. Immigration and Naturalization Service (hereafter "INS"), *Operations Instructions and Interpretations* (Washington, D.C., 1971-482-319/SC-6), sec. 349.1(f)(3)(i); 8 I. & N. Dec. 317 (1959); *Tanaka v. Immigration & Naturalization Service*, 346 F.2d 438 (2d Cir. 1965). With thanks to Marian L. Smith for guiding me to these sources.

59. *Afroyim v. Rusk*, 387 U.S. 253, 257 (1967). *Afroyim* overturned *Perez v. Brownell*, 356 U.S. 44, 61 (1958). See INS, *Operations Instructions and Interpretations*, sec. 349.1(d)(2); and Harvey, "Expatriation Law"; Herzog, *Revoking Citizenship*, 82–86; P. Weil, *Sovereign Citizen*.

60. On dual citizenship, see chapter 2, note 53. It has also become part of a competition for citizens. Cook-Martín, *Scramble for Citizens*.

61. Borchard, "Decadence," 315.

62. Iridell in *Talbot v. Jansen*, 3 U.S. 133, 165 (1795); Theodore Roosevelt, "When is an American Not an American," *Metropolitan Magazine*, June 1915, in 351.117/50, General Records of the Department of State, Decimal Files, Record Group 59, 1910-1929, National Archives at College Park, MD; preamble to the 1930 Hague Convention on Certain Questions Relating to the Conflict of Nationality Laws, confirmed in the 1963 European Convention on Reduction of Cases of Multiple Nationality—both reiterated the norm of single citizenship—in Barry, "Home and Away,"43n124. Only in 1977 was a European protocol signed accepting plural nationality.

63. Neuman, *Strangers to the Constitution*. On "external citizenship," see Barry, "Home and Away"; and Bauböck, "Towards a Political Theory," 715.

64. A useful source for these debates is *AARO News*. See also Michaux, *Unknown Ambassadors*. Cf. Sophia Yan, "A Record 3,415 Americans Ditch Their Passports," CNN, February 17, 2015, http://money.cnn.com/2015/02/12/pf/americans-expat-citizenship-passports/index.html; Robert W. Wood, "Americans Renouncing Citizenship Hits New Record," *Forbes*, November 3, 2017, https://www.forbes.com/sites

/robertwood/2017/11/03/americans-renouncing-citizenship-hits-new-record-tax-bill-wont-change-that/#1a1ce2885f85.

CHAPTER FOUR

1. "L'émigrant est un type d'humanité qui plaît peu à la masse, considéré qu'il est souvent, au départ, comme un déserteur, ou du moins un égoïste; à l'arrivée, comme un concurrent, encombrant, ou un paria à exploiter." Gonnard, *Essai sur l'histoire de l'émigration*, 16–17.

2. Green and Weil, *Citizenship and Those Who Leave*; Dufoix, Guerassimoff, and de Tinguy, *Loin des yeux, près du cœur*; Green and Waldinger, *Century of Transnationalism*; Zahra, *Great Departure.*

3. Mols, "Population in Europe," 32. Mols quotes Bodin in French.

4. A Gentleman of the City of New York [S. Johnson], *An Inquiry into the Natural Rights of Man as Regards the Exercise of Expatriation, Dedicated to All the Adopted Citizens of the United States* (New York: Pelsue and Gould, 1813), 10, 11, 5. See chapter 3 above.

5. United Nations, Universal Declaration of the Rights of Man art. 13 (December 10, 1948), http://www.un.org/en/universal-declaration-human-rights/.

6. Brettell and Hollifield, *Migration Theory*. See chapter 2 above.

7. Higham, "Strange Career."

8. Cf. Noiriel, *Le creuset français.*

9. Eckstein and Najam, *How Immigrants Impact Their Homelands*; Chu, *Cosmologies of Credit*; Waldinger, *Cross-Border Connection.*

10. Even in the field of political science, Jim Hollifield noted, there is a dearth of literature on the rules of exit. Hollified, "Politics of International Migration," 173. See note 2 above and chapter 3, note 10.

11. For a useful brief overview of different types of contemporary emigration, see Weiner, *Global Migration Crisis*, 29–44. See also Zahra, *Great Departure.*

12. Miller, *Emigrants and Exiles*; Green, "Modern Jewish Diaspora"; Hoerder and Rössler, *Distant Magnets.*

13. For recent work on the interstices of movement and *lieux de passages*, see chapter 2, note 78.

14. Sayad, "Les trois âges de l'émigration algérienne"; Sayad, *La double absence.*

15. Tapinos, *L'immigration étrangère en France.* Cf. the different interpretations of Rempel and Lobdell, "Role of Urban-Rural Remittances";

and Collier and Lal, "How Poor People Get Rich." See also Hatzipanayotou, "International Migration and Remittances"; Keely and Tran, "Remittances from Labor Migration"; and Stahl and Arnold, "Overseas Workers Remittances in Asian Development."

16. See, however, e.g., Lessinger, "Nonresident-Indian Investment"; and Khadria, *Migration of Knowledge Workers*; see also Waldinger, *Cross-Border Connection*; and Eckstein and Najam, *How Immigrants Impact Their Homelands.*

17. Thistlethwaite, "Migration from Europe Overseas"; B. Thomas, *Economics of International Migration*; Hoerder, *Labor Migration.*

18. See discussion of Germany, Italy, and Hungary below.

19. Torpey, *Invention of the Passport*; Robertson, *Passport in America.*

20. In contrast to this idea of shifting attitudes about the right to leave over time, cf. a United Nations study that (during the Cold War) argued that the right to emigrate is a natural right, with references ranging from Socrates, Grotius, and the Great Charter of 1215 (admitting that the pertinent article was eliminated the following year), to article 13 of the 1948 Universal Declaration of the Rights of Man. Inglés, *Étude des mesures discriminatoires*, 1–4. Frederick C. Whelan, on the other hand, argued that the right to leave is a new concept dating to 1948: "Citizenship and the Right to Leave." Torpey, *Invention of the Passport*, dates it to the French Revolution. More generally, see Green, "Location, Location, Location."

21. Schmitter-Heisler, "Sending Countries." See also Ewa Morawska, "East European Migrations 1880s–1914: Contexts and Actors" (paper presented at the Conference on "Migration Controls in 19th-Century Europe and America," Paris, Sorbonne, June 25–26, 1999).

22. This persisted into midcentury as American soldiers did the reverse, trying to avoid enrollment in the Civil War by (re)claiming their British ancestry/citizenship. See Schuck and Smith, *Citizenship without Consent.*

23. Cassano, *Procès-verbaux sommaires.*

24. On municipal concerns and business interests, see Maire, *En route pour l'Amérique*; Keeling, *Business of Transatlantic Migration*; Gammeltoft-Hansen and Sørensen, *Migration Industry.*

25. Green, *Repenser les migrations*, chap. 4.

26. "dérogation au principe de la liberté d'industrie." Chandèze, *Surveillance des agences d'émigration*; Chandèze, *L'émigration*; Green,

"'Filling the Void'"; François Weil, "Quitter la France, XIX-XXe siècle. Essai de synthèse" (paper presented at "Les Français aux Amériques," École des Hautes Études en Sciences Sociales, December 11–14, 2002).

27. Baghdasarian, *L'émigration européenne*, esp. 134–36.

28. See, e.g., Hay, *Treatise on Expatriation*, 22; Zolberg, "Exit Revolution."

29. The phrase was used by Charles Buller to describe Robert Wilmot Horton's emigration scheme. Johnston, *British Emigration Policy*, 168. See also Hvidt, *Flight to America*, 21–23, on Danish parishes' financing of paupers (and convicts) to go to America; it was cheaper than providing poor relief. Hvidt adds that such export was not a Danish or British specialty and cites examples ranging from Westphalia to Norway to France.

30. Cf. Siegelbaum and Moch, "Transnationalism in One Country?" On empire and transnationalism, see Kramer, "Power and Connection."

31. Feldman and Baldwin, "Emigration and the British State."

32. As Jean-François Féraud pointed out ten years earlier, "émigrant," "émigration," and "émigrer" were new words. *Dictionaire critique de la langue française* (Marseille: Mossy, 1787–88), http://portail.atilf.fr/cgi-bin/dico1look.pl?strippedhw=%E9migrant&headword=&docyear=ALL&dicoid=ALL&articletype=1. The term "réfugié" was used for the Huguenots who fled France after the Revocation of the Edict of Nantes, and the term "émigré" for the nobility who took flight during the French Revolution.

33. See F. Weil, "French Migration to the Americas"; F. Weil, "French State and Transoceanic Emigration"; Gonnard, *Essai*, 17, 271–74. He adds: "Du reste, la France, au lieu d'exporter des hommes, exporte des idées. . . ." (165).

34. Heurtier, *Rapport à Son Excellence*. See also Maire, *En route pour l'Amérique*.

35. P. Weil, *Qu'est-ce qu'un Français?*

36. Bade, *Vom Auswanderungsland zum Einwanderungsland?*; Bade, *Deutsche im Ausland*; Bretting and Bickelmann, *Auswanderungsagenturen und Auswanderungsvereine*; Brubaker, *Citizenship and Nationhood*; Fahrmeir, *Citizens and Aliens*; Hoerder, Rössler, and Blank, *Roots of the Transplanted*; Moltmann, *Deutsche Amerikaauswanderung*; Gabaccia, Hoerder, and Walaszek, "Emigration and Nation-Building."

37. See, e.g., Harzig, *Peasant Maids, City Women*.

38. Fahrmeir, "From Economics to Ethnicity," 183.

39. Fahrmeir, 183.

40. Cinel, *National Integration*, chap. 4; Douki, "L'État libéral italien"; Foerster, *Italian Emigration*, chap. 23; Gabaccia, *Italy's Many Diasporas*, 136-141; Baily, "Village Outward Approach"; Choate, *Emigrant Nation*; Tintori, "L'Italie et ses expatriés"; Tintori, "Italy: The Continuing History."

41. Foerster, *Italian Emigration*, 477.

42. Tommaso Tittoni, Foreign Minister, cited in Foerster, *Italian Emigration*, 477–78.

43. Douki, "L'État libéral italien."

44. The poet Edmondo De Amicis, quoted by Cinel, *National Integration*, 74.

45. See also Douki, "'Return Politics.'"

46. Puskás, *From Hungary to the United States*, 92–115, provides a particularly interesting analysis of emigration. See also Puskás, *Overseas Migration*, and articles by Tajták and Glettler in Puskás, *Overseas Migration*.

47. Puskás, *From Hungary to the United States*, 107.

48. Puskás, 107.

49. The novelist and nationalist Enrico Corradini, cited in Foerster, *Italian Emigration*, 494.

50. *Allgemeine Zeitung* (Augsburg), December 9, 1816, cited in Hansen, *Atlantic Migration*, 3.

51. Blum, *Strength in Numbers*. Blum concludes with the observation that France however turned to Malthusianism (like other European countries) during the nineteenth century, only to return to natalism at the end of that century. For the later period, see Charbit, *Du Malthusianisme au populationnisme*; Klaus, *Every Child a Lion*; Rosental, *L'intelligence démographique*.

52. Marchese di Cosentino, cited in Cinel, *National Integration*, 75.

53. See, e.g., [L'abbé] P. Labrune, *L'émigration* (Aubusson: A. Bouyet, 1869).

54. "une perte sèche pour le pays." Cited by Chevalier, "L'émigration française," 166 (in quotation marks but with no reference). Leroy-Beaulieu, *De la colonisation*, 607, cites Say via Wilhelm Roscher. More generally, see Gonnard, *Essai*, 281–86; and Stangeland, *Pre-Malthusian Doctrines*. Vauban, instigator of the first French population census of

1694, wrote: "The greatness of kings is measured by the number of their subjects." Cited in Blum, *Strength in Numbers*, 8.

55. "[N]ulle perte n'est plus fâcheuse pour la patrie abandonnée." Say, *Traité d'économie politique*, bk. 1, chap. 20, 239. "Toutes les lois contre l'émigration sont iniques.... Lorsqu'on empêche une population surabondante de sortir par la porte des frontières, elle sort par la porte des tombeaux." Say, *Cours complet d'économie politique pratique*, 6th pt., chap. 6, 151. Here, as elsewhere, Say argues that it is good laws and good institutions that create prosperity, not the number of individuals in and of themselves.

56. Gentleman of New York, *An Inquiry*, 6.

57. Horton, *Causes and Remedies of Pauperism*, 8, 13. In their correspondence, Tanneguy Duchatel admitted that, given the choice between emigration and extreme misery, "it must be considered as a happier lot, to live in comfort in one's native country, than in a distant colony; but better to live in comfort in a distant colony, than to endure in one's native country the bitter condition of pauperism." Horton, 14.

58. Puskás, *From Hungary to the United States*, 92–115; cf. Leroy-Beaulieu, *De la colonisation*, 626–27.

59. Georges de Pardonnet, *Émigration au Kansas, États-Unis d'Amérique du Nord. Le Kansas, ses ressources et produits, ses concessions gratuites de terres. Conseils pratiques aux émigrants* (Montbéliard: Imprimerie de Henri Barbier, n.d. [ca. 1873]), 3–4, 35–37; Pardonnet, *Amérique du Nord et du Sud, Renseignements généraux sur les diverses contrées où se dirige l'émigration européenne. Conseils pratiques aux émigrants* (Paris: 72, bd Haussmann [address of the Agence générale maritime], n.d. [ca. 1878]), 40–42.

60. Hirschman, *Exit, Voice, and Loyalty*.

61. E.g., Dufoix, *Politiques d'exil*.

62. Gonnard, *Essai*, 285ff. Malthus himself was in fact uncertain that emigration would provide any relief. Malthus, *Essay*, vol. 1, book 3, chap. 4, "Of Emigration." This would change as France became obsessed by its demographic lag by the late nineteenth century.

63. Bielik, Hogh, and Števrteckà, "Slovak Images"; Cygan, "Polish Women."

64. Foerster, *Italian Emigration*, 495, citing Enrico Corradini.

65. Gabaccia, Hoerder and Walaszek, "Emigration and Nation-Building."

66. "esprit de fraternité"; "remplir une mission élevée, sublime: une mission de civilisation." S. Linstant, *De l'émigration européenne dans ses rapports avec la prospérité future des colonies* (Paris: France [*sic*], Editeur], 1850), 45.

67. E.g., Linstant, 45.

68. Cited in Gabaccia, *Italy's Many Diasporas*, 139.

69. E.g., Duval, *Histoire de l'émigration européenne*, vi. Duval considered that emigration had always existed; the only thing new was the increase in its proportions. Duval, x. On Duval, see Charbit, *Du Malthusianisme au populationnisme*, chap. 8.

70. Puskás, *From Hungary to the United States*, 110.

71. Torpey, *Passport*; Whelpley, *Problem of the Immigrant*, 194–95.

72. Hvidt, *Flight to America*, 23–25; Zolberg, "Exit Revolution."

73. Cf. Torpey, *Passport*, pointing out the former; and Fahrmeir, "From Economics to Ethnicity," emphasizing the latter.

74. Puskás, *From Hungary to the United States*.

75. Fahrmeir, "From Economics to Ethnicity"; Eagle Glassheim, commenting at the conference "Unsettling Europe," Davis Center for Historical Studies, Princeton University, May 3, 2002. As Thomas Kleven cogently pointed out, the paradox of the contemporary liberal state is that international law favors emigration on the basis of individual rights but argues for barriers to immigration on the grounds of collective self-determination. Kleven, "Why International Law Favors Emigration."

76. Zolberg, "Exit Revolution"; Zolberg, "Archaeology of 'Remote Control.'"

77. Cf. Dowty, *Closed Borders*, esp. 26, and, more generally, chap. 2.

78. Fahrmeir et al., *Migration Control*; Neuman, *Strangers to the Constitution*.

79. Leroy-Beaulieu, *De la colonisation*, xi–xiv (intro. to 2nd ed.), 611, and 626n1. Indeed he suggested that those turbulent elements ill-suited to the Old World could find good use for their energies in the New (624–25).

80. Chu, *Cosmologies of Credit*, 126.

81. The US has always been one of the only countries in the world that taxes its citizens on their worldwide income no matter where they reside. US citizens are supposed to file tax declarations from wherever they may be domiciled.

CHAPTER FIVE

1. Green, *Other Americans in Paris.* Americans in Paris were not Americans in Mexico or China, where colonial relations and extraterritorial relations were more transparent. Scully, *Bargaining with the State*, 59, argues that the US had three tiers of attitudes toward Americans abroad, depending on where they were: Western Europe, Latin America, non-Western countries. More explicitly neocolonial situations pertained, for example, in Mexico and China. Hart, *Empire and Revolution*; Langley and Schoonover, *Banana Men*; Schell, *Integral Outsiders.*

2. Rosenberg, *Spreading the American Dream*; cf. De Grazia, *Irresistible Empire.*

3. For other, more contemporary examples, see, e.g., Ong, *Flexible Citizenship*; Tarrius, *Les fourmis d'Europe*; Tarrius, *Les nouveaux cosmopolitismes*; Turner, "Diasporic Tension." More generally, see chapter 2 above.

4. See chapter 2 above, and E. Cohen, "Expatriate Communities"; Fechter and Walsh, "Examining 'Expatriate' Continuities"; Klekowski von Koppenfels, *Migrants or Expatriates?*; Expatriate Archive Centre, accessed September 3, 2018, https://xpatarchive.com/.

5. Joe Costanzo and Amanda Klekowski von Koppenfels, "Counting the Uncountable: Overseas Americans," Migration Information Source, May 17, 2013, http://www.migrationpolicy.org/article/counting-uncountable-overseas-americans.

6. De Grazia, *Irresistible Empire.*

7. See chapter 3, note 57.

8. E.g., Blower, *Becoming American in Paris*; Gopnik, *Americans in Paris*; McCullough, *Greater Journey*; Stovall, *Paris Noir*; and chapter 3, note 4.

9. Green, *Other Americans.*

10. Archives of the Law Offices of S.G. Archibald (hereafter "SGA")—alas, now defunct; Class 3—Protection in France of private and national interests of the United States, 351.11 decimal files, General Records of the Department of State, Decimal Files, Record Group 59 (hereafter "RG59"), 1910–1929 and 1930–1939, National Archives at College Park, MD. (hereafter "NACP").

11. See chapter 3 above.

12. VD28, Archives 490, Mrs. Moulton, SGA.

13. Gertrude Moulton to her lawyer, S.G. Archibald, June 21, 1931; Gertrude Moulton to her brother, Feb. 17, 1933; Gertrude Moulton to her lawyer, July 10, 1935, VD28, Archives 490, Mrs. Moulton, SGA.

14. VD19, Archives 383, Mrs. Steichen, SGA.

15. Clara Steichen to Herman F. Gadd (lawyer in the Archibald firm), August 7, 1933; Clara Steichen to Gething Miller (also of the Archibald firm), October 5, 1933, VD19, Archives 383, SGA. See also Clara's letters to Alfred Stieglitz, YCAL MSS 85, Beinecke Rare Book and Manuscript Library, Yale University.

16. Tilly, "Citizenship, Identity and Social History," esp. 7–8.

17. Edward Cummings to President Woodrow Wilson, December 8, 1917, 351.112B81, RG59, NACP. See also cummings, *Enormous Room*, vii–ix.

18. Barry, "Home and Away."

19. For a history of the US consular service, see Barnes and Morgan, *Foreign Service*; Foster, *Practice of Diplomacy*, 216–42; Lee, *Consular Law and Practice*; Michael, *History of the Department of State*; Moore, *Digest of International Law*, vol. 5, chap. 16; Plischke, *U.S. Department of State*; G. Stuart, *American Diplomatic and Consular Practice*.

20. *Blackmer v. United States*, 284 U.S. 421 (1932); "Exile's Return," *Life*, October 10, 1949.

21. Lee, *Consular Law and Practice*, 3; see also 59, 187–93.

22. Foster, *Practice of Diplomacy*, 216–42; G. Stuart, *American Diplomatic and Consular Practice*, 168; Plischke, *U.S. Department of State*, 46–51, 80–90, 140–55, 210–24, 311–24, 333–35; Moore, *Digest of International Law*, vol. 5, chap. 16; Barnes and Morgan, *Foreign Service*; Michael, *History of the Department of State*, 52. The 1853 convention was replaced by a convention of July 18, 1968.

23. The Moses-Linthicum Act of 1931 further professionalized the foreign service. Plischke, *U.S. Department of State*, 221, 224, 311–14; G. Stuart, *American Diplomatic and Consular Practice*, 192–94. Although eligible as of 1924 as career officers, very few women were appointed until after World War II. Plischke, *U.S. Department of State*, 324.

24. E.g., G. Stuart, *American Diplomatic and Consular Practice*, 351ff.

25. G. Stuart, 372, 379.

26. Young, *Around the World*, 1:139.

27. Root, "Basis of Protection"; Borchard, *Diplomatic Protection*, v. See chapter 3 above.

28. Lee, *Consular Law*, 116–18. "As to the question whether consular protection may be forced upon nationals who, for political or other reasons, refuse to have any dealings with their consuls, there is no unanimity of views" (119).

29. G. Stuart, *American Diplomatic and Consular Practice*, 395.

30. G. Stuart, 398–99.

31. Katz, *From Appomattox to Montmartre*, 31, 47.

32. Torpey, *Invention of the Passport*; Robertson, *Passport in America*; cf. Fahrmeir, "Governments and Forgers."

33. From *The Life and Letters of Walter H. Page*, cited in Barnes and Morgan, *Foreign Service*, 190.

34. 351.11/365 [1914], RG59, 1910-1929, NACP.

35. Letter and memorandum, Ambassador to Secretary of State, November 12, 1914, 351.11/512, RG59, 1910-1929, NACP.

36. American Consul-General to Secretary of State, concerning "Whereabouts of Miss Alice B. Toklar [*sic*]," September 27, 1915, 351.11/943, RG59, 1910-1929, NACP; G. Stein, *Autobiography of Alice B. Toklas*, 161.

37. Letter, L.D. Clark to State Department, August 28 [1914], 351.11/685, RG59, 1910-1929, NACP (emphasis in original).

38. US Embassy in Paris to Secretary of State, June 24 and June 30, 1915, 351.11/816, 351.11/821 and 351.11/838, RG59, 1910–1929, NACP.

39. E.g., Secretary of State to Ambassador in Paris, September 9, 1914, 351.11/290a, RG59, 1910–1929, NACP.

40. Westinghouse Air Brake Company to Secretary of State, March 9, 1916, and related documents, including newspaper articles, 351.11/1082 and 351.11/1134 Westinghouse/Trube, RG59, 1910–1929, NACP; Donald Harper to Secretary of State, July 31, 1918, 351.11/1788, ibid.; and 351.11/1307 and 1899 (February 2, 1919), ibid.

41. Memorandum on the Citizenship of Mr. Emile Supper, July 27, 1915, from the American Consulate in Lyon to the Secretary of State, Washington, 351.11/890, RG59, 1910-1929, NACP. Files on Supper continue in 351.11/1105 and 351.11/1227.

42. The consulate was given instructions to give her such assistance as may be possible and proper. Office of the Solicitor to the Consular Bureau, June 5, 1916, and letter from Mme. Jan Haeften-Hatch to Secretary of State, May 16, 1916, 351.11/1161, RG59, 1910–1929, NACP (all spellings are original).

43. Protection certificates are held in Record Group 84 (RG84), Class 300—Protection of Interests—1940, NACP. For some examples, see Green, *Other Americans*, 241–42.

44. Lodge & Shipley Machine Tool Co., Cincinnati, to State Department, January 2, 1917 (and passim), 351.11/1347, re Harry Jones, RG59, 1910–1929, NACP.

45. All quotes except the last are from Osborne, American Consulate, Le Havre, to Secretary of State, April 7, 1913, 351.111B81, RG59, 1910–1929, NACP; last quote, Mr. Brown to Department of State, November 18, 1913, ibid.

46. All of the above are from Vice Consul John R. Wood, "Summary of Protection Cases Handled by the Consulate General at Paris, France, during the Year, 1925," February 20, 1926, 351.11/2003, RG59, 1910–1929, NACP. For other custody cases, see, e.g., 351.1115/15 and /19, RG59, 1930–1939, NACP.

47. Wood, "Summary of Protection Cases."

48. Wood, 7, 16, 24.

49. See in general: 351.117, RG59, 1910–1929, NACP, concerning men of French parentage—Frenchmen born in France and naturalized in the US or those born in the US of French parents—who were considered American in the US but would be considered French according to the Napoleonic Code and therefore liable to military service if they traveled to France. See, in particular, the case of P. A. Lelong, Jr., 351.117/48, 49a, 50, 51; and Flournoy, "Problems of Dual Nationality."

50. And beyond for those who married Asians. See chapter 3, note 9 above.

51. Robertson, *Passport in America*, 2, 152–59, and chap. 11; Torpey, *Invention of the Passport*, 94–96, 159–60.

52. John de Kay to Ambassador William G. Sharp, January 31, 1917, 351.114K18, RG59, 1910–1929, NACP.

53. Affidavit, February 25, 1908, 351.112G93, RG59, 1910–1929, NACP. See chapter 1 above.

54. Eli Joseph to US Ambassador, August 6, 1927, 351.1156 J77, RG59, 1910–1929, NACP.

55. See, e.g., 850.4 Robbins, Betty Page, and 851.2 in RG84-2513, NACP.

56. Grace V. Carpenter to Ministry of Foreign Affairs [*sic*], Washington, D.C., August 10, 1938, 351.1115-Carpenter Grace V. (Miss), RG59, 1930–1939, NACP.

57. 351.1115 Blandy, Mildred Arden, RG59, 1930–1939, NACP.

58. E.g. 850.4 Goldschmidt, Bruno (representing Meskin Brothers Fur Corporation), 1935, RG84-2513, NACP.

59. It turned out that foreign domestics following their masters who were themselves foreigners did not need work contracts E.g., 850.4, RG84-2513.

60. "Demands Swoboda's Trunks," *New York Times*, April 3, 1916; Stovall (Berne, Switz.) to Secretary of State, December 5, 1915; transcript, dated December 18, 1915, enclosed with cover letter dated December 20, 1915, all in 351.112Sw7, RG59, 1910–1929, NACP.

61. Seckler-Hudson, *Statelessness*, 102, 101; Flournoy, "Naturalization and Expatriation," 848, 851, 857; Borchard, *Diplomatic Protection*, 552–53.

62. Mrs. G. R. Wood to Secretary of State, April 10, 1938, 351.1115–Wood, Charles M./6, RG59, 1930–1939, NACP.

63. Wood, "Summary of Protection Cases," 24.

64. Milton L. Schmitt, Attorney at Law, San Francisco, to William W. Corcoran, American Vice Consul, Boulogne-sur-Mer, May 19, 1925, 351.1115-Noonan, Louella, RG59, 1910–1929, NACP.

65. Wm. H. Berry, Collector, to Secretary of the Treasury, September 3, 1918, reporting on letter from Herman Birnbrauer, 351.11/1805, RG59, 1910–1929, NACP.

66. Frank H. Mason to Secretary of State, July 27, 1911, 351.112C18/5, RG59, 1910–1929, NACP.

67. Frank Mason, farewell speech, American Chamber of Commerce in Paris, *Bulletin*, no. 119 (November 1913): 155.

68. In the end, the consulate admitted that the alterations were probably "without criminal intent." 351.1121 Turner, Blanche M., RG59, 1930–1939, NACP.

69. Root, "Basis of Protection," 526.

70. Leading to a last appeal in which the writer complained that his letters were surely being intercepted. 351.111D28, RG59, 1910–1929, NACP.

71. E.g., 351.1115 Bodge, Daisy Dean; and 351.11/1682, March 6, 1918, RG59, 1910–1929, NACP. American consuls are supposed to aid citizens in distress, "short of direct cash," and they are discouraged from extending personal loans. Lee, *Consular Law and Practice*, 132.

72. On loan recovery issue: 351.11/783a, 351.11/784a, RG59, 1910–1929, NACP; 351.11/869; continuing into early 1916, e.g., 351.11/1056 (January 21,

1916 letter). List of seventy-three persons owing money to the Treasury is under letter from Embassy to Secretary of State, July 12, 1916, 351.11/1200, RG59, 1910–1929, NACP; and into the mid-1920s. For the Shanghai example: 351.11/1764, 1918.

73. Putnam, *Paris Was Our Mistress*, 48.

74. But see, e.g., William O. Bullard to Secretary of State, August 10, 1915, quoted in Lloyd, *Eugene Bullard*, 41; and 351.1141—Mikell, Grace, RG59, 1930–1939, NACP.

75. The two women eventually got off with a fine and a one-month suspended sentence. Correspondence, 1926, 351.1115-Weitzenhoffer, Rosa and Julia Kaufman, RG59, 1910–1929, NACP.

76. A. Gaulin, American Consul General, to Secretary of State, December 5, 1927, 351.1115 Benjamin, George H., Mrs./4, RG59, 1930–1939, NACP; Ambassador Jesse Isidor Strauss to Gov. Herbert H. Lehman, December 21, 1935, ibid.

77. Contrary to my initial thoughts in an earlier version of this chapter: "Americans Abroad and the Uses of Citizenship: Paris, 1914–1940," *Journal of American Ethnic History* 31, no. 3 (2012): 5–32.

CONCLUSION

1. Keeling, *Business of Transatlantic Migration*, 37.

2. Alain Tarrius reminds us of the fatigue and the constraints of movement in *Les fourmis d'Europe*; Tarrius, *Les nouveaux cosmopolitismes*.

3. Communication with the author, email, September 18, 2013; see also Gabaccia, "Thoughts."

4. Y. Thomas, "*Origine*" *et* "*commune patrie*."

5. Goldberg, "Historical Reflections on Transnationalism," 213.

6. "Are There Costs to "Internationalizing" History?" (AHA Annual Meeting, 2013), https://aha.confex.com/aha/2013/webprogram/Session7432.html (and ibid, Session7638.html) (consulted April 22, 2015).

7. I am reminded of the stimulating discussions that occurred in June 1998 in Amsterdam and Cambridge (UK), thanks to David Thelen's convening of scholars that resulted in the special issue of the *Journal of American History*, December 1999, "The Nation and Beyond."

8. Dirk Hoerder has pointed out that if immigration societies contest the "nation" in nation-state, the state itself "remains highly pertinent to migration regimes and options for insertion." "Recent Methodological and Conceptual Approaches," 83.

9. D. A. Bell, "Questioning the Global Turn," 4; cf. Goldstein, "Future of French History."

10. Hunt, "Prospects of the Present," 29.

11. Subrahmanyam, "Histoire globale de la première modernité," November 28, 2014, http://www.college-de-france.fr/site/sanjay-subrahmanyam/inaugural-lecture-2013-11-28-18h00.htm.

Bibliography

Ackerman, Alissa R., and Rich Furman, eds. *Sex Crimes: Transnational Problems and Global Perspectives*. New York: Columbia University Press, 2015.

"AHR Conversation: On Transnational History." *American Historical Review* 111, no. 5 (2006): 1441–64.

"AHR Exchange." *American Historical Review* 112, no. 5 (2007): 1414–32.

"AHR Forum: Historiographic 'Turns' in Critical Perspective." *American Historical Review* 117, no. 3 (2012): 698–813.

"AHR Forum: Transnational Lives in the Twentieth Century." *American Historical Review* 118, no. 1 (2013): 1–139.

Alba, Richard D., and Victor Nee. "Rethinking Assimilation Theory for a New Era of Immigration." *International Migration Review* 31, no. 4 (1997): 826–74.

Alba, Richard, and Nancy Foner. *Strangers No More: Immigration and the Challenges of Integration in North America and Western Europe*. Princeton, NJ: Princeton University Press, 2015.

Aleinikoff, T. Alexander. "Theories of Loss of Citizenship." *Michigan Law Review* 84 (1985–86): 1471–1503.

Aleinikoff, T. Alexander, and Douglas Klusmeyer, eds. *Citizenship Today: Global Perspectives and Practices*. Washington, DC: Carnegie Endowment for International Peace, 2001.

________, eds. *From Migrants to Citizens: Membership in a Changing World*. Washington, DC: Carnegie Endowment for International Peace, 2000.

Allain, Jean-Claude. *Joseph Caillaux*. Vol. 1, *Le défi victorieux, 1863–1914*. Paris: Imprimerie nationale, 1978.

Anderson, Benedict R. O'G. *Long-Distance Nationalism: World Capitalism and the Rise of Identity Politics*. Amsterdam: Centre for Asian Studies Amsterdam, 1992.

Appadurai, Arjun. "Global Ethnoscapes: Notes and Queries for a Transnational Anthropology" [1991]. In *Modernity at Large: Cultural Dimensions of Globalization*, chap. 3. Minneapolis: University of Minneapolis Press, 1996.

________. "The Production of Locality." In *Counterworks: Managing the Diversity of Knowledge*, edited by Richard Fardon, 204–55. London: Routledge, 1995.

Bade, Klaus, ed. *Deutsche im Ausland—Fremde in Deutschland: Migration in Geschichte und Gegenwart*. Munich: Verlag C. H. Beck, 1992.

________. *Vom Auswanderungsland zum Einwanderungsland?* Deutschland 1880–1980 Berlin: Colloquium-Verlag, 1983.

Baghdasarian, S. *L'émigration européenne au XIXe siècle: Italie, Autriche-Hongrie, Russie, Grande-Bretagne, Allemagne*. Basel: Werner-Riehm, 1910.

Baily, Sam L. "The Village Outward Approach to the Study of Social Networks: A Case Study of the Agnonesi Diaspora Abroad, 1885–1989." *Studi emigrazione* 29 (March 1992): 43–68.

Balsan, Consuelo Vanderbilt. *The Glitter and the Gold*. New York: Harper, 1952.

Barkan, Elliott R. "Immigration, Incorporation, Assimilation, and the Limits of Transnationalism." *Journal of American Ethnic History* 25, nos. 2–3 (Winter–Spring 2006): 7–32.

Barnes, William, and John Heath Morgan. *The Foreign Service of the United States*. Washington, DC: US Department of State, 1961.

Barry, Kim. "Home and Away: The Construction of Citizenship in an Emigration Context." *New York University Law Review* 81, no. 1 (2006): 11–59.

Bauböck, Rainer. "Towards a Political Theory of Migrant Transnationalism." *International Migration Review* 37, no. 3 (2003): 700–723.

Bauböck, Rainer, and Thomas Faist, eds. *Diaspora and Transnationalism: Concepts, Theories and Methods*. Amsterdam: Amsterdam University Press, 2010.

Belich, James, et al., eds. *The Prospect of Global History*. Oxford: Oxford University Press, 2016.

Bell, David A. "Questioning the Global Turn: The Case of the French Revolution." *French Historical Studies* 37, no. 1 (2014): 1–24.

Bell, Lilian Lida. *The Expatriates: A Novel*. New York: Harper and Brothers, 1900.

Bender, Thomas. *A Nation among Nations: America's Place in World History*. New York: Hill and Wang, 2006.

________, ed. *Rethinking American History in a Global Age*. Berkeley: University of California Press, 2002.

Benstock, Shari. *Women of the Left Bank: Paris, 1900–1940*. Austin: University of Texas Press, 1986.

Berenson, Edward. *The Trial of Madame Caillaux*. Berkeley: University of California Press, 1992.

Bechtel, Guy. *1907: La grande révolte du midi*. Paris: Robert Laffont, 1976.

Bielik, František, Horst Hogh, and Anna Štvrteckà. "Slovak Images of the New World: 'We Could Pay Off Our Debts.'" In *Roots of the Transplanted*, edited by Dirk Hoerder and Inge Blank, 1:377–90. Boulder, CO: East European Monographs, 1994.

Blanc-Chaléard, Marie-Claude. "Transnationalism and Migration in the Colonial and Postcolonial Context." In Green and Waldinger, *Century of Transnationalism*, 236–60.

Bloch, Marc. "Pour une histoire comparée des sociétés européennes" [1928]. In *Mélanges historiques*, 1:16–40. Paris: EHESS, 1983.

Blower, Brooke. *Becoming American in Paris: Transatlantic Politics and Culture Between the World Wars*. New York: Oxford University Press, 2011.

Blum, Carol. *Strength in Numbers: Population, Reproduction and Power in Eighteenth-Century France*. Baltimore: Johns Hopkins University Press, 2002.

Bodnar, John. *The Transplanted: A History of Immigrants in Urban America*. Bloomington: Indiana University Press, 1987.

Borchard, Edwin M. "The Citizenship of Native-Born American Women Who Married Foreigners before March 2, 1907, and Acquired a Foreign Domicile." *American Journal of International Law* 29, no. 3 (1935): 396–422.

________. "Decadence of the American Doctrine of Voluntary Expatriation." *American Journal of International Law* 25, no. 2 (1931): 312–16.
________. *The Diplomatic Protection of Citizens Abroad, or the Law of International Claims*. New York: Banks Law, 1915.
________. "The Question of Expatriation in America Prior to 1907." *American Journal of International Law* 37, no. 3 (1943): 540–42.
Bourdelais, Marjorie. "Les immigrants français à La Nouvelle-Orléans au XIXe siècle: Une longue stabilité des formes d'intégration." *Annales de Démographie historique* (2000–2001): 27–42.
Bourne, Randolph. "Trans-national America." *Atlantic Monthly* 118 (July 1916): 86–97.
Bouvier, Pierre. *De la socioanthropologie*. Paris: Galilée, 2011.
Boyden, Michel, Hans Krabbendam, and Liselotte Vandenbussche, eds. *Tales of Transit: Narrative Migrant Spaces in Atlantic Perspective, 1850–1950*. Amsterdam: Amsterdam University Press, 2013.
Braudel, Fernand. *The Mediterranean and the Mediterranean World in the Age of Philip II*. 2 vols. Translated by Siân Reynolds. London: Collins, 1972–73. First published 1949.
Bredbenner, Candice Lewis. *A Nationality of Her Own: Women, Marriage, and the Law of Citizenship*. Berkeley: University of California Press, 1998.
Bredin, Jean-Denis. *Joseph Caillaux*. Paris: Hachette, Folio Histoire, 1980.
Brettell, Caroline B., and James F. Hollifield, eds. *Migration Theory: Talking Across Disciplines*. 3rd ed. New York: Routledge, 2015.
Bretting, Agnes, and Hartmut Bickelmann. *Auswanderungsagenturen und Auswanderungsvereine im 19. und 20. Jahrhundert*. Stuttgart: Franz Steiner Verlag, 1991.
Brinkmann, Tobias, ed. *Points of Passage: Jewish Transmigrants from Eastern Europe in Scandinavia, Germany, and Britain, 1880–1914*. New York: Berghahn Books, 2013.
Brochmann, Grete, and Tomas Hammar, eds. *Mechanisms of Immigration Control: A Comparative Analysis of European Regulation Policies*. Oxford: Berg, 1999.
Brubaker, Rogers. *Citizenship and Nationhood in France and Germany*. Cambridge, MA: Harvard University Press, 1992.
________. "The Return of Assimilation? Changing Perspectives on Immigration and its Sequels in France, Germany and the United States." *Ethnic and Racial Studies* 24, no. 4 (2001): 531–48.

________. *Trans: Gender and Race in an Age of Unsettled Identities.* Princeton, NJ: Princeton University Press, 2016.

Caillaux, Joseph. *Mes mémoires.* Vol. 1, *Ma jeunesse orgueilleuse, 1863–1909.* Paris: Plon, 1942.

Camilleri, Joseph A. *Civilization in Crisis: Human Prospects in a Changing World.* New York: Cambridge University Press, 1976.

Caplan, Jane, and John Torpey, eds. *Documenting Individual Identity: The Development of State Practices in the Modern World.* Princeton, NJ: Princeton University Press, 2001.

Cassano, Prince de. *Procès-verbaux sommaires du Congrès international de l'intervention des pouvoirs publics dans l'émigration et l'immigration, tenu à Paris du 12 au 14 août 1889.* Paris: Imprimerie nationale, 1890.

Castells, Manuel. *The Rise of the Network Society.* Malden, Mass.: Blackwell, 1996.

Cavaillé, Jean-Pierre, Simona Cerutti, Robert Descimon, Christian Jouhaud, Judith Lyon-Caen, and Dinah Ribard. "Production locale du supralocal." In Zuñiga, *Pratiques du transnational*, 197–208.

Chandèze, Gustave. *L'émigration: Intervention des pouvoirs publics au XIXe siècle.* Paris: Imprimerie Paul Dupont, 1898.

________. *Surveillance des agences d'émigration.* Paris: Bibliothèque des Annales économiques, 1890.

Charbit, Yves. *Du Malthusianisme au populationnisme, les économistes français et la population, 1840–1870.* Paris: INED Travaux et documents no. 9, Presses Universitaires de France, 1981.

Chartier, Roger. "La conscience de la globalité (commentaire)." *Annales* 56, no. 1 (2001): 119–23.

Chevalier, Louis. "L'émigration française au XIXe siècle." *Études d'histoire moderne et contemporaine* 1 (1947): 127–71.

Choate, Mark I. *Emigrant Nation: The Making of Italy Abroad.* Cambridge, MA: Harvard University Press, 2008.

Chu, Julie Y. *Cosmologies of Credit.* Durham, NC: Duke University Press, 2010.

Cinel, Dino. *The National Integration of Italian Return Migration, 1870–1929.* New York: Cambridge University Press, 1991.

Clavin, Patricia. "Introduction: Defining Transnationalism." *Contemporary European History* 14, no. 4 (2005): 421–39.

Cohen, Deborah. *Braceros: Migrant Citizens and Transnational Subjects in the Postwar United States and Mexico*. Chapel Hill: University of North Carolina Press, 2011.

Cohen, Deborah, and Maura O'Connor, eds. *Comparison and History: Europe in Cross-National Perspective*. New York: Routledge, 2004.

Cohen, Erik. "Expatriate Communities." *Current Sociology* 24, no. 3 (1977): 5–90.

Cohen, Robin. *Global Diasporas: An Introduction*. Seattle: University of Washington Press, 1997.

Cohen, Yves. "Circulatory Localities: The Example of Stalinism in the 1930s." *Kritika: Explorations in Russian and Eurasian History* 11, no. 1 (2010): 11–45.

Collier, P., and D. Lal. "How Poor People Get Rich: Kenya (1960–1979)." *World Development* 12 (1984): 1007–18.

Connolly, Brian. "Intimate Atlantics: Toward a Critical History of Transnational Early America." *Common-Place* 11, no. 2 (2011), http://www.common-place-archives.org/vol-11/no-02/connolly/.

Conzen, Kathleen, et al. "The Invention of Ethnicity: A Perspective from the U.S.A." *Journal of American Ethnic History* 12, no. 1 (1992): 3–41.

Cook-Martín, David. *The Scramble for Citizens: Dual Nationality and State Competition for Immigrants*. Stanford, CA: Stanford University Press, 2013.

Cornelius, Wayne A., Philip L. Martin and James F. Hollifield, eds. *Controlling Immigration: A Global Perspective*. Stanford, CA: Stanford University Press, 1994.

Cott, Nancy F. "Marriage and Women's Citizenship in the United States, 1830–1934." *American Historical Review* 103, no. 5 (1988): 1440–74.

________. *Public Vows: A History of Marriage and the Nation*. Cambridge, MA: Harvard University Press, 2000.

________. "Revisiting the Transatlantic 1920s: Vincent Sheean vs. Malcolm Cowley." *American Historical Review* 118, no. 1 (2013): 46–75.

Cowley, Malcolm. *Exile's Return: A Literary Odyssey of the 1920s*. New York: W. W. Norton, 1934.

Cowling, Keith, and Roger Sugden. *Transnational Monopoly Capitalism*. Sussex, UK: Wheatsheaf Books, 1987.

cummings, e.e. *The Enormous Room*. Mineola, NY: Dover, 2002. First published 1922.

Curtin, Philip D. *Cross-Cultural Trade in World History*. Cambridge: Cambridge University Press, 1984.

Cygan, Mary Eleanor. "Polish Women and Emigrant Husbands." In *Roots of the Transplanted*, edited by Dirk Hoerder and Inge Blank, 1:377–74. Boulder, CO: East European Monographs, 1994.

Dahinden, Janine. "The Dynamics of Migrants' Transnational Formations: Between Mobility and Locality." In Bauböck and Faist, *Diaspora and Transnationalism*, 51–72.

Daniel, Dominique. "Automatic Birthright Citizenship: Who is an American?" In *Federalism, Citizenship, Collective Identities in U.S. History*, edited by C. Van Minnen et al., 245–67. Amsterdam: VU University Press, 2000.

Dauvergne, Catherine. *Making People Illegal: What Globalization Means for Migration and Law*. New York: Cambridge University Press, 2008.

________. *The New Politics of Immigration and the End of Settler Societies*. Cambridge: Cambridge University Press, 2016.

Davis, Natalie Zemon. *Trickster Travels: A Sixteenth-Century Muslim Between Worlds*. New York: Hill and Wang, 2006.

De Grazia, Victoria. *Irresistible Empire: America's Advance through 20th-Century Europe*. Cambridge, MA: Harvard University Press, 2005.

Deacon, Desley, Penny Russell, and Angela Woollacott, eds. *Transnational Lives: Biographies of Global Modernity, 1700–present*. Basingstoke, UK: Palgrave Macmillan, 2010.

Diminescu, Dana. "The Connected Migrant: An Epistemological Manifesto." *Social Science Information* 47 (2008): 565–79.

Dolis, John. *Transnational Na(rra)tion: Home and Homeland in Nineteenth Century American Literature*. Rutherford, NJ: Fairleigh Dickinson University Press, 2015.

Dodd, Anna Bowman. "The Expatriates: The American Colony in Paris." *Bookman* 25 (May 1907): 247–66.

Douki, Caroline. "L'Etat libéral italien face à l'émigration de masse (1860–1914)." In Green and Weil, *Citizenship and Those Who Leave*, 91–113.

________. "The 'Return Politics' of a Sending Country: The Italian Case, 1880s–1914." In Green and Waldinger, *Century of Transnationalism*, 35–55.

Douki, Caroline, and Philippe Minard. "Histoire globale, histoires connectées: un changement d'échelle historiographique?" *Revue d'histoire moderne et contemporaine* no. 54-4bis (2007-5): 7–21.

Dowty, Alan. *Closed Borders: The Contemporary Assault on Freedom of Movement*. New Haven, CT: Yale University Press, 1987.

Dufoix, Stéphane. *Diasporas*. Translated by William Rodarmor. Berkeley: University of California Press, 2008.

________. *Politiques d'exil: Hongrois, Polonais et Tchécoslovaques en France après 1945*. Paris: Presses universitaires de France, 2002.

Dufoix, Stéphane, Carine Guerassimoff, and Anne de Tinguy, eds., *Loin des yeux, près du cœur: Les États et leurs expatriés*. Paris: Presses de la Fondation nationale des sciences politiques, 2010.

Dunbar, Ernest, ed. *The Black Expatriates: A Study of American Negroes in Exile*. New York: Dutton, 1968.

Durand, Jorge. "Mexican Policy and the Asymmetry of Power: The Mexican Case, 1900–2000." In Green and Weil, *Citizenship and Those Who Leave*, 224–42.

Duval, Jules. *Histoire de l'émigration européenne, asiatique et africaine au XIXe siècle: Ses causes, ses caractères, ses effets*. Paris: Librairie de Guillaumin et Cie., 1862.

Earnest, Ernest. *Expatriates and Patriots: American Artists, Scholars, and Writers in Europe*. Durham, NC: Duke University Press, 1968.

Eckstein, Susan Eva, and Adil Najam, eds. *How Immigrants Impact their Homelands*. Durham, NC: Duke University Press, 2013.

Endy, Christopher. *Cold War Holidays: American Tourism in France*. Chapel Hill: University of North Carolina Press, 2004.

Enright, D. J. "Expat." *Times Literary Supplement*, August 10, 1962.

Fabre, Michel. *From Harlem to Paris*. Urbana: University of Illinois Press, 1991.

Fahrmeir, Andreas. *Citizens and Aliens: Foreigners and the Law in Britain and the German States, 1789–1870*. New York: Berghahn Books, 2000.

________. "From Economics to Ethnicity and Back: Reflections on Emigration Control in Germany 1800–2000." In Green and Weil, *Citizenship and Those Who Leave*, 176–91.

———. "Governments and Forgers: Passports in Nineteenth-Century Europe." In *Documenting Individual Identity: The Development of State Practices in the Modern World*, edited by Jane Caplan and John Torpey, 218–34. Princeton, NJ: Princeton University Press, 2001.

Faist, Thomas. "Transnationalization in International Migration: Implications for the Study of Citizenship and Culture." *Ethnic and Racial Studies* 23, no. 2 (2000): 189–222.

Faist, Thomas, and Peter Kivisto, eds. *Dual Citizenship in Global Perspective: From Unitary to Multiple Citizenship*. Basingstoke, UK: Palgrave Macmillan, 2007.

Fechter, Anne-Meike, and Katie Walsh, eds. "Examining 'Expatriate' Continuities: Postcolonial Approaches to Mobile Professionals." Special issue, *Journal of Ethnic and Migration Studies* 36, no. 8 (2010).

Feldman, David, and M. Page Baldwin. "Emigration and the British State, c.1815–1925." In Green and Weil, *Citizenship and Those Who Leave*, 135–55.

Field, James A., Jr. "Transnationalism and the New Tribe." *International Organization* 25, no. 3 (1971): 353–72.

Fishkin, Shelley Fisher. "Crossroads of Cultures: The Transnational Turn in American Studies: Presidential Address to the American Studies Association, November 12, 2004." *American Quarterly* 57, no. 1 (2005): 17–57.

FitzGerald, David. "150 Years of Transborder Politics: Mexico and Mexicans Abroad." In Green and Waldinger, *Century of Transnationalism*, 106–31.

FitzGerald, David, and David Cook-Martín. *Culling the Masses: The Demographic Origins of Racist Immigration Policy in the Americas*. Cambridge, MA: Harvard University Press, 2014.

Flanner, Janet. *Paris Was Yesterday, 1925–1939*. London: Virago, 2003.

Flournoy, Richard W., Jr. "Naturalization and Expatriation." *Yale Law Journal* 31 (1921–22): 702–719, 848–868.

———. "Problems of Dual Nationality in Time of War." *New York Times*, September 12, 1915.

Foerster, Robert F. *The Italian Emigration of Our Times*. 2nd ed. Cambridge, MA: Harvard University Press, 1924.

Foner, Nancy. *From Ellis Island to JFK: New York's Two Great Waves of Immigration*. New Haven, CT: Yale University Press, 2000.

________. "Transnationalism Old and New." In *In a New Land: A Comparative View of Immigration*, chap. 3. New York: New York University Press, 2005.

Fones-Wolf, Ken. "Immigrants, Labor and Capital in a Transnational Context: Belgian Glass Workers in America, 1880–1925." *Journal of American Ethnic History* 21, no. 2 (2002): 59–80.

Foster, John W. *The Practice of Diplomacy as Illustrated in the Foreign Relations of the United* States. Boston: Houghton Mifflin, 1906.

Frader, Laura. "French History: Old Paradigms, Current Tendencies, New Directions." *French Politics, Culture, and Society* 32, no. 2 (2014): 21–33.

________. *Peasants and Protest: Agricultural Workers, Politics, and Unions in the Aude, 1850–1914*. Berkeley: University of California Press, 1991.

Friedman, Jonathan, and Shalini Randeria, eds. *Worlds on the Move: Globalization, Migration, and Cultural Security*. London: I. B. Tauris, 2004.

Gabaccia, Donna R. *Foreign Relations: American Immigration in Global Perspective*. Princeton, NJ: Princeton University Press, 2012.

________. *Italy's Many Diasporas*. London: UCL Press, 2000.

________. "Thoughts on the Future of Transnational History." In *Yearbook of Transnational History*, vol. 1, edited by Thomas Adam, 11–42. Vancouver: Fairleigh Dickinson University Press, 2018.

________. "Time and Temporality in Migration Studies." In Brettell and Hollifield, *Migration Theory*, 37–66.

Gabaccia, Donna R., Dirk Hoerder and Adam Walaszek. "Emigration and Nation-Building during the Mass Migrations from Europe." In Green and Weil, *Citizenship and Those Who Leave*, 63–90.

Gammeltoft-Hansen, Thomas, and Ninna Nyberg Sørensen, eds. *The Migration Industry and the Commercialization of International Migration*. London: Routledge, 2013.

Gardner, Martha. *The Qualities of a Citizen: Women, Immigration, and Citizenship, 1870–1965*. Princeton, NJ: Princeton University Press, 2005.

Gerber, David A. "Theories and Lives: Transnationalism and the Conceptualization of International Migrations to the United States." *IMIS-Beiträge* 15 (2000): 31–53.

Gerstle, Gary. *American Crucible: Race and Nation in the Twentieth Century*. Princeton, NJ: Princeton University Press, 2001.

Gilpin, Robert. "The Politics of Transnational Economic Relations." *International Organization* 25, no. 3 (1971): 398–419.

Gilroy, Paul. *The Black Atlantic: Modernity and Double Consciousness*. Cambridge, MA: Harvard University Press, 1993.

Gjerde, Jon. "The Scandinavian Migration from Local and Transnational Perspectives." *Journal of American Ethnic History* 27, no. 2 (2008): 85–90.

Glick Schiller, Nina, Linda Basch, and Cristina Blanc-Szanton, eds. *Towards a Transnational Perspective on Migration: Race, Class, Ethnicity, and Nationalism Reconsidered*. New York: New York Academy of Sciences, 1992.

Glick Schiller, Nina, and Georges Eugene Fouron. *Georges Woke up Laughing: Long-Distance Nationalism and the Search for Home*. Durham, NC: Duke University Press, 2001.

Goldberg, Barry. "Historical Reflections on Transnationalism, Race, and the American Immigrant Saga." In Glick Schiller, Basch, and Blanc-Szanton, *Towards a Transnational Perspective*, 201–15.

Goldstein, Jan. "The Future of French History in the United States: Unapocalyptic Thoughts for the New Millennium." *French Historical Studies* 24, no. 1 (2001): 1–10.

Gonnard, René. *Essai sur l'histoire de l'émigration*. Paris: Librairie Valois, 1928.

Gopnik, Adam, ed. *Americans in Paris: A Literary Anthology*. New York: Library of America, 2004.

Gould, Eliga H. "Entangled Histories, Entangled Worlds: The English-Speaking Atlantic as a Spanish Periphery." *American Historical Review* 112, no. 3 (2007): 764–86.

Green, Nancy L. "'Filling the Void': Immigration to France Before World War I." In *Labor Migration in the Atlantic Economies*, edited by Dirk Hoerder, 143–61. Westport, CT: Greenwood Press, 1985.

———. "Forms of Comparison." In *Comparison and History: Europe in Cross-National Perspective*, edited by Deborah Cohen and Maura O'Connor, 41–56. New York: Routledge, 2004.

———. "French History and the Transnational Turn." *French Historical Studies* 37, no. 4 (2014): 551–64.

________. "Location, Location, Location: We Are Where We Write?" *American Historical Review* 119, no. 3 (2014): 809–16.

________. "The Modern Jewish Diaspora: East European Jews in New York, London, and Paris." In *European Migrants: Global and Local Perspectives*, edited by Dirk Hoerder and Leslie Page Moch, 263–81. Boston: Northeastern University Press, 1996.

________. *The Other Americans in Paris: Businessmen, Countesses, Wayward Youth, 1880–1941*. Chicago: University of Chicago Press, 2014.

________. *Repenser les migrations*. Paris: Presses Universitaires de France, 2002.

________. "Trans-frontières: Pour une analyse des lieux de passage." *Socio-anthropologie*, no. 6 (2d semester 1999): 33–48.

Green, Nancy L., and Roger Waldinger, eds. *A Century of Transnationalism: Immigrants and Their Homeland Connections*. Urbana: University of Illinois Press, 2016.

Green, Nancy L., and François Weil, eds. *Citizenship and Those Who Leave: The Politics of Emigration and Expatriation*. Urbana: University of Illinois Press, 2007.

Gruzinski, Serge. *Les Quatre parties du monde: Histoire d'une mondialisation*. Paris: Éditions de la Martinière, 2004.

Guarneri, Carl J. *America in the World: United States History in Global Context*. Boston: McGraw-Hill Higher Education, 2007.

________, ed. *America Compared: American History in International Perspective*. 2 vols. Boston: Houghton Mifflin, 1997.

Guarnizo, Luis Eduardo. "The Economics of Transnational Living." *International Migration Review* 37, no. 3 (2003): 666–99.

Gueydan, B. E. [Berthe]. *Les rois de la République*. 3rd ed. 2 vols. Paris: Perrin, 1925.

Guiraudon, Virginie. *Les politiques d'immigration en Europe*. Paris: L'Harmattan, 2000.

Hagan, John. *Northern Passage: American Vietnam War Resisters in Canada*. Cambridge, MA: Harvard University Press, 2001.

Hammar, Tomas. *Democracy and the Nation State*. Aldershot: Avebury, 1990.

________. "Dual Citizenship and Political Integration." *International Migration Review* 19, no. 3 (1985): 438–50.

Handlin, Oscar. *The Uprooted*. Boston: Little, Brown, 1973. First published 1951.

Hannerz, Ulf. *Transnational Connections: Culture, People, Places.* London: Routledge, 1996.

Hansen, Marcus Lee. *The Atlantic Migration, 1607–1806.* Cambridge, MA: Harvard University Press, 1941.

Hansen, Randall, and Patrick Weil, eds. *Dual Nationality, Social Rights, and Federal Citizenship in the U.S. and Europe.* New York: Berghahn Books, 2002.

Harper, Marjory, ed. *Emigrant Homecomings: The Return Movement of Emigrants, 1600–2000.* Manchester: Manchester University Press, 2005.

Hart, John Mason. *Empire and Revolution: The Americans in Mexico since the Civil War.* Berkeley: University of California Press, 2002.

Hartman, Andrew. "The Internationalization of the U.S. History Curriculum—and Its Discontents." *American Historian*, February 2015, 39–42.

Harvey, Gerald C. "Expatriation Law in the United States: The Confusing Legacy of *Afroyim* and *Bellei.*" *Columbia Journal of Transnational Law* 13, no. 3 (1974): 406–35.

Harzig, Christiane, ed. *Peasant Maids, City Women: From the European Countryside to Urban America.* Ithaca, NY: Cornell University Press, 1997.

Hatzipanayotou, Panos. "International Migration and Remittances in a Two-Country Temporary Equilibrium Model." In Vertovec and Cohen, *Migration, Diasporas and Transnationalism*, 50–63.

Haupt, Heinz-Gerhard, and Jürgen Kocka, eds. *Comparative and Transnational History: Central European Approaches and New Perspectives.* New York: Berghahn Books, 2009.

Hay, George. *A Treatise on Expatriation.* Washington, DC: A and G Way, 1813.

Heather, P. J. (Peter J.). *The Fall of the Roman Empire: A New History of Rome and the Barbarians.* New York: Oxford University Press, 2006.

Heine, Jorge, and Ramesh Thakur, eds. *The Dark Side of Globalization.* New York: United Nations University Press, 2011.

Herzog, Ben. *Revoking Citizenship: Expatriation in America from the Colonial Era to the War on Terror.* New York: New York University Press, 2015.

Heurtier, Nicolas. *Rapport à Son Excellence le ministre de l'Agriculture, du Commerce et des Travaux Publics fait au nom de la Commission chargée d'étudier les différentes questions qui se rattachent à l'émigration européenne*. Paris: Imprimerie impériale, 1854.

Higham, John. "The Strange Career of Strangers in the Land." *American Jewish History* 76 (December 1986): 214–26.

________. *Strangers in the Land, Patterns of American Nativism, 1860–1925*. New York: Atheneum, 1985. First published 1955.

Hirschman, Albert O. *Exit, Voice, and Loyalty*. Cambridge, MA: Harvard University Press, 1970.

Hoerder, Dirk. *Cultures in Contact: World Migrations in the Second Millennium*. Durham, NC: Duke University Press, 2002.

________. "Historians and Their Data: The Complex Shift from Nation-State Approaches to the Study of People's Transcultural Lives." *Journal of American Ethnic History* 25, no. 4 (2006): 85–96.

________, ed. *Labor Migration in the Atlantic Economies*. Westport, CT: Greenwood Press, 1985.

________. "Recent Methodological and Conceptual Approaches to Migration: Comparing the Globe or the North Atlantic World?" *Journal of American Ethnic History* 29, no. 2 (2010): 79–83.

________. "Transnational—Transregional—Translocal: Transcultural." In *Handbook of Research Methods in Migration*, edited by Carlos Vargas-Silva, 69–91. Cheltenham: Edward Elgar, 2011.

Hoerder, Dirk, and Horst Rössler, eds. *Distant Magnets: Expectations and Realities in the Immigrant Experience, 1840–1930*. New York: Holmes and Meier, 1993.

Hoerder, Dirk, Horst Rössler, and Inge Blank, eds. *Roots of the Transplanted*. 2 vols. Boulder, CO: East European Monographs, 1994.

Hoffnung-Garskof, Jesse. *A Tale of Two Cities: New York and Santo Domingo since 1950*. Princeton, NJ: Princeton University Press, 2008.

Horton, Robert Wilmot. *Causes and Remedies of Pauperism: Containing Correspondence with M. Duchatel*. Paris: J. Smith, 1830.

Howard, Michael C. *Transnationalism in Ancient and Medieval Societies: The Role of Cross-border Trade and Travel*. Jefferson, NC: McFarland, 2012.

Hunt, Lynn. "Les Cultural Studies (1970–2010)." In *1970–2010: Les sciences de l'homme en débat*, edited by Yann Brailowsky and Hervé Inglebert, 189–202. Nanterre: Presses Universitaires de Paris Ouest, 2013.

________. "The Prospects of the Present." *Perspectives on History*, December 2012.

Hvidt, Kristian. *Flight to America: The Social Background of 300,000 Danish Emigrants*. New York: Academic Press, 1975.

"Immigration, Incorporation, Integration, and Transnationalism: Interdisciplinary and International Perspectives." Special issue, *Journal of American Ethnic History* 25, no. 2–3 (2006).

Inglés, José D. *Étude des mesures discriminatoires dans le domaine du droit qu'a toute personne de quitter tout pays, y compris le sien, et de revenir dans son pays*. New York: United Nations, 1963.

Iriye, Akira. *Cultural Internationalism and World Order*. Baltimore: Johns Hopkins University Press, 1997.

________. "The Internationalization of History." *American Historical Review* 94, no. 1 (1989): 1–10.

________. "Transnational History." *Contemporary European History* 13, no. 2 (2004): 211–22.

________. "The Transnational Turn." *Diplomatic History* 31, no. 3 (2007): 373–76.

Iriye, Akira, and Pierre-Yves Saunier, eds. *The Palgrave Dictionary of Transnational History*. Basingstoke, UK: Palgrave Macmillan, 2009.

Jacobson, Matthew Frye. "More 'Trans-' Less 'National.'" *Journal of American Ethnic History* 25, no. 4 (2006): 74–84.

James, Alan G. "Expatriation in the United States: Precept and Practice Today and Yesterday." *San Diego Law Review* 27 (1990): 853–905.

Johnson, Christopher H., et al. *Transregional and Transnational Families in Europe and Beyond: Experiences since the Middle Ages*. New York: Berghahn Books, 2011.

Johnston, H. J. M. *British Emigration Policy, 1815–1830, "Shovelling Out Paupers."* Oxford: Clarendon Press, 1972.

Joppke, Christian. "Citizenship between De- and Re-Ethnicization." *Archives européennes de sociologie* 44, no. 3 (2003): 429–58.

Karst, Kenneth L. *Belonging to America: Equal Citizenship and the Constitution*. New Haven, CT: Yale University Press, 1989.

Katz, Philip. *From Appomattox to Montmartre: Americans and the Paris Commune*. Cambridge, MA: Harvard University Press, 1998.

Kastoryano, Riva. "Vers un nationalisme transnational: Redéfinir la nation, le nationalisme et le territoire." *Revue française de science politique* 56, no. 4 (2006), 533–53.

Katzenstein, Peter J., Robert O. Keohane, and Stephen D. Krasner. "International Organizations and the Study of World Politics." *International Organization* 52, no. 4 (1998): 645–85.

Kazal, Russell A. "Revisiting Assimilation: The Rise, Fall, and Reappraisal of a Concept in American Ethnic History." *American Historical Review* 100, no. 2 (1995): 437–71.

Keeling, Drew. *The Business of Transatlantic Migration between Europe and the United States,* 1900–1914. Zurich: Chronos, 2012.

Keely, Charles B., and Bao Nga Tran. "Remittances from Labor Migration: Evaluations, Performance and Implications." In Vertovec and Cohen, *Migration, Diasporas and Transnationalism*, 64–89.

Keohane, Robert O., and Joseph S. Nye, Jr., eds. "Transnational Relations and World Politics." Special issue, *International Organization* 25, no. 3 (1971). Republished as *Transnational Relations and World Politics*. Cambridge, MA: Harvard University Press, 1972.

Kerber, Linda. "The Meanings of Citizenship." *Journal of American History* 84, no. 3 (1997): 833–54.

________. *No Constitutional Right to be Ladies: Women and the Obligations of Citizenship*. New York: Hill and Wang, 1998.

________. "The Stateless as the Citizen's Other: A View from the United States." *American Historical Review* 112, no. 1 (2007): 1–34.

Kettner, James H. *The Development of American Citizenship, 1608–1870*. Chapel Hill: University of North Carolina Press, 1978.

Keyssar, Alexander. *The Right to Vote*. New York: Basic Books, 2000.

Khadria, Binod. *The Migration of Knowledge Workers: Second-Generation Effects of India's Brain Drain*. New Delhi: Sage, 1999.

Khagram, Sanjeev, and Peggy Levitt, eds. *The Transnationalism Studies Reader: Intersections and Innovations*. New York: Routledge, 2008.

Klaus, Alisa. *Every Child a Lion: The Origins of Infant Health Policy in the United States and France, 1890–1920*. Ithaca, NY: Cornell University Press, 1993.

Klekowski von Koppenfels, Amanda. *Migrants or Expatriates? Americans in Europe*. Basingstoke, UK: Palgrave Macmillan, 2014.

Kleven, Thomas. "Why International Law Favors Emigration over Immigration." *Inter-American Law Review* 33 (Spring 2002): 69–100.

Kocka, Jürgen. "Comparison and Beyond." *History and Theory* 42, no. 1 (2003): 39–44.

Kramer, Paul A. "The Geopolitics of Mobility: Immigration Policy and American Global Power in the Long Twentieth Century." *American Historical Review* 123, no. 2 (2018): 393–438.

________. "Power and Connection: Imperial Histories of the United States in the World." *American Historical Review* 116, no. 5 (2011): 1348–91.

Krasner, Stephen D. "State Power and the Structure of International Trade." *World Politics* 28 (1976): 317–47.

Kuhn, Philip A. *Chinese Among Others: Emigration in Modern Times*. Lanham, MD: Rowman and Littlefield, 2008.

Lachance, Paul F. "The Foreign French." In *Creole New Orleans: Race and Americanization*, edited by Arnold R. Hirsch and Joseph Logsdon, 101–30. Baton Rouge: Louisiana State University Press, 1992.

Laney, Al. *Paris "Herald": The Incredible Newspaper*. New York: Appleton-Century, 1947.

Lang, Michael. "Globalization and Its History." *Journal of Modern History* 78, no. 4 (2006): 899–931.

Langley, Lester D., and Thomas Schoonover. *The Banana Men: American Mercenaries and Entrepreneurs in Central America, 1880–1930*. Lexington: University Press of Kentucky, 1994.

Lee, Luke T. *Consular Law and Practice*. London: Stevens and Sons, 1961.

Lentz-Smith, Adriane. *Freedom Struggles: African Americans and World War I*. Cambridge, MA: Harvard University Press, 2009.

Lepenies, Wolf, ed. *Entangled Histories and Negotiated Universals: Centers and Peripheries in a Changing World*. Frankfurt-am-Main: Campus Verlag, 2003.

Leroy-Beaulieu, Paul. *De la colonisation chez les peuples modernes*. 3rd ed. Paris: Guillaumin et Cie., 1886. First published 1874.

Lessinger, Johanna. "Nonresident-Indian Investment and India's Drive for Industrial Modernization." In Vertovec and Cohen, *Migration, Diasporas and Transnationalism*, 90–111.

Levenstein, Harvey. *Seductive Journey: American Tourists in France from Jefferson to the Jazz Age*. Chicago: University of Chicago Press, 1998.

________. *We'll Always Have Paris: American Tourists in France since 1930*. Chicago: University of Chicago Press, 2004.

Levitt, Peggy. *The Transnational Villagers*. Berkeley: University of California Press, 2001.

Lindsay, Lisa A., and John Wood Sweet, eds. *Biography and the Black Atlantic*. Philadelphia: University of Pennsylvania Press, 2013.

Liu, Haiming. *The Transnational History of a Chinese Family: Immigrant Letters, Family Business, and Reverse Migration*. New Brunswick, NJ: Rutgers University Press, 2005.

Lloyd, Craig. *Eugene Bullard: Black Expatriate in Jazz-Age Paris*. Athens: University of Georgia Press, 2000.

Lucassen, Jan, and Leo Lucassen, eds. *Migration, Migration History, History*. Bern: Peter Lang, 1997.

Lucassen, Leo. "The Gulf Between Long Term and Short Term Approaches in Immigration Studies: A Reassessment of the Chicago School's Assimilation Concept." *IMIS-Beiträge*, no. 5 (1997): 5–23.

________. "Working Together: New Directions in Global Labour History." *Journal of Global History* 11 (2016): 66–87.

MacDonald, John S., and Leatrice D. MacDonald. "Chain Migration: Ethnic Neighborhood Formation and Social Networks." *Milbank Memorial Fund Quarterly* 42, no. 1 (1964): 82–97.

Maier, Charles S. *Once within Borders: Territories of Power, Wealth, and Belonging since 1500*. Cambridge, MA: Harvard University Press, 2016.

Maire, Camille. *En route pour l'Amérique: L'odyssée des émigrants en France au XIXe siècle*. Nancy: Presses universitaires de Nancy, 1993.

Malthus, T. R. *An Essay on the Principle of Population*, edited by Patricia James. Cambridge: Cambridge University Press, 1989. First published 1803.

Manning, Patrick. *Migration in World History*. New York: Routledge, 2005.

Marciniak, Marta. *Transnational Punk Communities in Poland: From Nihilism to Nothing Outside Punk*. Lanham, MD: Lexington Books, 2015.

Marshall, T. H. *Citizenship and Social Class and Other Essays*. Cambridge: University Press, 1950.

McCarthy, Harold T. *The Expatriate Perspective: American Novelists and the Idea of America*. Rutherford, NJ: Fairleigh Dickinson University Press, 1974.

McCullough, David. *The Greater Journey: Americans in Paris*. New York: Simon and Schuster, 2011.

McKeown, Adam. *Chinese Migrant Networks and Cultural Change: Peru, Chicago, Hawaii, 1900–1936*. Chicago: University of Chicago Press, 2001.

________. "Global Migration 1846–1940." *Journal of World History* 15, no. 2 (2004): 155–89.

________. *Melancholy Order: Asian Migration and the Globalization of Borders*. New York: Columbia University Press, 2008.

________. "Transnational Chinese Families and Chinese Exclusion, 1875–1943." *Journal of American Ethnic History* 18, no. 2 (1999): 73–110.

Michael, William H. *History of the Department of State of the United States*. Washington, DC: Government Printing Office, 1901.

Michaux, Phyllis. *The Unknown Ambassadors: A Saga of Citizenship*. Bayside, NY: Aletheia, 1996.

Milbank, David L. *International and Transnational Terrorism: Diagnosis and Prognosis*. Washington, DC: Central Intelligence Agency, 1976. Available through DOCEX, Library of Congress.

Miller, Kerby A. *Emigrants and Exiles: Ireland and the Irish Exodus to North America*. New York: Oxford University Press, 1985.

Mols, Roger. "Population in Europe 1500–1700." In *The 16th and 17th Centuries*, edited by Carlo M. Cipolla, 15–82. Vol. 2 of *The Fontana Economic History of Europe*. London: Collins, 1973.

Moltmann, Günter, ed. *Deutsche Amerikaauswanderung im 19. Jahrhundert: Socialgeschichtliche Beiträge*. Stuttgart: J. B. Metzler, 1976.

Montgomery, Maureen F. *"Gilded Prostitution": Status, Money and Transatlantic Marriages, 1870–1914*. New York: Routledge, 1989.

Moore, John Bassett. *A Digest of International Law*. Vol. 5, chap. 16, "Consuls." Washington, DC: Government Printing Office, 1906.

________. "The Doctrine of Expatriation." *Harper's Magazine* 110, no. 656 (1905): 225–36.

Morawska, Ewa. "Disciplinary Agendas and Analytic Strategies of Research on Immigration and Transnationalism. Challenges of Interdisciplinary Knowledge." *International Migration Review* 37, no. 3 (2003): 611–40.

________. "Immigrants, Transnationalism, and Ethnicization: A Comparison of This Great Wave and the Last." In *E Pluribus Unum?*, edited by John Mollenkopf and Gary Gerstle, 175–212. New York: Russell Sage Foundation, 2002.

________. "In Defense of the Assimilation Model." *Journal of American Ethnic History* 13, no. 2 (1994): 76–87.

Motomura, Hiroshi. *Americans in Waiting: The Lost Story of Immigration and Citizenship in the United States.* Oxford: Oxford University Press, 2006.

Moya, José. "The Historical Emergence and Massification of International Families in Europe and its Diaspora." In Johnson et al., *Transregional and Transnational Families*, 22–40.

________. "Modernization, Modernity, and the Trans/formation of the Atlantic World in the Nineteenth Century." In *The Atlantic in Global History: 1500–2000*, 2d ed., edited by Jorge Canizares-Esguerra and Erik Seeman, 187–207. Oxford: Routledge, 2018.

Moya, José, and Adam McKeown. "World Migration in the Long Twentieth Century." In *Essays on Twentieth-Century History*, edited by Michael Adas, 9–52. Philadelphia: Temple University Press, 2010.

Neuman, Gerald L. "Back to Dred Scott." *San Diego Law Review* 24, no. 2 (1987): 485–500.

________. *Strangers to the Constitution: Immigrants, Borders, and Fundamental Law.* Princeton, NJ: Princeton University Press, 1996.

Ngai, Mae M. *Impossible Subjects: Illegal Aliens and the Making of Modern America.* Princeton, NJ: Princeton University Press, 2004.

________. "Promises and Perils of Transnational History." *Perspectives on History*, December 2012.

Noiriel, Gérard. *Le creuset français: Histoire de l'immigration XIXe-XXe siècles.* Paris: Seuil, 1988.

________. *La tyrannie du national, Le droit d'asile en Europe 1793–1993.* Paris: Calmann-Lévy, 1991.

Nordman, Daniel. *Frontières de France: De l'espace au territoire: XVIe-XIXe siècle.* Paris: Gallimard, 1998.

Ong, Aihwa. *Flexible Citizenship: The Cultural Logics of Transnationality*. Durham, NC: Duke University Press, 1999.

O'Rourke, Kevin H., and Jeffrey G. Williamson. *Globalization and History: The Evolution of a Nineteenth-Century Atlantic Economy*. Cambridge, MA: MIT Press, 1999.

Panagakos, Anastasia N., and Heather A. Horst. "Return to Cyberia: Technology and the Social Worlds of Transnational Migrants." *Global Networks* 6 (2006): 109–24.

Parker, Kunal M. *Making Foreigners: Immigration and Citizenship Law in America, 1600–2000*. New York: Cambridge University Press, 2015.

Paul, Harry. *Science, Vine, and Wine in Modern France*. Cambridge: Cambridge University Press, 1996.

Pech, Rémy. *Entreprise viticole et capitalisme en Languedoc Roussillon: du Phylloxera aux crises de mévente*. Toulouse: Association des publications de l'Université de Toulouse-Le Mirail, 1975.

Peraldi, Michel, ed. *Cabas et containers: Activités marchandes informelles et réseaux migrants transfrontaliers*. Paris: Maisonneuve et Larose, 2001.

Pereira, Victor. "Portuguese Migrants and Portugal: Elite Discourse and Transnational Practices." In Green and Waldinger, *Century of Transnationalism*, 56–83.

Plischke, Elmer. *U.S. Department of State: A Reference History*. Westport, CT: Greenwood Press, 1999.

Portes, Alejandro, Luis E. Guarnizo, and Patricia Landolt. "The Study of Transnationalism: Pitfalls and Promise of an Emergent Research Field." *Ethnic and Racial Studies* 22, no. 2 (1999): 217–37.

Potot, Swanie. "Les mutations européennes au prisme des migrations : Un regard sociologique au-delà des frontières." Habilitation thesis, Université Paris Diderot, 2016.

Przeworski, Adam, and Henry Teune. *The Logic of Comparative Social Inquiry*. New York: John Wiley and Sons, 1970.

Puskás, Julianna. *From Hungary to the United States (1880–1914)*. Budapest: Akadémiai Kiadó, 1982.

________, ed. *Overseas Migration from East-Central and Southeastern Europe, 1880–1940*. Budapest: Akadémiai Kiadó, 1990.

Putnam, Samuel. *Paris Was Our Mistress: Memoirs of a Lost and Found Generation*. New York: Viking Press, 1947.

Raj, Kapil. "Go-Betweens, Travelers, and Cultural Translators." In *The Blackwell Companion to the History of Science*, edited by Bernard Lightman, 39–57. Chichester, UK: Wiley-Blackwell, 2016.

________. *Relocating Modern Science: Circulation and the Construction of Knowledge in South Asia and Europe, 1650-1900*. Basingstoke, UK: Palgrave Macmillan, 2007.

Reichel, Philip, et al. *Handbook of Transnational Crime and Justice*. Thousand Oaks, CA: Sage, 2005.

Rempel, H., and R. Lobdell. "The Role of Urban-Rural Remittances in Rural Development." *Journal of Development Studies* 14 (1978): 324–41.

Revel, Jacques, ed. *Jeux d'échelles: la micro-analyse à l'expérience*. Paris: Gallimard-Le Seuil "Hautes Études," 1996.

Robertson, Craig. *The Passport in America: The History of a Document*. New York: Oxford University Press, 2010.

Roche, John P. "The Expatriation Decisions: A Study in Constitutional Improvisation and the Uses of History." *American Political Science Review* 58, no. 1 (1964): 72–80.

Rodgers, Daniel T. *Atlantic Crossings: Social Politics in a Progressive Age*. Cambridge, MA: Harvard University Press, 1998.

Root, Elihu. "The Basis of Protection to Citizens Residing Abroad." *American Journal of International Law* 4 (1910): 517–28.

Rosenberg, Emily S. *Spreading the American Dream: American Economic and Cultural Expansion, 1890–1945*. New York: Hill and Wang, 1982.

Rosental, Paul-André. *Les sentiers invisibles: Espace, familles et migrations dans la France du 19e siècle*. Paris: EHESS, 1999.

________. *L'intelligence démographique: sciences et politiques des populations en France,1930–1960*. Paris: O. Jacob, 2003.

Sabah, Lucien, ed. *Journal de Gueydan "de" Roussel 1940–1944: Un agent de la BN [Bibliothèque nationale] et de la Gestapo*. Paris: Klincksieck, 2000.

Sahlins, Peter. *Boundaries: The Making of France and Spain in the Pyrenees*. Berkeley: University of California Press, 1989.

Salyer, Lucy E. *Laws Harsh as Tigers: Chinese Immigrants and the Shaping of Modern Immigration Law*. Chapel Hill: University of North Carolina Press, 1995.

________. *Under the Starry Flag: How a Band of Irish Americans Joined the Fenian Revolt and Sparked a Crisis over Citizenship*. Cambridge, MA: Harvard University Press, 2018.

Sassen, Saskia. *Territory, Authority, Rights: From Medieval to Global Assemblages*. Princeton, NJ: Princeton University Press, 2006.

Saunier, Pierre-Yves. "Learning by Doing: Notes about the Making of *The Palgrave Dictionary of Transnational History*." *Journal of Modern European History* 6, no. 2 (2008): 159–80.

________. *Transnational History*. Basingstoke, UK: Palgrave Macmillan, 2013.

________. "Transnationalism." In Iriye and Saunier, *Palgrave Dictionary*, 1047–55.

Say, Jean-Baptiste. *Cours complet d'économie politique pratique*. 3rd ed. 1852. Reprint, Osnabrück: Otto Zeller, 1996.

________. *Traité d'économie politique*. 6th ed. Paris: Guillaumin, 1841.

Sayad, Abdelmalek. *La double absence, Des illusions de l'émigré aux souffrances de l'immigré*. Paris: Seuil, 1999.

________. "Les trois âges de l'émigration algérienne." *Actes de la Recherche en Sciences Sociales*, no. 15 (1977): 59–79.

Schaffer, Simon, et al., eds. *The Brokered World: Go-Betweens and Global Intelligence, 1770–1820*. Sagamore Beach, MA: Watson, 2009.

Schain, Martin. *The Politics of Immigration in France, Britain, and the United States: A Comparative Study*. New York: Palgrave Macmillan, 2008.

Schell, William, Jr. *Integral Outsiders: The American Colony in Mexico City, 1876–1911*. Wilmington, DE: SR Books, 2001.

Schmitter-Heisler, Barbara. "Sending Countries and the Politics of Emigration and Destination." *International Migration Review* 19 (Fall 1985): 469–84.

Schneider, Dorothee. "The United States Government and the Investigation of European Emigration in the Open Door Era." In Green and Weil, *Citizenship and Those Who Leave*, 195–210.

Schuck, Peter H., and Rogers M. Smith. *Citizenship Without Consent: Illegal Aliens in the American Polity*. New Haven, CT: Yale University Press, 1985.

Scott, Rebecca J., and Jean M. Hébrard. *Freedom Papers: An Atlantic Odyssey in the Age of Emancipation*. Cambridge, MA: Harvard University Press, 2012.

Scully, Eileen. *Bargaining with the State from Afar: American Citizenship in Treaty Port China, 1844–1942*. New York: Columbia University Press, 2001.

Seckler-Hudson, Catheryn. *Statelessness: With Special Reference to the United States (A Study in Nationality and Conflict of Laws)*. New York: Kraus, 1971. First published 1934.

Sewell, William H., Jr. "Marc Bloch and the Logic of Comparative History." *History and Theory* 6, no. 2 (1967): 208–18.

Shklar, Judith. *American Citizenship: The Quest for Inclusion*. Cambridge, MA: Harvard University Press, 1991.

Siegelbaum, Lewis H., and Leslie Page Moch. "Transnationalism in One Country? Seeing and Not Seeing Cross-Border Migration within the Soviet Union." *Slavic Review* 75, no. 4 (2016): 970–86.

Smith, J. Harvey. "Agricultural Workers and the French Wine-Growers Revolt of 1907." *Past and Present* 79 (1978): 100–125.

________. "La crise d'une économie régionale: La monoculture viticole et la Révolte du Midi (1907)." *Annales du Midi* 92, no. 3 (1980): 317–34.

Smith, Marian L. "'Any woman who is now or may hereafter be married . . .' Women and Naturalization, ca. 1802–1940." *Prologue Magazine* 30, no. 2 (1998).

Smith, Michael Peter, and Luis Eduardo Guarnizo, eds. *Transnationalism from Below*. New Brunswick, NJ: Transaction, 1998.

Smith, Robert C. "Diasporic Memberships in Historical Perspective: Comparative Insights from the Mexican, Italian and Polish Cases." *International Migration Review* 37, no. 3 (2003): 724–59.

Smith, Rogers M. *Civic Ideals: Conflicting Visions of Citizenship in U.S. History*. New Haven, CT: Yale University Press, 1997.

Soysal, Yasemin Nuhoglu. *Limits of Citizenship: Migrants and Postnational Membership in Europe*. Chicago: University of Chicago Press, 1995.

Spiro, Peter J. *At Home in Two Countries: The Past and Future of Dual Citizenship*. New York: New York University Press, 2016.

Stahl, Charles, and Fred Arnold. "Overseas Workers Remittances in Asian Development." In Vertovec and Cohen, *Migration, Diasporas and Transnationalism*, 170–96.

Stangeland, Charles Emil. *Pre-Malthusian Doctrines of Population: A Study in the History of Economic Theory*. New York: Columbia University Press, 1904.

Stanziani, Alessandro. *Histoire de la qualité alimentaire, XIX-XXe siècle*. Paris: Seuil, 2005.

Stearns, Harold. "Apologia of an Expatriate." *Scribner's Magazine* 85, no. 3 (1929): 338–41.

Stein, Gertrude. *The Autobiography of Alice B. Toklas*. New York: Vintage Books, 1990. First published 1933.

Stein, Sarah Abrevaya. *Plumes: Ostrich Feathers, Jews, and a Lost World of Global Commerce*. New Haven, CT: Yale University Press, 2008.

Stovall, Tyler. *Paris Noir: African-Americans in the City of Light*. Boston: Houghton Mifflin, 1996.

Struck, Bernhard, Kate Ferris, and Jacques Revel. "Introduction: Space and Scale in Transnational History." *International History Review* 33, no. 4 (2011): 573–84.

Stuart, Amanda Mackenzie. *Consuelo and Alva Vanderbilt: The Story of a Daughter and Mother in the Gilded Age*. New York: Harper Perennial, 2005.

Stuart, Graham H. *American Diplomatic and Consular Practice*. New York: D. Appleton-Century, 1936.

Subrahmanyam, Sanjay. "Between a Rock and a Hard Place: Some Afterthoughts." In Schaffer et al., *Brokered World*, 429–40.

________. "Connected Histories: Notes Towards a Reconfiguration of Early Modern Eurasia." *Modern Asian Studies* 31, no. 3 (1997): 735–62.

________. *Three Ways to be Alien: Travails and Encounters in the Early Modern World*. Waltham, MA: Brandeis University Press, 2011.

Suri, Jeremi. "Transnational Influences on American Politics." In *The Concise Princeton Encyclopedia of American Political History*, edited by Michael Kazin, Rebecca Edwards, and Adam Rothman, 559–65. Princeton, NJ: Princeton University Press, 2011.

Susman, Warren Irving. "Pilgrimage to Paris: The Backgrounds of American Expatriation, 1920–1934." Ph.D. thesis, University of Wisconsin, 1957.

"Symposium: A Tribute to the Work of Kim Barry: The Construction of Citizenship in an Emigration Context." *New York University Law Review* 81, no. 1 (2006).

Talleyrand-Périgord, Charles-Maurice de. *Mémoires 1754–1815*, edited by Paul-Louis and Jean-Paul Couchoud. 1957. Reprint, Paris: Librairie Plon, 1982.

"Transnational Migration: International Perspectives." Special issue, *International Migration Review* 37, no. 3 (2003).

Tapinos, Georges. *L'immigration étrangère en France, 1946–1973*. Paris: INED Travaux et Documents no. 71, Presses Universitaires de France, 1975.

Tarrius, Alain. *Les fourmis d'Europe: Migrants riches, migrants pauvres et nouvelles villes internationales*. Paris: L'Harmattan, 1992.

________. *La mondialisation criminelle*. La Tour d'Aigues: Éd. de l'Aube, 2015.

Tarrius, Alain (with Lamia Missaoui). *Les nouveaux cosmopolitismes: mobilités, identités, territoires*. La Tour-d'Aigues: Éd. de l'Aube, 2000.

Thelen, David, ed. "The Nation and Beyond: Transnational Perspectives on United States History." Special issue, *Journal of American History* 86, no. 3 (1999).

Thiel, Markus. *The Limits of Transnationalism: Collective Identities and EU Integration*. New York: Palgrave Macmillan, 2011.

Thistlethwaite, Frank. "Migration from Europe Overseas in the 19th and 20th Centuries." In *Population Movements in Modern European History*, edited by Herbert Moller, 73–92. New York: Macmillan, 1964.

Thomas, Brinley, ed. *The Economics of International Migration*. London: Macmillan, 1958.

Thomas, Yan. *"Origine" et "commune patrie": Étude de droit public romain (*89 *av. J.-C.*—212 *ap. J.-C.)*. Rome: École Française de Rome, 1996.

Tilly, Charles. "Citizenship, Identity and Social History." *International Review of Social History* 40, supp. 3 (1995): 1–16.

Tintori, Guido. "L'Italie et ses expatriés: une perspective historique." In Dufoix, Guerassimoff, and de Tinguy, *Loin des yeux*, 79–104.

________. "Italy: The Continuing History of Emigrant Relations." In *Emigration Nations: Policies and Ideologies of Emigrant Engagement*, edited by Michael Collyer, 126–52. Basingstoke, UK: Palgrave Macmillan, 2013.

Topp, Michael Miller. "The Transnationalism of the Italian-American Left: The Lawrence Strike of 1912 and the Italian Chamber of

Labor of New York City." *Journal of American Ethnic History* 17, no. 1 (1997): 39–63.

Torpey, John. *The Invention of the Passport: Surveillance, Citizenship and the State*. Cambridge: Cambridge University Press, 2000.

Trivellato, Francesca. *The Sephardic Diaspora, Livorno, and Cross-Cultural Trade in the Early Modern Period*. New Haven, CT: Yale University Press, 2009.

Tsiang, I-Mien. *The Question of Expatriation in America Prior to 1907*. Baltimore: Johns Hopkins University Press, 1942.

Turner, Simon, ed. "Diasporic Tension: The Dilemmas and Conflicts of Transnational Engagement." Special issue, *Journal of Ethnic and Migration Studies* 34, no. 7 (2008).

Tyrrell, Ian. "American Exceptionalism in an Age of International History." *American Historical Review* 96, no. 4 (1991): 1031–55.

________. "Reflections on the Transnational Turn in United States History: Theory and Practice." *Journal of Global History* 4, no. 3 (2009): 453–74.

________. *Reforming the World: The Creation of America's Moral Empire*. Princeton, NJ: Princeton University Press, 2010.

________. *Transnational Nation: U.S. History in Global Perspective since 1789*. Basingstoke, UK: Palgrave Macmillan, 2007.

________. "What Is Transnational History?" Last accessed September 8, 2018. http://iantyrrell.wordpress.com/what-is-transnational-history/.

VanDaele, Jasmien. "Engineering Social Peace: Networks, Ideas, and the Founding of the International Labour Organization." *International Review of Social History* 50, no. 3 (2005): 435–66.

Vecoli, Rudolph J. "'Contadini' in Chicago: A Critique of *The Uprooted*." *Journal of American History* 54 (1964): 404–17.

Veenswijk, Virginia Kays. *Coudert Brothers: A Legacy in Law: The History of America's First International Law Firm, 1853–1993*. New York: Truman Talley, 1994.

Vertovec, Steven. *Transnationalism*. London: Routledge, 2009.

Vertovec, Steven, and Robin Cohen, eds. *Migration, Diasporas and Transnationalism*. Cheltenham, UK: Edward Elgar, 1999.

Vidal, Laurent, and Alain Musset, eds. *Les territoires de l'attente: Migrations et mobilités dans les Amériques, XIXe-XXIe siècle*. Rennes: Presses universitaires de Rennes, 2015.

Viet, Vincent. *La France immigrée, Construction d'une politique, 1914–1997*. Paris: Fayard, 1998.
Wagner, Anne-Catherine. *Les nouvelles élites de la mondialisation: Une immigration dorée en France*. Paris: Presses Universitaires de France, 1998.
Waldinger, Roger. *The Cross-Border Connection: Immigrants, Emigrants, and Their Homelands*. Cambridge, MA: Harvard University Press, 2015.
Waldinger, Roger, and David FitzGerald. "Transnationalism in Question." *American Journal of Sociology* 109, no. 5 (2004): 1177–95.
Warner, Charles K. *The Winegrowers of France and the Government since 1875*. New York: Columbia University Press, 1960.
Weil, François. "French Migration to the Americas in the 19th and 20th Centuries as a Historical Problem." *Studi Emigrazione* 33 (September 1996): 443–60.
________. "The French State and Transoceanic Emigration." In Green and Weil, *Citizenship and Those Who Leave*, 114–31.
________. "Les migrants de France et leurs rêves américains au XIXe siècle." *Diasporas*, no. 9 (2007): 32–42.
Weil, Patrick. *La France et ses étrangers, L'aventure d'une politique d'immigration, 1938–1991*. Paris: Calmann-Lévy, 1991.
________. *Qu'est-ce qu'un Français? Histoire de la nationalité française depuis la Révolution*. Paris: Grasset, 2002.
________. *The Sovereign Citizen: Denaturalization and the Origins of the American Republic*. Philadelphia: University of Pennsylvania Press, 2013.
Weiner, Myron. *The Global Migration Crisis: Challenge to States and to Human Rights*. New York: HarperCollins College, 1995.
Werner, Michael, and Bénédicte Zimmermann, eds. *De la comparaison à l'histoire croisée*. Paris: Seuil, 2004.
Westwood, Sallie, and Annie Phizacklea. *Trans-Nationalism and the Politics of Belonging*. London: Routledge, 2000.
Whelan, Frederick G. "Citizenship and the Right to Leave." *American Political Science Review* 75, no. 3 (1981): 636–53.
Whelpley, James Davenport. *The Problem of the Immigrant*. London: Chapman and Hall, 1905.
White, Richard. *The Middle Ground: Indians, Empires, and Republics in the Great Lakes Region, 1650–1815*. Cambridge: Cambridge University Press, 1991.

Williams, Phil, and Ernesto U. Savona, eds. *The United Nations and Transnational Organized Crime*. London: F. Cass, 1996.

Williams, Roger N. *The New Exiles: American War Resisters in Canada*. New York: Liveright, 1971.

Wimmer, Andreas, and Nina Glick Schiller. "Methodological Nationalism and Beyond: Nation State Building, Migration and the Social Sciences." *Global Networks: A Journal of Transnational Affairs* 2, no. 4 (2002): 301–34.

Wyman, Mark. *Round-Trip to America: The Immigrants Return to Europe, 1880–1939*. Ithaca, NY: Cornell University Press, 1993.

Young, John Russell. *Around the World with General Grant*. 2 vols. New York: American News, 1879.

Yun-Casalilla, Bartolomé (with Angeles Redondo). "'Localism,' Global History and Transnational History: A Reflection from the Historian of Early Modern Europe." *Historisk Tidskrift* 127, no. 4 (2007): 659–78.

Zahra, Tara. *The Great Departure: Mass Migration from Eastern Europe and the Making of the Free World*. New York: W. W. Norton, 2016.

Zolberg, Aristide. "The Archaeology of 'Remote Control.'" In *Migration Control in the North Atlantic World*, edited by Andreas Fahrmeir, Olivier Faron, and Patrick Weil, 195–222. New York: Berghahn Books, 2003.

________. "The Exit Revolution." In Green and Weil, *Citizenship and Those Who Leave*, 33–60.

________. *A Nation by Design: Immigration Policy in the Fashioning of America*. Cambridge, MA: Harvard University Press, 2006.

Zuñiga, Jean-Paul. "L'histoire impériale à l'heure de 'l'histoire globale': Une perspective atlantique." *Revue d'histoire moderne et contemporaine*, no. 54-4bis (2007/5): 54–68.

________, ed. *Pratiques du transnational: Terrains, preuves, limites*. Paris: La Bibliothèque du Centre de Recherches Historiques, 2011. http://hal.archives-ouvertes.fr/docs/00/65/00/24/PDF/CRH_pratiques-du-transnational.pdf.

Index

41088134R00128

Printed in Poland
by Amazon Fulfillment
Poland Sp. z o.o., Wrocław